I Was Told There'd Be a Village

I Was Told There'd Be a Village

Transforming Motherhood Through the Power of Connection

MELISSA WIRT

GRAND
CENTRAL

New York Boston

Grand Central Publishing
Hachette Book Group
1290 Avenue of the Americas, New York, NY 10104
grandcentralpublishing.com
@grandcentralpub

First Edition: April 2025

Grand Central Publishing is a division of Hachette Book Group, Inc. The Grand Central Publishing name and logo is a registered trademark of Hachette Book Group, Inc.

The publisher is not responsible for websites (or their content) that are not owned by the publisher.

The Hachette Speakers Bureau provides a wide range of authors for speaking events. To find out more, go to hachettespeakersbureau.com or email HachetteSpeakers@hbgusa.com.

Grand Central Publishing books may be purchased in bulk for business, educational, or promotional use. For information, please contact your local bookseller or the Hachette Book Group Special Markets Department at special.markets@hbgusa.com.

Print book interior designed by Bart Dawson.

Library of Congress Cataloging-in-Publication Data

Names: Wirt, Melissa, author.
Title: I was told there'd be a village : transforming motherhood through the power of connection / Melissa Wirt.
Description: First edition. | New York : GCP, [2025] | Includes bibliographical references. |
Identifiers: LCCN 2024050298 | ISBN 9781538759059 (hardcover) | ISBN 9781538759097 (ebook)
Subjects: LCSH: Motherhood. | Mothers—Social networks. | Parents—Social networks.
Classification: LCC HQ759 .W545 2025 | DDC 306.874/3—dc23/eng/20241213
LC record available at https://lccn.loc.gov/2024050298

ISBNs: 9781538759059 (Hardcover); 9781538759097 (ebook)

Printed in the United States of America

LSC-C

Printing 1, 2025

For Lindi, thank you

Contents

PART III
So You Think You Might Have a Village (Maybe). Now What?

Introduction

Is There Anybody Out There?

When I sat down to write this book, I had barely begun to type before I was paralyzed by self-doubt. I heard my inner mean girl laughing at me: "You want to write about community in motherhood? You're not a psychologist or a social worker or an anthropologist. You've never written anything longer than a blog post. There are days when you don't even feel like you *have* any friends. *You* are going to write a book about connection? Good luck with that." A hot flash of shame burned down my body. My inner mean girl was right. Who was I to position myself as someone who could offer advice to my fellow moms? I was hardly anyone's idea of a social butterfly. The progress I've made toward finding a village has been what people politely call hard-won, meaning I have stumbled clumsily along the way and occasionally gotten emotionally bruised. I wondered if there was something else I should be writing about. Maybe a business book for women entrepreneurs? Or a handbook for breastfeeding moms? Or, I don't know, a guide to fixing Xerox machines? The idea of tackling the topic of finding friendship and community as a mom filled me with anxiety. But why? It's not as if I am timid about sharing details about my personal life. I host a podcast where I talk openly about many of the embarrassing parts of motherhood, like how often I have sex with my husband now that I'm a mom, how our family dog ate our pet guinea pig, and how my body has changed post-kids. Why was I more comfortable talking about things like my weak pelvic floor than I was talking about how alone I sometimes feel as a mom?

My fear and shame were telling me something. The fact that copping to my isolation gave me a pukey feeling wasn't a sign that I should find a new subject; it was a sign that it was the *perfect* subject.

Every mom I know feels overwhelmed by the demands of being a mother today. When I first learned about Eve Rodsky's "Shit I Do" list, which catalogs the hundreds of tasks that moms handle every day, I felt a wave of kinship. What mom hasn't tallied up the time she's spent doing the invisible work of motherhood? These invisible tasks include things like searching for the number for poison control, emailing teachers about junior's food allergies, labeling the kid's shoes and lunch boxes and jackets so they don't get lost at school, and listening to parenting podcasts to improve our emotional regulation skills. We all share the knowledge that we are doing a lot. We also share the feeling that it would be embarrassing, an admission of failure, to ask for help. We'd never call a friend to ask if she could watch our baby for an hour while we run to the grocery store, even though it would be nine thousand percent easier to navigate the aisles without a baby strapped to our body. We wouldn't dream of organizing a Meal Train for ourselves after we've had outpatient surgery. Most of us won't even talk honestly with our mom friends about how we feel when our kids are struggling and we don't know what the heck to do to help them. We've gotten the message that we are not supposed to ask for help with any of these things. Not in twenty-first-century America, anyway. And so we continue momming in isolation instead of leaning on one another for support.

The more I thought about it, the more I realized that it wasn't just me. We are in the midst of a crisis in motherhood—and we're not talking about it. That changes now.

If you're a mom, I'm willing to bet you've fantasized about a world where you had a network of people you coparented with, a cohort who could transform motherhood into a group project. I'm also willing to bet that you feel awkward admitting you need help. I know I do. The idea of texting a friend to request a favor is as nerve-racking as the prospect of asking a boss for additional vacation time. It's like admitting that you can't hack it. But *of course* you need help. It is an enormous amount of work to keep our children fed, clothed, bathed, educated, and on their way to becoming decent human beings (who don't litter and who are kind to animals and who cover their mouths when they cough). Still, we parents are expected to do this work all by ourselves. The America we live in today tells us that good parents put our kids' needs, happiness, and success ahead of everything else—including our own needs. This attitude has left many of us on the verge of breaking down.

~

Back in 2019, our family was living in my husband's childhood home near Richmond, Virginia. Our kids were at their happiest playing in the surrounding cul-de-sac, but with five children under eight years old, space was pretty tight, especially because it was never just our family in the house. Doors slammed throughout the day as my kids' friends ran in and out. At the time, I was in the early stages of building my business, Latched Mama, which sells clothes for nursing mothers. I squeezed in calls to the supplier between taking the kids to the dentist and their swim meets. I was in the thick of parenting, and I couldn't see my way through to the end of each day. I was very much in a deal-with-whatever-issue-is-erupting-in-front-of-me mode, and there were so many issues. Keeping my own kids in line, and ensuring that they were kind to one another, was hard enough. Then add another handful of kids to the mix, many of them siblings themselves, and I had to stop what I was doing every five minutes to play referee. I'd take work calls while wearing the toddler, nursing the infant, and peering out the kitchen window to make sure that whatever fort was being made outside was either built at ground level or engineered in such a way that when it fell to the ground, bones would not be broken. I'd gotten to the point where my space, and my life, no longer felt like my own.

Each day, just before dinner, a couple of moms would stop by to pick up their children, often sitting down to chat. We talked about all the things moms talk about—how our kids were doing, who was being extra clingy or going through a sleep regression, who was having a growth spurt—all topics of conversation that I had once loved. However, increasingly, as these women sat in my kitchen, rather than enjoying our bonding time, I found myself watching the clock, calculating how long they could stay before the night's schedule would be thrown into chaos. There was a time when I had looked forward to seeing other moms around the neighborhood. They were my people, fellow travelers keeping me company on my motherhood journey. We met up for coffee and walks and lingered to talk whenever we ran into each other around town. But now that I owned my own business and was a mom of five, talking to other moms felt like a luxury I couldn't afford. I needed to get Nathan, our oldest, to martial arts, give the rest of the kids their baths, and somehow find the time to make a healthy dinner that would satisfy seven people. I fell into bed each night completely wrung out.

Even though I was fortunate to be able to afford babysitters who could pitch in with the day-to-day demands of childcare, I still felt too overwhelmed by my family's needs to let myself make time to connect. As those very nice moms, many of whom I considered my friends, shared their daily concerns, I'd stare at the clock behind them, sending telepathic messages: "I wish I had time to listen to your story, but I just don't. Isn't that your kid I hear telling you it's time to go?"

Truth is, I didn't know how good I had it. Those moms I was so quick to shoo out had made my parenting easier in ways I was too blinkered to see. When I caught the dreaded norovirus and couldn't shake it, one of them drove me to the hospital for fluids so my husband, Eric, could stay home with the kids. Another mom texted me to ask if I needed any groceries while she was at the store. Another left broth on my doorstep the next day. I *had* a village. I just couldn't see it.

Back then, I was convinced I would stop feeling so overwhelmed if our family could escape from the nonstop company and move to a bigger house. By the time it was 2020: the pandemic was just getting underway, and more space seemed like a good idea. One afternoon, I expanded my search parameters on Zillow, and a property I'd never seen before appeared. When I clicked on it, I got goose bumps. It had a house and an enormous barn, which I fantasized could act as a warehouse for my business. All my problems—my exhaustion, my overwhelm, my feeling that I had lost myself—would be solved. *Hallelujah!*

The moment Eric and I pulled down the long driveway for the viewing, we knew it was our forever home. The promise of more space felt like salvation, but if I am honest, the beautiful property also felt like a much-needed affirmation that I was pulling it off—I had my life together enough to provide everything my family needed. Things couldn't be that bad if we had a house like *this.*

For the first few months after we moved in, I rejoiced *Oh, my gosh, do you hear that quiet? This is what heaven sounds like.* Those early days on the farm were intoxicating. Zoning laws prevented us from using the barn for my business, so it became an oasis for the Wirt clan. The kids could run through pastures pretending to be wood nymphs or, let's be real, Transformers. We might have been in lockdown, but there would not be eight hours of screen time a day for us! We were going to the school of life, and it would be bloody glorious. (If only I'd known how quickly those naive feelings of self-satisfaction would evaporate.) Without any other families around, my kids looked to me to keep them occupied. At first, this was fantastic. We were like *Little House on the Prairie*—or one of those homesteading families on Instagram. We could find joy in the simple things with just one another for company. Give us a shovel and a pail, and we'd be set for hours.

I baked. I made homemade Play-Doh. I watched over my children with great care. My life narrowed to focus exclusively on my own brood and the business that supported us. I had solitude galore. I could parent my kids exactly as I liked with no interruptions. *See?* I thought as I crawled into bed each night. *Look at me. I have the house, the job, the family. My business is holding on. Who says you can't have it all?*

But after the initial high, the isolation began to take its toll. I hadn't anticipated how it would feel to spend the day playing pioneer or supermarket or train station with five kids while feeding them and making sure they were logging in for remote learning and getting them to bed on time, all with Eric as the only other adult around to talk to. Instead of feeling liberated by our solitude, I felt suffocated by it. Despite getting exactly what I wanted—an insular bubble, without anyone to mom next to—I soon found myself miserable and more overwhelmed than ever. To my shock, I realized that I was missing the continual flow of neighbor kids passing through the house, and, more to the point, I really missed catching up with their moms. It felt bananas to complain when so many other people had things tougher than we did, but an unsettling feeling that I may have made a mistake—a very expensive mistake—by moving us out of our old neighborhood crept in, and I couldn't dislodge it.

I'd been duped by the big lie about contemporary motherhood—that the ideal mother will turn all her energy and attention inward to her own family unit, everything else be damned. Nearly every mom I know has bought into this mentality. Increasingly, we all seek out our metaphorical farms—cocoons sheltering the family, free from the ties that bind us to other people—and, as a result, we are pretty damn lonely.

In my defense, putting our own families first makes sense. After all, what is more important than protecting and raising the next generation? The fate of the entire species depends upon it. So with the best of intentions, as modern parents, we turn ourselves into child-optimizing machines. While not everyone goes as far as I did by picking up and moving to a remote farm, we concentrate the laser focus of our attention on our children. We enroll in Baby

Einstein classes, puree our veggies into homemade baby food, jockey for a place in the best schools, and hound teachers about our children's performance. We chauffeur our kids from piano to soccer to cheer squad, reading articles about attachment parenting on our phones as we wait in the car by ourselves. We operate out of a fear of messing up our kids' childhoods.

In our quiet moments, we know something is amiss. At the end of each activity-filled day, we collapse into bed, bodies limp, minds processing tomorrow's to-do list. We are told we can "do hard things," but what is left unsaid is that we'll do them unsupported and alone. Is the word for what we're feeling *languishing*? Is it *burnout*? Is it *mom rage*—or maybe *dumpster fire*? We knew raising kids would be difficult, but was it supposed to be *this* difficult? Or this lonely? Hadn't someone, somewhere, said that it takes a village to raise a child?

For millennia, there *were* villages, large groups of people woven together in communities of around twenty individuals linked by proximity and dependent upon one another. They hunted for food together, protected one another, and shared responsibility for tending to children, a structure called alloparenting. They lived in a web of extended families united by their common need to survive.[1] This period of history, when raising kids was a group effort among several generations of a family, with friends, neighbors, and even other children pitching in, lasted tens of thousands of years.

But now, the idea of a village is as foreign to us as the idea of commuting by horseback. If you had set out to design a society that keeps people away from one another, you might have come up with one that looks a lot like the world we live in today. We cram our schedules so full that we rush from activity to activity with no opportunity for serendipitous meetups. Instead of venturing out into markets, we have food delivered to us. We order our Q-tips, clothes, and movies online. We check Yelp instead of reaching out to a friend to ask for a restaurant recommendation. Everything about our society is engineered to keep us apart from anyone outside the nuclear family.

Beginning in the Middle Ages, as society began the process of shifting from intermingled groups to smaller family units living side by side, the social mindset shifted from communal to individualistic. Our current hyper-individualist mindset in the West wouldn't be so bad if we lived in a society with a strong social support system and robust family-friendly policies and institutions. However, for those of us who have become mothers in twenty-first-century America, the message we get from our government is very much *You're on your own. Good luck!*

The US government's failure to support mothers begins early, with childbirth, an event that is more likely to kill women in the United States than in any other developed country—and the risk is three times higher for Black women.[2] After giving birth, we have a quick session at the hospital with a lactation consultant, and then we are sent home, where we are left to google "good latch" and "mastitis" while a Niagara Falls of hormones cascades through our bodies. We try desperately to remember the swaddle the nurse showed us and turn to the internet for advice to help our babies learn to sleep through the night.

Because Americans still (still!) don't have a good national paid parental leave program, a few weeks later, many moms have to go back to work before they are ready, forcing them to spend a gigantic percentage of their household income on childcare. If a mom decides to breastfeed, she'll have to finagle a way to pump her breast milk, usually at a workplace that isn't equipped with a private room. Pumping during the first year of life can take as many as 1,800 hours, an amount of time that is within spitting distance of the 1,960 hours you'd work at a full-time job in that same year. In the years that follow, families in the United States continue to feel this dearth of support in the lack of universal pre-K and subsidized childcare. Simply put, we are left to lone wolf our way through parenting.

If I have learned one thing from watching the Latched Mama community of half a million mothers bravely share their triumphs and heartbreak online, it is that every mom out there is dealing with these challenges.

In an ideal world, there would be a committee of highly trained experts working day and night to nudge our society back to a more natural and beneficial state of connectedness. But the hard truth is that there is no incentive for anyone else to fix our culture of isolation. It's working for everyone else that moms bear the brunt of child-rearing labor. In no household anywhere is the non-lead parent thinking, *Gosh, I really wish I could do more of the scheduling, meal planning, and pesticide-intake monitoring.*

Things have gone on this way for so long that we assume "hard" is just the way things are.

But it doesn't have to be this way.

A NETWORK OF SLEEPER CELLS

What if we had the power to make a change? What if there was already a network of support out there? What if it turned out that we moms are our own greatest resource? I believe we are. After all, who runs the world? Moms. We are a group of highly capable, motivated women who know how to tend and befriend—and we are *everywhere*, hiding in plain sight like sleeper cells just waiting to be activated. What if we could show up for one another and collectively lighten our loads by offering logistical and emotional support? Yes, we can protest and advocate for institutional change, and we should. But protesting doesn't get my kid to swim practice while I'm at work. Maybe someday there will be an effective, centralized organization creating better maternal support policies. Wouldn't that be nice? In the meantime, in this book, I want to address how we can cope *right now*. I'm convinced that one of the best solutions is leaning on one another. We mothers can show up, not just for our kids but also for other moms—and for ourselves.

Consider yourself activated.

This quiet revolution is already brewing. Not just on the margins, where people are co-living and forming mommunes (which are great, but not always a realistic option), but also in our living rooms, where a number of parents are opening their doors to a more porous way of parenting. When moms step up for one another, the result is awesome. I've seen that if we let go of the mindset that we must do it all ourselves, we can embrace a village mindset and become what I call *village moms.*

In a world populated by village parents, moms will join forces to help one another thrive. Village moms show up for others with understanding and without judgment. They know that we are all fighting the same battle and feel safe and open enough to host a playdate without thinking twice about the fact that the dog peed on the floor earlier that day. A village mom also takes care of herself by calling on her resources for help—she might drop her kids

---

*   A quick note: a village mindset is not the exclusive property of moms. Dads, uncles, aunts, friends, and grandparents are welcome recruits to the cause. I'm addressing moms in particular here because the crisis in parenting falls most heavily on our shoulders.

off at a friend's house, go grab a cup of coffee and head to Target, or get her nails done, then come back and pick up those fed and happy kids three hours later. And she will return this favor for her fellow moms.

Village parenting is already happening out there. Through my work at Latched Mama, I've watched moms create community in ways that are beautiful and inspiring. It's happening in PTAs, grocery aisles, and boardrooms, where moms have one another's back, stick up for one another, lend a hand, and appreciate the heck out of how hard it is to be a mom in America today. It's time for it to happen for you. For all of us.

HOW TO USE THIS BOOK

Becoming a village mom starts with embracing a village mindset. How we *think* about the possibilities of parenting together has an enormous impact on how we parent. Moms today are more isolated than ever before, thanks to a perfect storm of technology, lifestyle patterns, and a lack of institutional resources. However, by challenging the assumption that it is *normal* to live this way, we can begin to make change.

The best part? The village mindset is contagious. Once you start to build your village, I think you'll find, as I have, that the energy you put into it inspires other people and spreads like wildfire. After I told one mom about the subject of this book, she decided to take a friend's son with her on vacation so her friend could stay home with her dying dog. I discussed villages with another mom friend who started a monthly Zoom for parents of kids with learning challenges so they could share resources and support.

Each chapter in this book begins with a mindset shift that I encourage you to embrace to get you thinking like a village mom. That's right: we're going to deprogram decades of isolationist thinking. I'll address the struggle to accept vulnerability, the challenge of relearning friendship against the chaotic backdrop of motherhood, and the importance of maintaining your sense of self post-kids. The way you spend your time and energy reflects your values. I'm going to ask you to divert some of those limited and precious resources to building a village, and I promise you, the return on investment will be worth it. At the end of each chapter, I'll also include practical suggestions that will make a difference. I know that not everyone is ready to take big, bold steps, so I've tried to include suggestions that will seem doable, not daunting.

Too often, we feel panicky and ashamed when we think about confronting our isolation—as I did when I set out to write this book—but we can't fix what we won't talk about. I want to normalize talking about how hard it is to find a village. I want to bring the problem out of obscurity and make it an essential part of the motherhood conversation. We need more stories of struggle, and we need more stories of success. Throughout the book, I'll share the stories of moms who have found the courage to change their mindsets and their actions and experienced the power of a village.

Every mom has a story. The ones I've included are gleaned from the Latched Mama community, my own circle, and from dozens of interviews with women who generously allowed a glimpse into their lives. Names, locations, and narrative details have been adjusted to provide privacy for these women and ensure that their stories resonate.

I'll also share my own story of falling into a pit of despair after I cut myself off from my community when I moved to the farm.

As friendless and alone as a person has ever felt, I gathered my courage, peeled myself up off the floor, and started building the connections that bolster me today. The village I'm working to create for myself gives me so much, and I give back. I am so much better off with the strength of my village behind me than I was when it was just me, Eric, and the kids in our beautiful, beautiful bubble.

I want to be clear: I'm not done yet. Not even close. The footprint is there, but my village is still very much a construction zone. I'm not positioning myself as a poster child for having a village. I am the in-progress child, right there in the muck with you. I'm learning to practice what I preach—that motherhood is better when we do it together.

Before we begin, let's address the elephant in the room: I know it feels like you don't have time. I felt that way, too. For some of us, the very idea of speaking to someone when you don't absolutely have to fills us with dread. But that's what got us to this place, walled off from one another, and the upsides are too great to deny with a barrage of "but, but, but." The truth is, if you want something to change, you have to move out of your comfort zone. But this will be worth it, because if you build a village, you will not only feel less alone, you will experience less stress, you will be healthier, and your kids will be better off.

I am now the mother of six children. As I navigate every messy, beautiful, and difficult day of parenthood, I continue to be inspired by the courageous women I meet. I am astonished by what I witness daily in my community when moms band together. It starts with simply sharing our stories. So, my fellow moms, let's do this thing. Let's join forces and fight back against a system that feels like it was designed to make us fail. Let's build a village.

I Was Told There'd Be a Village

PART I

You're Not Wrong— This Is Hard

Chapter 1

Parenting Culture Is Broken, and Moms Are Not Okay

ISOLATION MINDSET: I'm fine. Everything's fine. Parenting is supposed to be hard. I've got this.

VILLAGE MINDSET: Everything is not fine. This isn't normal. Being a mom shouldn't feel this hard or this isolating. We're being set up to fail, and we need to make a change.

For months after we moved to the farm, we continued to huddle together as a family, exploring the trails, testing our favorite picnic spots, voting on what our first farm animal would be (it was a cat—baby steps), and taking a lot of deep breaths. When you live somewhere without another house in sight, clothing is very much optional. Thanks to that freedom (and a few White Claws), baby number six was on the way by Christmas. Eric and I were overjoyed that we'd be welcoming a new baby into the world on the farm. Another happy member of our close-knit family! What could be better?

All through the winter, I fantasized about strolling through fields of wildflowers in the summer with a sweet-smelling newborn strapped to my chest. That reverie somehow chased away any worries I might have had about whether moving out of our old neighborhood had been a mistake.

On Christmas morning, when I was around three months pregnant, Eric and I snuggled on the couch, watching the kids open their presents. Underneath my cozy blanket, I was suddenly struck by a horrible feeling that something was wrong with my pregnancy. I wasn't bleeding, but this was far from my first rodeo, and I knew when my body felt off. The next day, I had some lab work done, hoping my spidey sense was out of whack. When the blood work came back, my heart sank. The HCG and progesterone levels were low. Really low. A second draw confirmed that the levels were dropping instead of doubling as they should have been. I'll never forget the feeling of hope duking it out with terror during my ultrasound. The result was heartbreaking: the fetus we'd been so eager to welcome into our lives was not viable. I stumbled out of the doctor's office feeling numb. In a daze, I shared the news with Eric before breaking down into racking sobs. I knew that it wasn't my fault, that there is no shame in a failed pregnancy, but knowing I shouldn't feel ashamed didn't stop me from feeling that way.

I spent the next two weeks totally cut off from the world. I had trouble forming thoughts, let alone words, to help me process the fact that the "farm baby" I'd hoped for would not be arriving. Eventually, I started bleeding. The flow was heavy enough for the midwife to prescribe Cytotec—a drug used to expel what was left of the unsuccessful pregnancy in my body. Around dinnertime, I locked myself in the bathroom to take my pills. As I slipped them into my cheek, I could hear the kids asking where I was and Eric trying to keep them interested in their mac and cheese and away from me.

A tiny but wise part of me whispered that I should find someone to keep me company during those hard hours. I picked up my phone and scrolled through my contacts. I rolled over screen after screen without stopping on a name. *Oh, wow.* There wasn't a single person in my network I felt safe enough with in that moment to call and say, "Hey, I'm really going through it. Can you just keep me company for a minute?" I had pushed so deep into my isolation that even though I had hundreds of contacts in my phone, I couldn't make myself hit Dial. I was afraid that no one would show up for me—not even if I asked.

I crumpled to the floor. My body felt like a deflated balloon. The miscarriage was soul-crushing, but feeling like there was no one I could reach out to made it even more devastating. Was I so unworthy of love that there was not one person in the whole world I could trust to be there for me? The feelings of loneliness and isolation I'd felt since we'd moved to the farm went from an addling fog to a debilitating lightning bolt. Where had everyone gone? I'd had friends at one point, hadn't I? Maybe—but I had also spent the better part of a year wholly focused on running my business and making sure all the members of my family had exactly what they needed—all the members except me, that is. I gritted it out alone on the cold tile of my bathroom floor thinking, *This can't be the way it's supposed to be.*

I couldn't have told you whom or what I needed the night I miscarried, but lying there on my bathroom floor, somewhere between the trips to the toilet and wishing someone would refill my water cup, I had a moment of deep knowing: motherhood is hard as hell, but motherhood without a village is damn near impossible.

I'M ALONE; YOU'RE ALONE; WE'RE ALL ALONE TOGETHER

I know I'm not the only one who has found herself stunned by how alone it often feels to be a mother. Moms are more disconnected from one another than they've been at any other time in history.

We have an epidemic of loneliness in the United States, and it is hitting mothers especially hard. A 2016 study of happiness levels shows that parents are less happy than childfree adults.[1] One survey found that 66 percent of mothers with children under five reported feeling lonely.[2] At Latched Mama, we have an online community that is five hundred thousand moms strong and has given me a front-row seat to just how hard isolation has hit us. Every day, I see posts that illustrate how much moms need more connection, community, and support. We post from our kitchens, our bedrooms, and our closets as we try to hold it all together. Women declare their isolation in posts like the ones below.

My husband & I have essentially lost all our close friends since becoming parents...I have managed "being at a time of my life when I don't have friends" fairly well for about 2 years (my daughter is 3). But not having friends is starting to really bother me. I'm lonely. I'm in my late 30s, both my husband & I have full time jobs outside our home, I'm a mom to a toddler, and I struggle with social anxiety. I don't even think I remember how to make friends. And even if I did...it feels so complicated to meet people, make a connection, & build trust to become friends.

I'm not looking for a "magic formula" to make friends as an adult but I'd love some ideas & even some success stories of making friends when you're a busy mom.

—*Anonymous*

This season of motherhood is really hard. It's lonely and sometimes isolating. It's okay to cry in your kitchen over spilled Froot Loops.

—*Irene*

Does anyone else wish they had someone to talk to? Someone to vent about daily struggles, anxieties, and feelings and have it be reciprocated? It can be so lonely sometimes. Hugs to all those who are struggling with this.

—*Cara*

Feeling lonely may sound like no big deal. It can even sound sort of cute and sweet, like a puppy waiting at the window for its owner to come home. But pervasive loneliness is not a small thing. A prolonged feeling of loneliness is a sign of need—and of that need going unfulfilled. When we experience loneliness, it's a signal letting us know that we are connection-deprived, the same way we feel thirst to let us know that we should drink some liquids before we end up dehydrated.

Think about your own life. When was the last time you called a friend just to talk? Or asked another mom how she was doing and really listened to the answer? I'm guessing you've filled up your car with gas more recently than you've made a date with a friend to grab a coffee. We've arrived at a point where we treat friendship and connection as luxuries when they are as essential to our survival as the food we eat. We are increasingly left to go it alone as parents, and it is taking an enormous toll on us mentally, emotionally, and physically.

My friend Lynn, mom to two-year-old Alice and five-year-old Dan, is a perfect example of how isolation can deal a blow to well-being in motherhood.

In 2021, Lynn left her job as a copywriter at an advertising agency in Philadelphia to give it a go as a freelancer. She had loved the camaraderie of working in an office. Most of her adult friendships had been formed during happy hours with her colleagues. But with Alice in preschool and Dan starting kindergarten, she and her husband, Caleb, decided it would make more sense—and save money on childcare—if she worked at the dining-room table in their suburban home while the children were in school. That way, she'd be able to pick them up and enjoy time with them in the afternoons. She figured she'd replace the chitchat she enjoyed at her office with some conversation during school pickup. As she got her business off the ground, postpandemic technology and shifts in work-culture norms made working from home even easier than she'd anticipated. Lynn was able to meet with clients over Zoom and then change from her blazer into a sweatshirt minutes after she hung up so she could head off to pick up the kids.

She loved the freedom that working for herself offered, but during the quiet of her days at home, she missed her former coworkers. She hadn't fully appreciated how much she relied on them for her social life. She was embarrassed to admit it, but she didn't have a lot of friends outside the office. She'd gradually lost touch with her friends from college as they disappeared into their own young families. She saw photos of their vacations and their kids' first days of school on social media, but she was startled to realize that it had been years since she'd met up with most of them in person. And until she became a freelancer, she hadn't spent a lot of time in her neighborhood getting to know the people who lived near her. The hours she wasn't working and commuting were spent doing her second shift as a mom, which kept her so busy preparing meals and making sure she was there for every single milestone the kids reached that she didn't have a lot of time for socializing. In fact, there were days when she did not say a single word to another human being between 8:05 a.m., when her kids left for school, and 3:20 p.m., when she got in line for pickup.

Her former coworkers continued to invite her when they went for after-work drinks, but since her old office was a thirty-minute drive away, going would mean missing the kids' bedtimes, which she feared would leave them feeling neglected, so she demurred. Her husband, Caleb, was stretched as thin as she was, so she didn't feel right asking for nights out with her old crew. Before long, she got dropped from the group text. She was a little hurt, but she understood. Why keep inviting someone who never shows up?

She guessed she'd need to find some new people to talk to.

When she quit her job, she assumed that she would make new friends whose lives were in sync with her new schedule, but she hadn't counted on what it meant to start from zero with a new crowd. The last time she had to make new friends was more than ten years previously, when she'd first been hired at the agency. At the start of the kids' school year, she had attended the meet-and-greets held for parents over Triscuits and cheddar cubes, but she had trouble finding other opportunities to talk to parents. It's hard to start a conversation from separate cars in a carpool line. Plus, whenever she did run into a group of parents at a school function, it seemed like the moms already knew one another. Had there been some sort of social hour she missed when everyone became besties? For the first time in her life, she felt like she was on the outside looking in.

As she approached Dan's school each day to pick him up, her heart raced, and her face felt flushed. Could everyone tell she felt like an outsider? She was a successful professional with a booming career—she was turning down gigs left and right—but she felt extremely self-conscious and sensed that she didn't belong with the parents she saw every afternoon. She wasn't working longer hours than she used to, but she felt increasingly run-down. She tossed and turned for hours each night before falling asleep.

So she did all the things you're supposed to do when you have sleep problems. She stopped drinking the fun stuff—coffee and alcohol. She turned off her phone at 9:00 p.m. and even left it in another room, but she couldn't turn off her brain. It was like she'd lost the ability to relax. She felt anxious and jittery. Nighttime thoughts of what she needed to take care of the next day, the next week, and the next decade scrolled through her mind. She wished she had someone to talk to, but it felt weird to call her old colleagues and confess how much she missed them.

She thought, *I'm fine. I'm better than fine. I know the names of all my kids' teachers. My clients love me; I make bank; I need to buck up. The kids are thriving. I'm doing great.*

Somehow, though, she didn't feel great. Her energy dragged, and it got harder for her to get out of bed in the morning. She withdrew from the world more each day, ordering her lunch from Grubhub rather than driving to Panera. She suspected this wasn't the best way to fix her sense of isolation, but with every passing day, the prospect of finding new friends felt more daunting. After a while, even making it to the mailbox to pay a bill required more energy than she had. Was this what depression felt like? She felt emptier than she'd ever felt in her life, like a dried-out sponge, drained of life and so brittle she feared she might break into a million useless pieces.

Yikes.

She scheduled an appointment with her doctor. After he had taken her vitals (her blood pressure was up, though it wasn't anything that required medication, at least not yet), her doctor typed into his monitor as he went through the checklist—family history, any change in medications—and then, in a robotic voice, he asked, "Do you ever have any feelings of depression or thoughts of self-harm?" He didn't even wait for an answer before saying, voice dripping with sarcasm, "Thank you for completing the mental health checklist mandated by the state of Pennsylvania."

Lynn was floored that her doctor couldn't tell she was barely holding it together. As she drove home, she figured out what had happened. He'd taken one look at the habitual smile plastered on her face and decided he probably needed to check her iron levels and send her on her way. It didn't occur to him that she was teetering on the precipice of depression. If he, with his many years of training and experience, couldn't spot that she was close to breaking down, then how could she expect her friends and family to notice?

Lynn was suffering from what I think of as the invisible isolation of motherhood. From the outside, her life appeared full to the brim with her busy career and healthy family, but the view from the inside could not have been different. To Lynn, her life felt hollow. Psychologist Susan Pinker explains in her book *The Village Effect* that sustained loneliness like Lynn's takes a terrible toll on our well-being, affecting our longevity, memories, and happiness.[3] It's time to bring the invisible isolation that so many of us moms suffer from into the light and make it visible so we can talk openly about how to fix it. The stakes are too high to keep it hidden.

THE COST OF BEING CUT OFF

I think I was in middle school when I learned that when we humans are threatened, or in a state of emergency, our primal brains go into fight-flight-or-freeze mode. But it wasn't until I was an adult and started looking into why my loneliness felt like a crisis that I learned that humans have evolved to interpret isolation as an emergency every bit as serious as being chased by a lion.

From the earliest days of humanity, to be on your own was to be vulnerable to starvation, dehydration, cold, and danger. So even today, loneliness feels like an emergency. When we experience isolation, our brains kick our nervous systems into high alert. Hormones surge; our pupils widen, the better to see those threats; cortisol courses through our veins; and our blood pressure and blood sugar skyrocket.[4] As Susan Pinker says, "As incredible as it sounds, feeling isolated creates a 'lonely' fingerprint on every cell." Which affects how the body responds to stress.[5]

The thing is, the fight-flight-or-freeze mechanism developed to deal with acute dangers. Once the immediate danger passed, our systems recalibrated, and our bodies returned to their resting states. Isolation and loneliness, however, are chronic states. We weren't meant to live with sustained stress, and as a result, protracted loneliness can lead to a harrowing list of long-term health problems, including heart disease, high blood pressure, dementia, depression, and anxiety. Lonely people have high levels of a blood protein that causes clotting, which puts them at risk for stroke.[6] To make matters worse, it also screws up our ability to get a good night's sleep and weakens our immune systems.[7] One study even found that people who were lonely reported feeling more symptoms of the common cold than other people.[8]

Given all that, it shouldn't be surprising that a 2009 study found that poor social connections pose a greater risk to your longevity than obesity, drinking, and not exercising.[9] In fact, not having a supportive social network is as bad for you as smoking fifteen cigarettes a day.[10] On top of that, loneliness *feels* bad. The parts of the brain where we feel emotional pain and the parts that register physical pain overlap, meaning that the emotional pain of being alone can cause our bodies to respond as if we have been injured.[11]

Our lack of connection is obviously really hurting us, and yet, as surgeon general Dr. Vivek H. Murthy pointed out in a *New York Times* article, while there are more adults in the United States suffering from loneliness than from diabetes, we spend far more money treating and preventing diabetes.[12]

The most shocking statistic I learned while researching this book is that the leading cause of death for mothers in the first year of a child's life is self-harm.[13] Once I knew that, I started seeing evidence that a lack of support can make a challenging situation far worse, like a devastating Latched Mama post from a member who wrote that she was so depressed after having her second child that she could barely function. She was lonely and anxious and unable to connect with her baby. It got so bad that she began to have thoughts of suicide.

The truth is glaringly obvious: loneliness in motherhood is a crisis.

THE SOLUTION IS FREE AND READILY AVAILABLE—BUT IT'S NOT EASY

One of the worst parts of all this is that our isolation mindset is so deeply entrenched that it causes us to perpetuate our own loneliness. Whether out of guilt or pride, we turn down offers of help. We soldier on when we get sick, plowing through our days fueled by cough drops and DayQuil. We opt to have dinner delivered instead of running the risk of bumping into a neighbor while we're on our third day of sweatpants. We choose to stay home and binge-watch Netflix instead of calling a friend for a walk.

I've noticed that many moms are afraid to admit that they don't have the connection and support they need. We hide our loneliness from our partners, our families, and sometimes even ourselves, but every once in a while, we catch a glimpse of another mom in the cereal aisle and have a flash of recognition: *Does she feel it, too? Is she like me? Is she overwhelmed, cut off from support—and, gulp, lonely?*

The answer is, in all likelihood, yes. You are not alone in feeling painfully lonely.

The good news is that we know exactly how to reverse all the negative effects of loneliness and isolation: connect with other people. The data is clear: having a supportive network of friends is one of the best things you can do for your health and happiness as a mom. Susan Pinker points out that people who invest in meaningful personal relationships with "lots of real social contact" are healthier than people who are isolated.[14] Researchers have found that having social connections lowers moms' stress levels.[15] We humans feel better together. Even hearing a loved one's voice can help regulate our emotions.[16] When we connect with another person, we feel less anxious and more secure.[17]

Studies have shown that connection increases your life-span and improves the years you spend on earth. Researchers at Harvard conducted the longest-ever study (eighty-four years and counting) of what brings people happiness, and their conclusion was breathtakingly simple. It isn't physical health, material wealth, or massive achievements that predict our chances for happiness and longevity.[18] As the lead investigators, Robert Waldinger, MD, and Marc Schulz, PhD, wrote in their book, *The Good Life*, the one thing that consistently proved the "power of its ties to physical health, mental health, and longevity [is] good relationships. Good relationships keep us healthier and happier."[19]

Could it really be that simple? Could the answer to our stress and sadness and feelings of being overwhelmed be...other people?

THE VILLAGE SOLUTION

After her disappointing doctor's visit, Lynn knew she couldn't continue going through her days without talking to another adult besides Caleb. She just needed to summon the energy—and the courage—to put herself out there.

For her job, Lynn regularly spoke to people who were at the top of their fields, but somehow talking to other parents felt far more intimidating. She pumped herself up by telling herself that if she could talk to a marketing director who managed a million-dollar budget, she could strike up a conversation about whether a two-year-old preferred bananas or oranges. She challenged herself to catch the eye of at least one mom the next time she ventured out.

One September afternoon while Dan was still in school, she took Alice to the playground after preschool. She set her belongings down and watched Alice waddle over to the sandbox where a boy around her age was playing. Another mom in a brown puffer coat hovered nearby. Lynn noticed that this mom was really dialed in to her kid. She wasn't on her phone or staring off into space, and Lynn liked that. She waited until their eyes met and then gave a little half smile.

Smiling back, the other mom pulled some snacks from her bag and asked, "Would your daughter like some goldfish? Would that be okay?"

Lynn fought her initial impulse to say, "No, thanks," and bury her head in her own bag to cut the conversation short. Instead, remembering her challenge to herself, she said, "Sure. This one is always hungry."

The other mom handed Alice a mini pouch of crackers. "I'm Addy, and this is Otto," she said, turning to Lynn. "We live around the block. How about you?" Lynn braced herself, knowing that she was about to embark on the playground equivalent of talking to the person next to her on an airplane. She felt deeply awkward, as if she had forgotten how to speak a language she once knew. But what the heck. Alice was occupied, and she couldn't sit in awkward silence forever. If she wanted to be one of those moms who laughed together as if they were part of a secret club, she was going to have to talk to another mom at some point. She told Addy she also lived a block away and asked how long they'd been in the neighborhood. They chatted for another fifteen minutes as the kids played. When Addy got ready to go, she said to Lynn, "You should give me your number."

Lynn couldn't believe how validated she felt by this simple request—like she'd been asked out on a date by her crush. She'd gotten the mom seal of approval, and it left her glowing. She texted Addy as soon as she got home to say that she was so happy that Addy asked for her number. Addy texted back right away to set up a playdate. The positive momentum was a rush.

On the day of the playdate, Lynn spent as much time getting dressed as she had getting ready for her senior prom. She tried to find an outfit that said, "Capable, approachable, normal." She was shockingly nervous as she rang the bell. What if she started to feel exhausted by having to be "on"? Before she could turn back, Addy opened the door and welcomed her in. Once inside, they set the kids down to play and let them range free while they drank the tea Addy had prepared. It was immediately obvious that Lynn had worried for nothing.

There was a lot of silence as the two kids parallel-played, but she found it suited her. She didn't feel pressure to sparkle. She could just enjoy being with another person. *Companionable* was the way she would have described it. She knew that this would be a regular occurrence.

The next time she planned to go to the playground, she texted Addy to let her know she'd be there. Addy and Otto joined them shortly after. Very quickly, almost effortlessly, they became friends, integrating their husbands into the mix. Within weeks, the two families were making themselves at home in each other's home. Lynn started to feel like herself again. One particularly pleasant afternoon, Lynn even broached the subject of how lonely she sometimes felt as a mom. She couldn't believe it when Addy confessed that she had been incredibly nervous to talk to Lynn at the playground that first time.

Eventually, Lynn even pushed herself to invite a couple of other moms and their kids from the playground over to her house. It felt so good when she recognized other people in the neighborhood as she ran errands. There was something comforting about knowing the names and faces of the people who lived near her. Her energy picked up, and her feelings of brittleness subsided.

The solution to the loneliness crisis among moms is easy to identify but not so easy to implement. I don't want to shoot sunshine and unicorns in your face. Sustaining friendships during motherhood is one of the hardest aspects of raising tiny humans. Friendships get harder when we're adults. You can't turn to the mom next to you and say, "I like your scrunchie" and then have a new bestie. Making friends is *hard*. Building a village is *hard*. My own journey has left me occasionally bruised and battered, but it has been worth it. So worth it. We all have the power to make a change. We can fight our isolation, one connection at a time.

THE FIVE C'S OF SUCCESSFUL VILLAGES

I want to acknowledge again that when you are overextended, the idea of making a change sounds exhausting. Still, I promise it's possible to push against the feelings of isolation and lean in to a village mindset. The idea of a village has fallen so far out of our collective consciousness that you may have little idea what I'm talking about. So I'm going to paint a picture for you, give you the blueprints. In my research and through my own journey, I've discovered that the most beneficial villages are cooperative, connected, consistent, compassionate, and concentric.

Cooperative. There's give-and-take in a village. You learn not only how to accept help but also how to ask for it. Radical notion, I know. At the same time, you'll strengthen ties and support other moms when you show up for them with helpful gestures grand and small.

Connected. Showing up is not just about bringing someone a tray of lasagna in the weeks after she gives birth. It's also about developing deep, trusting relationships that allow you to feel safe enough to open up and be vulnerable and connect to another perfectly imperfect person.

Consistent. A village is meant to be a familylike structure you can count on. Maintaining a village takes ongoing upkeep to help it thrive.

Compassionate. As members of a village, we cut one another some slack. We choose the most generous interpretation and give other people the benefit of the doubt. If another mom forgets to text back, we assume she was having a busy day, not that she is a total snob. This compassion extends to ourselves as well. We can't be a vital member of the community if we're always cutting ourselves down with negative self-talk.

Concentric. Villages are made up of a series of circles of people. There is an intimate, inner circle of the people we pour our hearts out to. Then there's a second circle of people with whom we enjoy social connections. Finally, there's an outer ring of people we may not invite over for dinner but with whom we have a shared sense of purpose and community.

When you have a village with these five elements, the impact can be transformational, even lifesaving. It's my hope that all of us can create a village with whatever version of these characteristics works for us.

HOW I SCRAPED MYSELF OFF THE FLOOR

I'd love to say that the day after I lost my pregnancy and cried a thousand tears on my bathroom floor, I woke up, grabbed my hard hat, and got to work building a village. That's not what happened. As I mentioned in the introduction, my village is still very much a work in progress.

Over the past few years, I have worked with intention to begin laying the foundation for a strong village. I have gathered a small but mighty group of women I trust to carry me through hard times and a larger group to whom I would gladly lend a hand without so much as a sigh.

When I was on that floor, though I felt deeply alone, I also knew full well that I wasn't carrying more than what was also being carried by most women in America. This is hard for everyone. We all have mess piled up between us and other people. Whether it is old mess, new mess, past mess, systemic mess, or psychological mess, it's all mess, and it all stands in the way of connection.

Let's start clearing away some of that mess in the next chapter.

Build Your Village

Below are a few ways to begin shifting from an isolation mindset to a village mindset.

- *Envision something different.* Take a moment to imagine what a village with all five *C*'s would look like for you. Really see yourself connecting with other people. What would that entail? A weekly walk with a friend? A group text with a few other moms? A network of parents in the neighborhood you could count on to keep an eye on your kid?
- *Identify what's holding you back.* There are six billion reasons why you might not have a village. Maybe you are consumed by your work. Maybe you live far from other people (I can relate!). Maybe your social skills are rusty and you don't trust yourself to act like a person in the presence of other people. Maybe you tried early in motherhood to make a new connection only to get hurt. What is the biggest barrier to creating connection? Can you think of one action you can take that would lower the barrier just a smidgen?
- *Establish your starting point.* You'll never reach your destination if you don't know where you're starting from. Be brutally honest with yourself about the state of your relationships. Can you name a friend you can call on for emotional support? How about one you would ask for a favor? When was the last time you enjoyed a moment of real connection with someone who was not your partner or a blood relative?

Chapter 2

The Cure for
Giving Tree Syndrome

ISOLATION MINDSET: Giving my time and energy to my children should be my top priority.

VILLAGE MINDSET: If we're going to be the moms we want to be, we must cure Giving Tree syndrome, our hard-to-kick habit of suppressing our needs in the service of everyone else's.

Sasha used to be fun. Really fun. When she was in her twenties, she had so much suck-the-marrow-out-of-life energy that for her thirtieth birthday, her friends had a shirt made for her that said I ♥ ACTIVITIES! She played basketball, went to art openings and concerts in the far reaches of Brooklyn, and threw dinner parties in her Harlem apartment, where everyone played parlor games until the sun started to lighten the sky the next morning. She was an extrovert and loved having a life that was full to the brim.

At thirty-two, she decided to start a family with her husband, Doug. They had two little girls, Chloe and Sophie, two years apart. During the girls' toddler years, Sasha hired babysitters on occasion so she could spend time with Doug and see her friends for some "activities!" after work, but as the kids grew, so did the number of activities on *their* schedules. As she entered middle school, Chloe wanted to learn to play chess and basketball, while third grader Sophie loved hockey and theater. Sasha didn't mind too much when she learned that Chloe's basketball would overlap with her regular book club meeting, because parenting involved sacrifice, right? Book club would be there when basketball season was over. Then the rehearsal schedule for Sophie's play was released, and Sasha saw that Sophie would need to be at the theater on the night she usually went to spin class. Well, okay, maybe Doug could cover rehearsals sometimes, and if not, she could wake up early to squeeze in a workout. No big deal.

She managed to keep a good attitude until she got the bad news about hockey practice. It was *before school* (ice time being a rarity). Okay. She could handle this. Her colleagues usually rolled into the office in the late morning, so she could make time to take Sophie to practice on the subway, drop her at school, and then lug the gear back home before she went in to work. So much for exercising in the morning—or getting a full night's sleep. When the new schedule began, she began to dread the rush to get ready for work, where she caught herself making mistakes because she was so tired.

The demands of motherhood had always been time-consuming, but now they seemed to be time-devouring. It felt like one of her girls needed her for something every second of every day. If she wasn't schlepping them to an activity, she was helping Sophie with her homework or making sure Chloe had the supplies she needed for her diorama or making the next round of doctor and dentist appointments or texting the girls' friends' parents to arrange for playdates for the upcoming weekend. She had become a full-time project manager for the world's cutest bosses.

It took Sasha a while to realize that the laws of the space-time continuum weren't going to bend and let her reclaim time for herself. There was no wormhole she could slip through that would allow her to be several places at once. As she tried to find time to fit in a weekly workout, she realized with a sinking feeling that there were no nights—none—blocked off on the calendar for *her.*

To make matters worse, the children's activities cut into the family's already tight budget, so with a heavy heart, she decided to skip her annual "girls' trip," when she met up with her college roommates. That was a tough decision for her, but she just didn't see another way. It wasn't like she was going to cancel her daughters' extracurriculars. They were loving them so much.

One night, just before Sasha was about to fall asleep, a text dinged on her phone. It was an old friend asking if she wanted to go see a local band that weekend. If Sasha had had the energy to do so, she would have laughed. There was no way she could make it. She had to get Sophie to a sleepover that night, which would take her an hour on the subway round-trip. A few short years before, going to a show was the kind of thing where she would have hit the auto reply "Let's do it" without a moment's hesitation. Now she couldn't remember the last time she'd been able to say "Let's do it." Heck, she couldn't remember the last time she'd left the house to do something for herself other than go to work. As if that even counted. How on earth had her life contracted so much?

GIVING TREE SYNDROME

Like so many of us moms, Sasha was suffering from what I call Giving Tree syndrome. On the off chance that you're not familiar with *The Giving Tree* by Shel Silverstein, the book tells the story of an extremely generous tree that grows alongside a boy as he becomes a man. The tree does it all—provides shade for the boy to sit under, branches for him to swing on, apples for him to sell, and wood so he can make a boat. The tree gives and gives and gives until in the end, it is reduced to a stump. It is the saddest, most messed-up book of all time. *The Giving Tree* was marketed as a children's book, but my gut says that its true audience, the reason it has sold more than ten million copies, is that the story hits moms where we live. Moms read it, and we see ourselves in the give-until-it-hurts behavior of the tree.

We moms put ourselves last in a thousand ways every day. This is a habit that begins when our children are infants and we shrug off advice to "sleep while the baby sleeps," choosing instead to scrub the counters or fold onesies while we have the chance. It's a hard habit to break. I bet you recognize this phenomenon in your own life.

Do any of the following Giving Tree tendencies sound familiar?

- Every member of your family is showered, fed, dressed, and out the door before you've had a chance to use the bathroom in the morning.
- You introduce yourself not by your name but as "X's mom."
- You listen lovingly and attentively to your child's play-by-play description of what happened at school and your partner's rant about the boss, but no one ever asks a single question inviting you to share details about your day.
- Your bedroom is your sanctuary, your refuge, your haven . . . until the kids build a fort in it that they absolutely forbid you to dismantle under penalty of death by a thousand meltdowns. The fort stays.
- You drop your kids off at a birthday party and suddenly have two free hours to yourself. You can't think of how to spend it, so you go grocery shopping and run errands for your family.
- You are up for a promotion, but you'll need to travel to mandatory training sessions to qualify. When you look at the dates for the sessions, you realize they conflict with your children's extracurriculars—so you consider waiting until next year.

I know I am guilty of putting myself last. In my first couple of years as a mom, I used to make dinner for my husband and kids before I left the house anytime I had evening plans. I made sure everyone had eaten a full meal, had brushed and flossed and pottied, and was on the way to bed with the next day's outfit folded on the dresser before I would dare sneak out the back door. That was my way of coping with the guilt of leaving my family behind. I wasn't worried that the kids wouldn't eat. I was worried I was failing because I wasn't the one providing the meal.

We take care of our people out of love. But there is love, and then there is obliterating our sense of self. When we neglect to give ourselves the love and care we deserve because we are tending to everyone else's needs before our own, we are sending the message "I don't matter." Sorry—what? We would never in a million trillion years let our children speak to themselves that way. So why do we send ourselves this message? Or model that behavior for our kids with our actions? It's the wrong bleeping message. We moms need to claim our right to show up as people with needs and wants and preferences—because our needs and wants and preferences are the very things that define us.

My worst bout of Giving Tree syndrome was probably the winter after I miscarried. I let my own needs slide so far down my to-do list that they nearly fell off completely. And it's no wonder—I was struggling with my mental health while trying to juggle my business and my family. And on top of that, we were in the midst of a global pandemic.

The kids were ages nine, seven, five, three, and one. The to-do list each day was mind-boggling. So many meals to shop for, prep, and cook. I needed to feed the picky eaters and then clean off the floor. Dishes, dishes, and more dishes. Diapers, bottles, laundry. Plus, we knew that we were supposed to be enriching our brood with an endless stream of stimulating activities, something that fell almost entirely on our shoulders since the pandemic had shut down so many outlets. In between diaper changes for our youngest, there were five sets of clothes the kids had outgrown that needed to be switched out. We patched together a learning plan for our older kids, who were homeschooled. Oh, and had anybody thought about taking the training wheels off the five-year-old's bike? Or whether our three-year-old should still be wearing a pull-up at night? Eric pitched in where he could, but he had a boss to answer to, so most of the weight fell on me.

My mind was constantly scanning, looking for the person I needed to help next. Was it my one-year-old with a wet diaper? My three-year-old with a skinned knee? My employee who needed a ride to the grocery store? I would help them all! Just line up and let me handle the situation. My mind was never still. But the thing about a mind constantly in motion is that it never sits with itself long enough to notice it is in crisis.

I was giving so much to other people that I saved nothing for myself. I felt absolutely wrecked. It was as if someone had been slowly but steadily siphoning off my life force while I slept.

It was clear to me that I needed to make some time for myself, if only to recharge, but that felt impossible as my list of worries grew ever longer. For one thing, our family had new money concerns. We were making much higher mortgage payments than we had been before, and it was hard to stay on top of them. For the first time since I started Latched Mama, I wondered if it had been wise to give up a stable career in real estate to start my own company. What if I had put our family at risk? Latched Mama was getting by, but the pandemic had thrown all our projections off. What was going to happen six months or a year into the future was anybody's guess. Even worrying about it felt self-indulgent. It never occurred to me to ask someone for guidance. I had gotten us into this situation, and I felt immense pressure to be the one to see us through safely.

I told myself I was on it. I was doing it all—an independent woman, large and in charge. Except that in the process of mothering my kids and my business, I completely forgot that I was also in charge of taking care of me.

On Latched Mama's Facebook page, I have seen posts from hundreds of women who, like Sasha and me, are giving until they have nothing left to give. From new moms who are struggling with the rigors of feed-on-demand and baby wearing to moms of toddlers confessing that they are ashamed about the relief they feel when they drop their children at pre-K each day, it seems to me that moms just want to know that they are not alone in feeling hollowed out by the endless giving. I can say with certainty they are not.

STRESS-CASE SCENARIO

Many of us feel like it is our responsibility to give endlessly to our families because their needs are endless. At baseline, we're responsible for keeping little ones fed, dressed, healthy, and civil. This requires an astonishing number of logistical maneuvers and superhuman levels of energy. Serving as CEO of Family, Inc., can be really, really stressful. Studies by the Pew Research Center found that 56 percent of moms felt stress about balancing work and family,[1] 41 percent of moms found being a mom tiring, and 29 percent found it stressful most of the time.[2]

On top of our own stresses, women tend to absorb most of the stress in our families. We're like a filter grabbing the gunk that weighs everyone else in the household down. The fight your kid had with her best friend, your mother's concern about your father's failing health, your partner's work stress—all that gets stuck in your system, which makes it difficult to function. As just one illustration of the toll all that stress takes, consider that eight in ten people who have an autoimmune disease to which stress is a contributing factor are women.[3]

STRESS IS A FAMILY AFFAIR

The irony of giving so much of ourselves—even out of love—is that it can harm our kids. As they develop, children use their parents as a lens to help them interpret experiences and learn to react to them. If that lens is clouded by anxiety, stress, and worry, they'll learn that the world is an unsafe place, which in turn affects their mental health. Children rely on the adults around them to teach them how to self-regulate and manage stress, in large part by example. We provide soothing through our loving touch, our steady voices, and our calm demeanor. If we are constantly stressed, it's difficult to perform those wonderful regulating actions consistently.

As Gabor Maté, child development expert and author of *The Myth of Normal*, has said, "When parents are stressed, kids are stressed."[4] Parental stress has a direct impact on children. In fact, research has shown that parents' stress levels affect kids' behavior more than the kids' own stress levels. Stress negatively affects our children's health, behavior, and cognitive development.[5]

That winter after my miscarriage, when I was giving every branch, twig, and leaf of myself to my kids, I was a perfect case study in how stress can spread through a family. I was short-tempered; the littlest things put me in a bad mood. I must have rolled my eyes at poor Eric a thousand times a day. My family walked on eggshells around me. Their sentences would start with, "Mom, I know you're tired, but..." I knew things were bad when the older kids would help the younger ones without being asked, hoping it would prevent me from snapping or raising my voice. It didn't work.

THE IDEAL PARENT IS NOT SO IDEAL

Sasha recognized that she, too, was struggling with unmanageable levels of stress. She'd been stressed before. But in the past, she could point to concrete reasons for the stress—a deadline, an illness in the family, a fender bender. Now when she tried to locate the source of her stress, the closest she could come was "societal expectations." She was killing herself trying to conform to our ideals of how a mother should behave. As sociologist Caitlyn Collins, author of *Making Motherhood Work*, pointed out, the cultural expectation is that parenthood should be "incredibly emotionally absorbing." In addition, she said, it "should be time-consuming, and it should be child-centered." Oh, and it "tends to be quite expensive."[6] That is a lot of pressure to put on parents. No wonder we are drowning.

Sasha didn't remember her own childhood requiring so much participation from her mother. Sure, she'd been on the swim team, but that was only in the summer. Mostly, she remembered tagging along as her mother went about her life, not her mother tagging along as Sasha lived hers. Nowadays, though, she would feel like a bad mom if she dragged the girls along with her as she shopped for shoes in a store. Instead, if she needs shoes, she quickly orders a pair online between meetings. There was so much emphasis on spending quality time with her kids, which meant focusing on them intensely. But whew—it wore her out.

The continual raising of expectations reminds me of a classic episode of *The Simpsons*. Homer gets a new job at a company called Globex. When he's looking to increase productivity, he asks his employees if they could just work harder. They say, "Sure thing, boss," and buckle down. Productivity goes up, so he asks again. And again, they work harder. This goes on until finally the workers have been stretched to the breaking point. Society is Homer-Simpsoning us moms, and if we don't do something about it, we are going to break down.

The expectation that we will keep giving of ourselves until there's nothing left often comes from our own families. Consider a post that appeared on the Latched Mama Facebook page. A pregnant mom was at her wit's end because she had fought with her husband over whether he could watch her toddler while she showered. He refused because he "helped out enough already." He told her that she knew what she signed up for when she became a stay-at-home mom, so she shouldn't complain about doing all of the housework and cooking, let alone ask for a little time to herself. She felt angry and defeated.

When I hear a story like that, I am full of mom rage. I want to run to the top of the nearest mountain and shout, "It's all too much!" Is it any wonder we moms are perpetually on the brink of a breakdown? We cannot be the kind of mothers—or people—we want to be if we don't take care of ourselves. We need to let go of the idea that we serve our families best by serving our families exclusively.

GETTING BUY-IN

The problem with our invisible isolation is that it is invisible to everyone else. Other people just don't see it. Even the most supportive partners and friends might not be champing at the bit to relinquish the time they spend with you. So the only way we are going to be able to create time and space for ourselves is if we claim it.

Sasha decided to do just that. She sat down with Doug and explained how stretched she felt by the kids' schedules. She told him that if she didn't manage to carve out some Sasha time, she wasn't sure how she was going to get through her days. Doug was understanding and said all the right things—all the right things except, "How can I help?" She almost let it go—just bringing up how upset she was had been hard enough—but when she thought about another month of scrambling from one kid activity to another, she dug in.

She said, "I'm glad you seem to understand the problem. I have an idea for something that would really help. I need time for myself so that I can recharge. Can we think of a couple of ways to carve some out for me?" Once she asked directly, Doug agreed to help out. Ultimately, he decided to ask his boss if he could shift his work schedule to two hours earlier twice a month so that he could cover taking Chloe to basketball while Sasha went to book club and so Sasha could have one other night to do whatever she darn well wanted to. She missed the special time with Chloe, but her heart was so much lighter because she had affirmed that spending time on herself was valuable.

We can set the stage for a transition to a village-focused life by being open and honest with the people in our lives who will be affected by the shift. We can say to our mothers, our sisters, our best friends, our partners, "Hey, you are amazing, and I cherish our relationship, but I've got some mom stuff to deal with. I might be a little less available for a while, but know that I love you, and I need this." It can be a terrifying conversation to have because we are so conditioned to give as unquestioningly as the Giving Tree did, regardless of the impact it's having on us. It takes courage to upset the status quo, even when you are talking to people who care deeply about you.

WALKING BACK TO MYSELF

I had to have my own hard conversation with Eric when I was ready to claim time for myself. During the worst of my invisible isolation, I was able to pinpoint my feelings of loneliness as the source of my stress. I knew I needed to get out and connect with other people, but I didn't feel ready to do so right away. Who would want to talk to the jittery, short-fused stress ball I had become? *I* didn't want to hang out with me. And I couldn't imagine asking another person to spend time with me in that state. Before I could connect with other people, I needed to connect with myself again.

It was time to put myself back on the list so I could feel worthy of connection. Not first on the list, maybe, but at least on it. I knew that in order to do so I would need to set a boundary with Eric and the kids. I decided that I was going to walk every single day in the morning by myself, for myself. I was going to have to get my family on board. I sat Eric down to tell him my plan. I was nervous. My palms were as sweaty as they would have been had I confessed that I'd forgotten to mail our mortgage payment and the bank was coming for the farm. That's how bad my Giving Tree syndrome was. I had trouble asking for even a small slice of time for myself. I was afraid that Eric would think I was slacking in my mothering duties.

Negotiating time for anything other than your family can be hard, especially if you've neglected yourself for so long that it has become a habit for you and an expectation for others. When I told Eric, "This is something I need to do for me," he bristled.

He complained that I was passing the buck to him, leaving him to oversee making breakfast for all five kids. I told him he was right. I *was* passing the buck, but it was one that I'd been holding on to for the past few years, and I was going to drop it if someone didn't help me manage all I was holding. I told him, gently, that I needed to let him take charge while I recharged. He agreed, though that didn't stop him from grumbling "Enjoy your me time" that first morning.

The kids didn't love it, either. They'd gotten used to knowing where I was at all times, a situation that was on me. I mean, I let them come in the bathroom with me. But in this case I was firm and told them, "No. This is my time." I left the house each day and walked a mile-and-a-half circuit through the fields around the farm. It was such a little thing, those thirty minutes each morning, but taking those steps is the perfect metaphor for the beginning of my journey toward a village.

It was January, and it was freezing out there, but it was also quiet and calm. I was able to be completely alone with my thoughts, which felt different from lonely. I played Taylor Swift's *Folklore* album on loop. Something about listening to that album pierced my emotional armor. It was as if she were giving me permission to see that I hadn't been fair to myself. Like many women, I'd based my personal value on how much I could give to other people, how valuable I was to them, but what if that was the wrong currency to measure? What if there was more to me than who I was to my family and my business? What would that even mean? Who was I beyond a mother, wife, and boss? For so long I'd depended on being a good girl—doing everything I was supposed to do—to show the world I was worthy, but I was starting to wonder whether channeling all my energy toward making everyone happy meant that I was doomed to unhappiness myself.

For the first time in ten years, I could hear myself think. I saw how I'd been numbing myself and my emotions, not with drugs or alcohol or even TV but by staying constantly busy—with work and with taking care of everyone's needs. I'd gotten so used to not feeling love for myself that when the feelings came back it hurt, as if blood were coming back into my leg after I'd been sitting on it too long. But I was ready to stop numbing myself. I didn't want to keep turning away. In those cold, quiet fields, I knew in my gut that I needed to reconnect with myself, not just so I could be a better parent but also so I could be a person who felt worthy of connecting to other people.

Each morning after my walk, I returned to my family with the same number of items on my to-do list but with less panic about whether doing them well would determine if I was lovable. I felt more grounded, centered. Life was coming back to my limbs.

Once Eric saw how much happier I was on the days I walked, he became a morning walk booster. He made sure I had an umbrella on rainy days and had coffee waiting for me when I returned.

CHOOSING ME TIME OVER FREE TIME

By going for those long walks, I had inadvertently made a wise choice. I was choosing to do something that filled me up instead of something that numbed me even more. It is so tempting to spend your precious free minutes chilling the heck out—and I want to be clear that there's nothing wrong with taking a break and doing absolutely nothing when you need to—but when you are feeling like an empty husk, rather than flopping down to watch Netflix and switching off your brain, it may be more beneficial to make time for something that reminds you of who you are, something that fills you up. Researcher Cassie Holmes, PhD, a professor of marketing and behavioral decision-making at UCLA Anderson School of Management, found that having between two to five hours of time during the day where you're doing something *you* want to be doing—whether it's fencing or playing the piano or sitting on the porch with a friend—is optimal for life satisfaction.[7] Two hours feels like a moon shot, but could you do twenty minutes a day? Or maybe a night once a week when you close the door to your room and read? Whatever shape it takes, claim that time with confidence, knowing that it's not only the right choice for you, it's also the right choice for your family.

Is clearing twenty minutes a day for yourself or asking for two free nights a month going to solve every problem you have? Probably not. But it will remind you of who you are and that you are someone worth connecting to. Coming back to ourselves helps enormously as we start the hard work of connecting to other people. We need to remind ourselves (and everyone else) that we matter. And we need to remember that tending to ourselves doesn't negate our ability to love and nurture our families. The next time you're tempted to bury your needs under everyone else's, say no to being a stump. Be a freaking tree. Let's cultivate a glorious forest where we can all grow together.

Build Your Village

Ready to tackle your Giving Tree syndrome? Below are few small steps you can take.

- *Investigate yourself.* If you're having trouble figuring out where to start as you rediscover who you are, imagine that you are a journalist tasked with the assignment of writing a profile of yourself. What would you include? How would you describe yourself? What are some of the things you do or think or enjoy that make you *you*? Are you someone who derives joy from the natural world? Do you feel most alive when you are intellectually engaged? Are you a foodie who gets a thrill from trying a new recipe?

- *Onboard your people.* Finding time for yourself needs to be a group effort. Make a list of reasons why doing so is important—essential, even—to your well-being. Then have conversations with the people who will be most affected by your (rightly!) prioritizing yourself once in a while. Explain to them why you need to make changes and then acknowledge that it will affect them. Take the time to get your partner and friends and family members on board with your village mission. Help them understand that while they might need to make some sacrifices—like spending less time with your wonderful self—the benefits to the family will be worth it. Time spent with other people is time you aren't spending with your partner, which can lead to anger and resentment. Creating a village is a group effort. The more you can get your people on board by being transparent about your efforts, the less resistance you'll meet.

- *Take twenty.* If you feel ready to banish Giving Tree syndrome and reconnect with yourself, carve out time to do something meaningful and self-affirming. Start by trying to set aside twenty minutes a day for me time. The rule is that this should not be something related to your kids or your partner or your identity as a mom. Don't worry—the kids will live. Twenty minutes away from their mom is not a scarring experience. In fact, it's a good experience for them. Your me time can be spent listening to a specially curated Spotify playlist, bird-watching in the park, or enjoying a slice of blueberry pie with no distractions. It can be spent writing a journal entry or clicking through old family photos on your phone or throwing a ball to your dog in the backyard. It doesn't matter what you are doing as long as you are doing something that fills you up.

Chapter 3

Making New Friends Just Sounds Like More Work

ISOLATION MINDSET: My life is so busy that I barely have time to put on pants every morning. And now you're telling me to make time for more people in my life? No, thank you.

VILLAGE MINDSET: The answer to feeling overwhelmed and isolated is not more pressure and isolation. Adding the right kind of connection will make our lives feel lighter, not heavier.

*B*efore I became a mom, I considered myself busy when I had a brunch and an engagement party to attend on the same weekend afternoon. I'd roll out of bed, enjoy a cup of coffee while still in my pajamas and last night's mascara, flip through a magazine, then spend twenty minutes in the shower before picking out a "look" that would work for both events. How was life ever so carefree and relaxing? How could a day have been so blissfully unproductive?

I remember those days fondly. And don't get me wrong: although I miss them, I love my life now. I love having a job that I'm passionate about and six kids who continually surprise and delight me. At the same time, my days feel *relentless*, as if there are only half as many hours as I need to complete the tasks that come down life's conveyor belt. I know I'm not the only one who looks back on preparenthood life through rose-colored mom goggles. According to research on how moms spend their days, we feel insanely busy because we *are* insanely busy.

There are 168 hours in a week. If we spend fifty-six of those hours asleep (Ha! As if any mom is getting eight hours a night), that leaves 112 hours to do everything we need to do each week—from work to filling the car up with gas to making dinner to scheduling a mammogram. The typical American mom with children under twelve years old spends approximately eight hours a day doing activities that are directly or indirectly related to childcare.[1] That's on top of any paid work she might do to support her family. One study found that moms with jobs outside the home put in ninety-eight hours of work a week between home and office. If you're keeping score, that is 2.5 full-time jobs' worth of work.[2] There's no denying it: the number of obligations and demands on moms just doesn't leave many of those 112 hours for finding and maintaining a village.

No wonder people roll their eyes when I tell them how important it is to make time to find their people. Connecting feels like another item on an endless to-do list. Time and energy are limited resources, and kids suck up the majority of those resources. Cultivating connection with other moms is an effort. Who wants to put on clean clothes to go out with friends or organize a book club when you are barely able to power through to the end of each day? Or when you're toggling so frantically between work and home that you feel like you're blowing it at both?

Being part of a village can feel like just one more obligation. One more ask when you're all asked out. We already have our kids, our partners, our extended families, and in some cases our work relationships to maintain, and we're also supposed to find energy for all the effort it takes to sustain connection? If you had asked me why I didn't have a village before I realized that I wouldn't survive motherhood without one, I would have simply said, "I don't have time or space for anyone else in my life."

The nonstop work that comes with being a mother can leave us feeling like the last thing we want to do is dig up the energy to talk with another person. This was the case for Alexis, a mom of two young boys who lives in suburban Iowa.

As the exhausted mom of three-year-old Sam and two-month-old Max, Alexis no longer recognized herself. When she looked in the bathroom mirror in the morning, instead of the bright, eager face that had looked back at her premotherhood, she saw a woman with frizzy hair and dark circles under her eyes. *She* was that woman?

She'd once been the queen of self-care. Not just the kind of basic maintenance that involved touching up her roots and making sure she was up-to-date on her dental visits but also the kind that kept her emotional system regulated. When she wasn't churning out press releases for the pharmaceuticals company she worked for, she did yoga. She made time to walk in the woods near her house a few times a week. She had long, in-depth conversations with friends at sidewalk cafés. But once she took her second maternity leave, she found the kind of person who was able to do all those things incredibly punchable. Woods? She would have loved to walk in the woods, but she knew that taking even a short walk with the boys would require her to prepare as if she were launching a minor military campaign. She'd need to equip herself with a baby carrier, countless stuffies, diapers, squeezie packs, teethers, burp cloths, extra clothes—and a strategic plan for a place to sit while breastfeeding Max.

The boys were joyous little creatures. Sweetly observant three-year-old Sam lit up anytime a cement mixer or garbage truck went by, and by two months old, Max was already smiling real smiles. One of those puppies could charge her heart's battery for days. But her kids' smiles didn't provide her with actual energy. As much as she loved them, the boys just needed *so much* from her. Now that she was home all day with Max, she and her husband, Joel, couldn't justify the cost of putting Sam in day care, so from 7:45 a.m., when Joel left for work, until 6:30 p.m., when he came home, it was the Alexis Show, up to her to keep the boys continually entertained and enriched.

She felt as if every moment of her days with the boys smashed into the next at full speed and, simultaneously, that time had never moved so slowly. She did everything the books and websites said to do. She made a point of speaking to Sam and Max while making good eye contact—she had read that it was important to build their budding vocabularies. She organized games like "smell the spices" to stimulate the formation of new neural pathways. She sang to them. And she kept them on a strict nap schedule. The Alexis Show also spilled over into the wee hours of the night, when she stumbled out of bed to nurse Max. The constant pressure to keep the boys fed might have been the worst of it. Why had no one warned her how draining feeding two young children would be? It seemed like she was serving, preparing, or cleaning up a meal every fifteen minutes. No sooner had she finished giving Sam his lunch than Max would wake up from his nap shrieking for milk. Milk, milk, milk. Grilled cheese, cheese quesadillas, cheese sticks. She felt like a one-woman dairy farm.

While a walk just for funsies felt off the table, she did force herself to leave the house with some regularity. In addition to making trips out for grocery shopping and construction-vehicle viewing, she was religious about attending the weekly Music Together class in her neighborhood with the boys. She felt good about the fact that the boys were socializing, and intellectually she knew those gatherings were a chance for her to socialize as well. There were a dozen other moms in the class wrangling their kids and gamely clapping along to "The Wheels on the Bus," and some of them had even flashed a welcoming smile when she'd met their eyes, but the thought of actually engaging with another mom while juggling her kiddos felt like it would break her. She came back from those outings zapped. Each night, as six thirty finally approached, she watched the clock intently, willing the minutes to tick by faster so that Joel could relieve her and at least hold one of the kids while she took a five-minute breather.

She often felt resentful, and she chastised herself for it. She knew that she should be relishing the sweetness of these days with the boys—"They go by so fast," everyone said. But she caught herself glowering at the carefree women she saw walking perkily by during her outings with the boys, carrying yoga mats and nothing else.

One frigid February morning as Alexis made breakfast, still bleary from the previous night's feedings, it began to snow. When she thought about the extra time it would take to cram snowsuits onto the squirming boys in order to get them to Music Together, her heart sank. Actually, every single molecule in her body sank as she realized she would have to wake them early from their naps, which meant they would be cranky. She pictured the roomful of parents and children she planned to join and felt repelled. She was not in the mood to socialize. She was not in the mood to make small talk about feeding schedules. She was not in the mood to meet new people. She was in the mood to sit down on her couch and never get up.

What had happened to her? She used to welcome the opportunity to interact with other people. But when was the last time she had spoken to another adult who wasn't her husband? Part of her reluctance to attend the class that day, she realized, was that in the nonstop managing of her children's needs, she had forgotten how to talk with other people like a normal human. She was out of practice, and the longer she went without talking with other adults, the harder it seemed. Something needed to change.

I can one hundred percent relate to that feeling. After my fifth child, Katherine, was born, we were still living in our old house, where there were moms aplenty nearby. However, between childcare tasks and my business, my life had become overfull. Pair that with my introverted nature, and the idea of socializing with another adult human started to feel like it would take herculean effort. I felt so needed by this little human and by all the other little humans who filled my days, but I didn't have a lot left in my tank for other people. There were moments when I felt like a helpless, sleep-deprived newborn myself, unaware of exactly what I needed, just hoping that someone would show up and mother *me* for a change. But when you're an adult, people expect you to use your words and tell them what you need and how they can help you. I couldn't come up with any words. Having to speak to anyone other than my sweet, needy baby had begun to fill me with dread and anxiety.

Each day, around three o'clock, as her siblings were at their peak rowdiness with their sitter, I'd strap Katherine in her car seat and travel to Starbucks. I'd look into the coffee shop through the window as I turned into the parking lot and see people sharing a table, heads leaning toward one another as they talked. Every once in a while, I'd have a pang of regret. *Maybe,* I'd think, *I should go inside and interact with other humans—or even invite a friend to join me.* But then I'd shake my head to rid it of that idea, deciding, *Those people must not be as busy taking care of a newborn baby as I am.* So instead of going inside, I'd pull around to the drive-through window, where I had cultivated my dream relationship with the staff. I would arrive at the window, smile without a word, and they would give me exactly what I thought I needed: my daily caffeine-and-sugar fix, a venti iced latte and two big chocolate chip cookies. I'd drive around to the back of the store and sit next to the retention pond watching the ducks while mainlining sugar. I felt so very vulnerable in my isolation, but there was also a sense of peace: for a few minutes, I didn't have to be anything to anyone. It was perfect. I didn't need a village; I needed my sugar fix. Now go away.

Like Alexis and me, you probably have 107 excuses for why you don't have the time and energy to waste on building your village—you're tired; you don't have a spare second to leave the house; you just want to sit there and watch your *Friends* marathon; you just want to be left alone.

I get it. It takes a lot of courage to introduce yourself to another mom at the playground or put in the extra effort required to transform someone from an acquaintance into a friend—especially when your kid is going through a sleep regression and you feel like the walking dead. Most of us assume that our "make new friends" stage is over after college. Still, as much as my afternoons with sugar and the ducks brought me momentary peace, sending a text while I drank my coffee or sharing those moments with another human being would have benefited me more. The cure for isolation and overwhelm is not to seek out more isolation so you can appreciate how overwhelmed you are. If you can get over that "I just don't wanna" feeling, you can reap the amazing benefits that come from cobbling together the beginnings of a village.

WHY IT'S WORTH THE EFFORT TO GET OFF THE COUCH AND START YOUR VILLAGE ALREADY

When you start building your village, the benefits add up pretty quickly. Even a village of just a few choice mom friends will help lighten your load and enrich your life. Below are just a few of the upsides of having a community to support you as you do the hard work of being a mother.

> *It's great for your health.* As I mentioned in chapter 1, increased connection helps you live longer and feel happier in the years you do have.

It keeps you in the know. Being around other moms allows you to tap into a flow of useful information. When you chat around the sandbox, you get the goods on which day care to avoid, which pediatricians will see you at a moment's notice, and the best kung fu program with an antibullying curriculum. Other moms are the ultimate resource.

It's good for your kid's brain and socialization. A 2019 study conducted at the University of Tennessee Health Science Center found that the children of moms with strong social connections had better cognitive development at two years old than the children of mothers with poor social connections.[3]

The study also found that the moms who socialized often did so with moms who have kids, offering opportunities for playdates, which helped their kids learn how to be around other kids.

It allows you access to the various versions of who you are. Humans are socially complex creatures. We bring many aspects of ourselves to our relationships with other people. With your friend from high school, you might be silly and nostalgic. Your neighbor might bring out the upright citizen in you. You might foreground your diligence and smarts around your coworkers. You contain multitudes, and being around many different people helps you remember parts of yourself that will wither up and die if you don't nourish them. Increasing the number of people you interact with will remind you of your astonishing range and talents.

PLOT TWIST:
ADD MORE MEANING,
FEEL LESS OVERWHELM

Even the above excellent reasons for building a village may not be enough to dislodge you from the couch cushions for a mom meetup. You still may feel like all the benefits in the world are not enough to motivate you because the weight of your responsibilities is simply too heavy. But what if I told you that having more people in your life will make you feel lighter and less overwhelmed?

This is the biggest reason to get yourself a village ASAP: *Having a village makes your life easier.*

Doing it all yourself is inefficient. Consider carpooling, for example. Half of parents spend five or more hours a week driving their kids from place to place.[4] Carpooling saves you time, energy, and money. Linking up with other parents will give you more breathing room in your life.

Not only will life be easier if you have a village, it will also feel easier.

Research has found that although we may think we crave uncluttered calendars, we are happier if we have some activity—as long as it's meaningful activity. And as we've already seen, there is no activity more meaningful than connecting with another human being. So while it might seem like a big "ugh" to add something else to your plate, that something else just might be the exact nourishment you need. "The goal is to make our time more fulfilling...not just full," according to Cassie Holmes. You may still have a jam-packed schedule, but by making your time feel more meaningful, you will also feel less mentally spent.[5]

IT DOESN'T HAVE TO BE DIFFICULT

When we're tuckered out and overwhelmed, often the last thing we feel like doing is reaching out to others. It takes So. Much. Effort. Like Alexis, many of us find ourselves carrying so much mental and emotional weight that the slightest additional burden feels as though it could break us. When we're in that dark place, the psychological lifting involved in communing with a fellow human can seem more exhausting than a two-hour spin class.

But if you are willing to look out for little moments where you can squeeze in connection, you will spot them—and they will almost definitely make you feel better. It is one of the great paradoxes of connection that the times when you least feel like making an effort may be the times when you'll derive the greatest benefit from making an effort.

A good way to help yourself get over that initial inertia is to make the lift a small one. There are dozens of painless ways to add connection without rearranging your entire life. Start small. You don't need to bare your soul to the mom sitting next to you during the PTA meeting, but you could compliment her on the smart question she asked. You don't need to volunteer to do in-home care for your neighbor who is recovering from breast cancer, but maybe you could bring her some soup next time you make a big pot. You don't need to go to every gathering held by the parents' meetup group in your neighborhood, but you could follow the social media account and comment now and then to get engaged in the conversation.

When poor exhausted Alexis realized that she needed to learn to talk to adults again, she started small. She decided to take advantage of an activity she already had in her schedule as an opportunity for connection—the weekly Music Together class.

She had noticed that some of the other moms didn't just plop their babies on a blanket and then wait for the teacher. They talked to one another before class—some even kept chatting during the music as their kids wiggled and jiggled. Where were these women getting this energy?

As tired as Alexis was, she had to admit that it would be more fun to be in a room where she knew the adults, not just their babies. She decided it was time to put some "together" in those Music Together classes. She resolved to meet at least one other person at her next session. When the time came, she thought of one mom in particular who seemed like she might be a good personality match. Karla came to class each week with a round-cheeked toddler named Evan, and she carried a tote bag from Alexis's favorite bookstore as her diaper bag, which felt like a promising sign.

At the next session, while the instructor greeted the latecomers, Alexis walked toward an open spot on the floor next to Karla. Max snoozed in his Ergo as she guided Sam by the hand. She was nearly overcome by bone-deep emotional fatigue when she imagined talking to a stranger. It could be so draining to put on a cheerful front. Or potentially awkward if she got snubbed. Or what if she felt pressure to talk to Karla every week when all she wanted was to get through class and go home? She nearly bailed, but at that moment, Karla looked up, and Alexis spit out, "Mind if we park here?" Karla smiled, and Alexis took that as her cue to sit down. Alexis pointed at the tote bag and said, "I've been meaning to get back there for weeks now. Have you read anything good lately?" Karla arched an eyebrow and said, "You mean other than *Goodnight Moon*?" That kicked off an exchange between the two moms that lasted through the class.

The following week, Alexis showed up early so she could have an extra five minutes to talk with Karla before the instructor arrived. She was delighted to find that Karla had saved her a space on the floor. The two moms didn't always have the world's most engaging conversations: let's face it—it's hard to find your soulmate while toddlers are tossing colorful handkerchiefs and shaking maracas between you. But she'd done it. She'd made the effort. And you know what? After she got over the hump of her social anxiety, it really wasn't that hard.

A few weeks later, Alexis found herself feeling even more grateful that she'd made an effort when Max blew out his diaper just as the teacher was starting Sam's favorite part of class. Alexis groaned. Karla stuck out her tongue playfully in a "yuck" face and told Alexis, "You go handle that situation. I've got Sam." Alexis grabbed Max and made a beeline for the bathroom while Sam danced happily. Karla's lending a hand was a small thing, but it was also huge. A diaper disaster was just the sort of event that might have crushed Alexis if she'd had to handle it by herself, but that day, she left class feeling light and happy.

PUT ON YOUR SNEAKERS

When she worked up the courage to talk to Karla, Alexis had what I call a "put on your sneakers" experience. This is moment when you get yourself to do one small thing—one really, really doable thing, like putting on your sneakers—to give yourself the push you need to do a bigger, more daunting thing, like going to the gym or getting out of the house in terrible weather to run an errand. You might not have the desire or energy to go out, but surely you can muster the can-do to put on your shoes, right? And then how about walking to the car? No big deal. The trick is to stay focused on the small immediate effort instead of cowering in front of the looming shadow of the long term. It's all about getting over the initial hump. Do one small thing at a time, and pretty soon, you're in the middle of doing the thing you've been dreading or putting off. Most of the time, that thing is actually kind of fun. (My friends and I joke about this when we talk about motivating ourselves to have sex in a long-term relationship, but it applies here, too!)

When you're trying to take that one small step, just remember that you are not necessarily hunting for the Thelma to your Louise. You're just coaxing open a few tendrils of connection that will give you a little support when life feels overwhelming.

HOW I LACED UP

During those long weeks postpartum, I knew pretty quickly that my daily Starbucks sugar fix was not the long-term cure for the bad case of extreme isolation I was experiencing, so when Katherine was around two months old, I put on my sneakers.

Years earlier, I'd put together a benefit for a friend who was fighting cancer. I had asked people to donate whatever items they could, and I planned to sell them at a yard sale and use the proceeds to help pay my friend's medical bills. I had good intentions, but I went overboard, trying to make it the World's Greatest Yard Sale. I rented a tent and tables and hired some of my Latched Mama employees to help out with sales. I imagined being able to present my friend with a hefty check by the end of the day. We had a nice flow of people, but not nearly enough to reach my overly ambitious goal. Not by a mile. By three o'clock on the afternoon of the event, all my employees had gone home, and I was left to deal with tables full of unpurchased donations to pack up and send to Goodwill. We actually *lost* money that day. Just then, as I was feeling like an idiot who couldn't do anything right, in walked Lindi with her twins.

Lindi was a former high school classmate—an incredible art-
ist I'd admired from afar. We weren't friends in high school. I
suspected she didn't even know who I was. I sure knew who she
was, though. I'd watched her work in art class, where everything
she touched turned out beautifully, as if making art were as easy
for her as breathing. I lost track of her after graduation, but now
here she was twenty years later, walking back into my life at that
low moment.

I wished the ground would swallow me so Lindi couldn't see
what a flop this yard sale had turned out to be—and by extension
what a failure I was—but I didn't have the energy to pretend that
I was happy with how things had turned out. I was in a moment
of utter vulnerability, and without even thinking, I blurted out,
"Hey, I'm Melissa. We used to sit next to each other in, like, an art
class." She did that pretend-excitement thing you do when someone remembers you and you definitely don't remember her.

"Melissa! From high school! What was your maiden name
again?" I told her, though her eyes showed zero recollection of who
I was. "It's great to see you again," I managed. I glanced down at
the three diaper covers she had in her hand and said ruefully, "Do
you want to look around a little more? We still have plenty of stuff
left. I think I *may* have overestimated how many people wanted to
buy used baby things." I pointed to the tables still piled high with
onesies and Moby Wraps. As she looked around, I asked, "What
have you been up to since I last saw you?" It turned out she was
a clothing designer, which was something we very much needed
at Latched Mama. I filed that info away, and to my surprise, she
asked to exchange numbers before we said goodbye.

We kept in touch, and once I saw her work, I began trying to
recruit her for my team. She wasn't able to join us until around a

year later, but when she did, we began a relationship that became the foundation of my village.

As we worked side by side, I saw that she was not only creative and hardworking but also very self-aware. She had more kids than I did (five to my three at the time), but she had the good sense to make herself a priority every once in a while. I knew I wanted this woman in my life outside of work, but the idea of making a new friend felt like a tall mountain to climb. I wasn't able to work up the courage to tell her I wanted her to be my friend—that was too hard, and I couldn't do it. But I could ask her to hang out outside of work once in a while. That was doable. But when? I was already struggling to find time to talk to Eric each day.

Then I hit upon a solution: I asked her to join me for a morning walk. I felt like a nervous teenager asking her for a date, and my heart did backflips when she agreed. I began showing up at her house on my way to the office. All I had to do was put Katherine in a carrier, put on my sneakers (literally), and go ring her doorbell. We'd walk for miles. Some days we didn't talk much. Some days we talked nonstop. As the number of morning walks increased, my afternoon Starbucks trips decreased, and so did my feeling of not measuring up as a mom. Things started feeling more manageable. Part of it was giving my body and hormones time to regulate. Part of it was moving my body (thank you, endorphins), but mostly it was the connection and happiness our daily conversations brought to my life. I didn't have to add anything extra to my to-do list. I just added the magic of connection, and it made a difference.

I know your day is already filled to bursting, but making a few small changes may be easier than you think. Put on your sneakers and get out there.

Build Your Village

Below are a few ways you can put on your sneakers.

- *Identify your options.* Make a list of the regular activities where you run into other people—maybe it's pickup from day care or taking your eighth grader to basketball practice—and make a point of showing up five minutes early or lingering for five minutes afterward to speak to another regular. You don't have to invite that person to your birthday party or get into a debate about the Middle East. Just engage in some small talk about the activity you're there for.
- *Make errands do double duty.* Errands. There are so damn many of them. We usually knock them off our lists solo, but if you are heading to Costco or Target or the dry cleaner, ask a friend if she would like to join you. Errands that require time but not a lot of brainpower are excellent opportunities to put on your sneakers. Next time you sit down to match a basket of socks, put a friend on speakerphone to keep you company as you work.
- *Work together.* If you work in an office, skip the sad desk lunch and either spend your lunch break eating with a coworker or writing an email to a friend. If you work from home, ask a friend or colleague if she would like to work out of your home, a sort of grown-up parallel play. If you stay home with your children, invite another mom over with her kids as you fold laundry or make lunch.
- *Assess your success.* Take an emotional inventory of how you feel before and after doing any of the above. Did adding a bit of connection drain your battery or charge it?

Chapter 4

Mom Friend Impostor Syndrome

ISOLATION MINDSET: I drop more balls than a basketball team. I have no idea what I'm doing as a mom. Who would want me as a friend?

VILLAGE MINDSET: I'm an imperfect work in progress, and so is everyone else. Perfectionism is a toxic force that keeps us apart when we need one another most.

*L*et me tell you about my friend Kim. I met Kim in my prenatal program in 2012, when I was pregnant with my first child, Nathan. She was my first mom friend.

You know how some women just seem to have been born comfortable with who they are? When I first met Kim, that was the impression she gave me. She radiated calm, like a walking meditation app. I never saw her get flustered or freaked out by the information the midwife shared with us about what was going on in our bodies or what we could expect when it was time for us to give birth. Kim was small and soft-spoken, but she had a strength, a solidity, that I was drawn to.

We got to know each other in the moments before and after class, and eventually, we started arranging to meet for coffee on the weekends (just one cup, of course!). During our talks, I learned that she came from a large family that had its share of strife. Her mom had died when she was young, so Kim didn't have many memories of her. Kim shared that information with me like it was no big deal. She seemed to have processed that trauma and found happiness in adulthood, which left me in awe. I didn't have anyone in my life like her.

Kim was just so...perfect. Even her home was perfect: the interiors were Instagram-worthy, with a midcentury-modern vibe. She was the kind of host who serves lemonade from a glass pitcher with lemon slices floating in it. Going to her house was like walking into a *Martha Stewart Living* spread. I was always afraid I would knock something over with my pregnant belly or spill something on her rug. Before we had our babies, she hosted gatherings for our prenatal group that could only be described as gracious. I had no idea that living, breathing people threw parties like these. They had color schemes. They had invitations. They had *themes*.

As our due dates approached, I pictured the two of us visiting each other's newborn and celebrating the miracle of our babies' births. We'd remain friends and meet up for brunch, glowing with contentment as our little angels slept in bassinets by our feet. We would drink mimosas and chat happily about how adorable our babies were.

I loved being around Kim, but at the same time, witnessing her excellence somehow made me feel bad about myself. It seemed like she was in charge of her life, while I was just pretending to be in charge of mine. I felt like a total impostor around her—a feeling shared by a lot of moms I know when other moms appear so much more put together. This feeling of not measuring up can really screw up our chances of connecting.

Even today, when faced with the prospect of making new mom friends, I struggle with a mean case of impostor syndrome. My mind starts a litany of self-criticism—*You don't do enough. You're blowing it at work* and *at home. Your house is a mess*—and it reminds me of the insecurity of my adolescent years, when it felt like no matter how hard I tried, I could never live up to the standards other girls seemed to meet effortlessly.

I'm feeling that impostor syndrome right now. What business do *I* have writing about how to build connection with other people when I have a hard time with it myself? I identify as an introvert—why should you listen to me? But, as I wrote above, I decided I am qualified to write about building connection precisely *because* I struggle with it, as we all do. I have all the same doubts you do about whether I have what it takes to surround myself with a vibrant community. I have sat among a group of women, sizing them up, and thought, *There are ten other people in this room who have brushed their hair, gotten their kids to swim practice on time, and cooked heathy dinners every night this week—none of which you have managed to do, Melissa. What makes you think you have anything to share with these obviously amazing people? Why would any of them want to speak with you?*

I started to let that kind of thinking get to me after Kim and I gave birth to our babies.

Nathan arrived in a hurry in the back of our SUV on the way to the hospital, while Kim labored with Evan all day and all night before she underwent a C-section. In hindsight, I can see that she was pretty devastated and overwhelmed by the experience. But at the time, you would never have known it, because it looked to me like she hadn't missed a beat as she stepped right back into her life. Her beautiful, beautiful life.

I thought that after she had her baby, Kim might take a hiatus from entertaining, but instead, baby in tow, she jumped right back into hosting, referring to her gatherings as "Mommy Marvel" parties. She diligently documented the events on Instagram. I'd scroll through the perfect shots of dimples and plump little thighs in the privacy of my home and feel a sense of despair because my postpartum life felt anything but Instagram-worthy. After Nathan was born, my house looked like a construction site with no construction going on. It was as if a hurricane had blown through, picking up every shred of peace and organization I had cultivated and smashing them into the walls, leaving debris everywhere. There was actual debris everywhere.

I was incapable of keeping house because Nathan had acid reflux and colic. (I can tell if your kid had colic by the way you responded to that sentence. If your reaction to the word *colic* was,

"Oh, so he cried a lot?" I envy you. But if, when you read that, the blood drained from your face and your stomach clenched as if someone just pulled a firearm from their waistband, I see you, sister.)

When my baby wouldn't stop crying, I did what I'd been trained to do. I read the books. I listened to the podcasts. I went down every rabbit hole on the internet, but nothing Eric and I tried seemed to help. There were nights when I ate my dinner with Nathan resting on my chest in the bathtub because that was the only way he would settle down. I felt outmatched, defeated.

I'd thought I would sit around sniffing my baby's sweet little head as he cooed. But he didn't coo—he cried. All. The. Time. I'd thought having a baby would be a beautiful, amazing experience where I fell cuckoo-banana-pants in love. Instead, I was walking around asking desperately, "Why is it crying?"

I felt totally alone. Based on what I could tell from our sporadic texts and phone calls, Kim was able to get baby Evan to nurse happily, sleep regularly, and make cute little noises. She'd gotten the baby we'd both expected to have, and I'd gotten a little Martian. I couldn't even begin to explain what life with Nathan was like to friends, least of all Kim. We tried to connect, but we went from walking together on the same path to being in different hemispheres. Her life hadn't stopped. She and her partner were going out and doing all the things with their baby that I had assumed I would be able to do—take walks in the park, visit friends, even eat in restaurants. She'd invite us, but we'd bail because we knew it would be miserable with Nathan. We did go out to dinner once so the boys could "meet." Evan slept through dinner and never woke up, and Nathan screamed the entire time.

Finally, I took Nathan to the pediatrician and said, "There is something wrong with my baby." The doctor examined Nathan and told me, "This is what babies do. You got a hard one. You just have to wait it out. Try to keep him entertained." Thanks a lot, Doc. Waiting it out sounds so simple, but when your child is screeching 24-7 in what sounds like pain, it is not simple at all.

One result of not being able to soothe Nathan was that I became extremely self-conscious about what people would think of me as a mom. I worried if I so much as stepped outside with my howler monkey, everyone would see what a bad mom I was. Judgment came from all corners—especially the internet, where no matter what approach you take to soothing your baby's reflux or colic, there is a flamethrower with your name on it. Just when I had convinced myself that I might be overly sensitive to the possibility of being scorned for my parenting, I heard an actress I respected on a podcast. She was laughing with the hosts, telling them that when she was feeling bad about her skills as a mom, she would go to the grocery store and see someone who was doing worse than she was and think, *At least I'm not that bad.* That confirmed my worst fears. If this woman, who had a reputation for being deeply kind, was admitting that she judged other moms in the grocery store, I was convinced that going out into the world would be inviting criticism. No, thank you. I'll just stay home.

Was this what the rest of my life was going to be? Was I going to be trapped alone with my child, just waiting for time to pass? Was *this* my future?

I wouldn't have dreamed of sharing my struggles with anyone, including Kim. How could I? Surely she of the clean house and adorable photos would never be able to relate. I felt so alone in my trouble. I couldn't even share how hard things were for me with my own mom, who was living in Florida at the time. When we caught up over the phone, I never let on that I was having a tough time. I didn't say a word to her about Nathan's colic or his reflux.

I don't think I have ever told my mom that anything in my life was hard.

Like so many women, I've always projected the image that everything is fine and I'm always great. And, like so many women, I dearly wanted my mother's approval. I felt like if I told her how unhappy I was, I would be admitting that I was failing at motherhood. I craved the chance to prove to everyone that I could do this.

When Nathan was around five months old, Kim threw a party—a Halloween party. It felt like a gauntlet thrown down. Here was my chance to show the world that I could do what other good moms were doing. I could get my baby out of the house and socialize like a normal human being. But I wasn't going to half-ass it. I wasn't after a participation trophy. I was going to win this game. I spent hours sewing a burlap sack and stuffing pantyhose with cotton balls to make a "sack of potatoes" costume for Nathan. (Have you ever tried to sew pantyhose material? Not easy.) I coaxed him into it in the car once we arrived, took a deep breath, and walked into the party. I could do this. Nathan had gotten drowsy on the drive over, and when I put him in his carrier, it seemed, blessedly, like he might just fall asleep. I pictured everyone commenting on how clever his costume was as he snoozed. Mom win!

I walked in to see that Kim had gussied up her already perfect home with A-plus decorations, including a Halloween-themed photo backdrop so that guests could take pictures of their babies to post on social media. Oh, no. An Instagram-worthy photo of Nathan? Nope, that wasn't going to happen for us. Over the previous few months, I had tried to get Nathan to pose for those one-week, one-month, two-months photos that everyone took. I attached a little sticker to his onesie that announced his age. But no dice. My baby was so colicky that the second we positioned him on his back, he would scream and start scratching his face. I tried propping him up with pillows to make him more comfortable, but he only screamed as if I had just dipped his feet in scalding water.

My confidence fizzled. I imagined the looks that would appear on the other moms' faces as soon as I set Nathan down for a picture and he started screaming. The idea of trying to fit in at this party suddenly seemed like a sick joke designed to publicly humiliate me. I quietly slipped back out the door and retreated home to my fortress of solitude.

PERFECTIONISM: ENEMY NUMBER ONE

The pressure to be perfect as a mom is overwhelming. Research has shown that women are particularly susceptible to perfectionism: more women than men report that they consistently fail to live up to their own standards both on the job and with their families.[1] There are a million ways to feel bad about your parenting each day. A friend's baby starts sleeping through the night at three weeks, while yours seems determined to set the record for most wake-ups in a ten-hour span. The mom on the blanket next to you at the beach brings tiny tins of perfectly sliced melon for her kids to snack on; meanwhile, you shove your half-eaten bag of Cheetos deeper into your tote. Someone else's kid goes to Kumon and can name all the state capitals, while yours thinks "the desert" is a continent. When we engage in this kind of comparison, we end up bulldozed by self-doubt. How does she get her baby to sleep when I can't? If I can't even keep the Cheerios out of the back seat of my car (or my hair), how can I be trusted with the care of a child?

According to Dr. Jen Douglas, licensed psychologist and former clinical assistant professor at Stanford University School of Medicine, people rely on perfectionism to cope in times of extreme stress—such as, oh, say, suddenly being responsible for a tiny human who cannot walk, speak, or feed itself.[2] Perfectionism rears up in times of transition and uncertainty because it gives us the illusion that we can control what is often uncontrollable. When we feel out of control, we figure that the answer must be to work harder and do more. To calm our churning self-doubt, we rely on what has helped us in the past—wrestling a problem to the ground through sheer force of intellectual effort, hard work, and research. We think, *If I check the boxes, put in the hours, I will crack the code*, as if spending ten hours searching for the perfect sleep sack will allow us to regain some measure of control. We also fall for the BS that if we do not mount an all-out campaign to buy the best of everything and be the best at everything, then we're not doing enough. A perfectionist's inner monologue says, *Something may go wrong, and if and when it does, it will be my fault. I will have failed this child, I will have failed as a mother, and I will* be *a failure.*

For many of us, becoming a parent is the first time we are confronted with an uncomfortable truth: we cannot achieve our way through this difficult time. We cannot parent perfectly. If you have a challenging class in college, you can stay up all night studying. You can hire a tutor. You can watch online seminars, and that extra work will probably pay off. If you are in debt, developing a budget and creating a careful financial plan can lead you in the right direction. But a baby is not a problem to be solved. A baby is a human being with complex needs and desires that are as mysterious as they are wonderful. You can read forty-five books on nutrition and still have a kid who only eats white rice.[3] As Dr. Douglas points out, this new miraculous being we created does not have a linear positive response to effort.

That was part of what was so hard for me in those early months of being a mom. Not being able to calm my baby down was a gut punch to my identity. I was an achiever! (Have you guessed this about me yet?) I could do hard things! Why couldn't I do this? I had landed my first job in real estate right out of college. From the time I was twenty-two, I was on full commission, making six figures. I was rookie of the year and subsequently the top sales rep in the southern Atlantic states. I sold millions of dollars' worth of real estate because I was good at my job. I'd been good at a lot of things. I expected to be good at this mom thing, too.

When we fall prey to perfectionism in motherhood, we often withdraw from situations where we can be judged as falling short, which is exactly what happened to me. I was so busy protecting myself from criticism that I lost out on the chance to connect with people like Kim—people who could have understood why I spent my days crying almost as hard and as long as Nathan did.

Mako, mom to Takumi, who lives in Colorado Springs, had a similar problem. From the time Taku was born, she craved mom friends, especially since most of her family lived in Sapporo, Japan, where she and her husband, Akira, had grown up. The couple had emigrated from Japan to the United States for college and gotten married soon after graduation. A few years later, Takumi was born. Mako had found a nice community of fellow moms in her neighborhood when Taku was an infant. They got together at the playground and in one another's home, and she loved feeling like she was part of a group of women who had so much in common. She prided herself on always managing to be on time for playdates and bringing Taku in color-coordinated outfits. He was quick to walk and quick to talk, which gave her a deep sense of satisfaction. Surely she'd had something to do with that. But then it came time for Taku to try potty training, and things did not go according to plan. She'd do a full-court press on going diaper-free, and for a week or two, it would seem like Taku was making progress. But then he'd say, "Okay, I think I'm done with potty training now. I'm ready for my diaper again."

For a while, Mako rolled with his reluctance, figuring he'd get to toileting when he was ready, but by the time he turned three and a half, she felt self-conscious about the fact that he still hadn't gotten it. She'd sheepishly hand over a supply of pull-ups to Taku's preschool teachers each week, apologizing and promising that they were working on it. When moms offered playdates on the weekend, Mako demurred. She worried that if she had another family over to her house, she'd be embarrassed by the fact that her little one was still in pull-ups. She wouldn't even consider taking him to someone else's house. What if he had an accident and she needed to change him while she was there? What would that say about her as a parent?

She decided she would have to wait for playdates until Takumi knew how to use the toilet like a pro. Her resolution held until Taku came home begging to invite his new friend Miles over. Mako saw how badly he wanted this, and frankly, she was dying to get to know Miles's mom, Alison, who always wore creative outfits to pick him up from day care and seemed like she'd be great to hang out with.

She arranged the playdate via text. The morning before Miles was supposed to arrive, she cleared the house of all evidence of an un-potty-trained kid. She hid Taku's pull-ups in the back of a drawer and even took the plastic sheet off his bed so it wouldn't make a telltale crinkling sound if the boys climbed up on the bed to play.

The boys ran straight into the backyard when Miles and Alison arrived. The moms followed close behind and sat on the back steps watching them chase each other around. At one point, Miles pulled at the waist of his pants and crowed to Taku proudly, "Look at my Minion underpants!" Without missing a beat, Taku tugged at his pants and shouted, "Look at my PAW Patrol pull-up!" Mako blushed furiously and started to explain herself to Alison: "It's a work in progress." But Alison didn't blink an eye. She waved her hands and said, "Eh, he'll figure it out. Are you guys planning on going to the school fair?" Mako felt a bit foolish. She'd worried for no reason. She'd almost denied Taku a chance to frolic with a friend and denied herself the chance to get to know Alison just because she was so tied to the idea that she had to be a perfect mom before she could handle something as simple as a no-stakes playdate.

ARE YOU STRUGGLING WITH PERFECTIONISM?

Perfectionism is a trap, but as Mako's story shows, it's not inescapable. The first thing you need to do to free yourself from the grip of perfectionism is recognize that you're in its clutches. And it's not your fault. We have become so accustomed as a society to holding moms to impossible standards that perfectionistic behavior feels like the natural response. We accept it as normal, and it's so commonplace that it can be difficult to distinguish perfectionism from simply doing your best.

According to Dr. Douglas, signs that you are suffering from perfectionism include the following:

> *Expending outsize effort.* Perfectionists often devote an outsize amount of time and energy to a task. A good example of this is product research. Due diligence is one thing, but if you find yourself on page 19 of the Amazon listings for car seats, and you've read all 358 reviews and created a chart of safety ratings, those are signs that you

are going overboard. Trust that you're not going to accidentally buy a car seat made out of tinfoil.

Spending all your downtime trying to perfect your parenting. When perfectionist moms finally get a moment to themselves, they often spend that time deep-cleaning the bathroom or making baby flash cards because they are so locked into the idea that more effort equals better results. If most of your time away from your child is spent trying to make your parenting perfect instead of recharging, you are probably falling into the trap of perfectionism.

Engaging in constant comparison. It's natural to want to see how other moms are dealing with the challenges of parenting, but constantly looking over your shoulder to see how you're doing compared to the next mom can quickly turn into an unwinnable game of one-upmanship. There is research that shows that the more we compare ourselves to others, the less content we are—even if we come out on top in the comparison.[4] What better reason to stop comparing yourself to other moms? You literally can't win.

Hiding out. If you find yourself avoiding other people because you reason that people can't judge you if they can't see you, that's a direct result of perfectionism.

ASK YOURSELF THE MAGIC QUESTION: IS THIS HOW YOU WANT YOUR KIDS TO LIVE?

There is no magic bullet that will slay the demon of perfectionism, alas. But Dr. Douglas says there is one question that sparks a change in her patients when she asks it: "Is this how you want your child to live?" What she means is: Do you want your kids to grow up believing *they* need to be perfect in order to deserve connection and companionship? Most parents, particularly of girls, immediately say, "Oh, no. I would never want that. Our daughter should know that she's loved unconditionally. She doesn't have to perform to have value on this earth."

It's not enough just to tell our kids that it's okay to be imperfect. Our kids will see right through us unless we also model this behavior and dare to be imperfect in front of them. To teach them, you must show them.

~

I wish I could tell you that when it came to saying goodbye to perfectionism, I experienced a liberating moment when I freed myself from its cage. In reality, perfectionism just became unsustainable for me. As my family and my business grew quickly, significantly, and simultaneously, hanging onto the perfectionism that kept me perpetually indoors and away from judgment became impossible.

By the time Latched Mama was ready to start selling products online, I had two kids. We were taking product shots with me as the model because we didn't have enough money to pay a real model. We set up shots in the living room, our studio MacGyvered together with fluorescent lights on a chain and white poster board on the wall to create a neutral backdrop (which would get dog hair all over it). Eric and I needed backup just to keep our toddlers out of the shots, so my mother-in-law came over to wrangle them. This was a woman who kept *her* house like a museum. I felt very aware that there were piles of toys and burp cloths everywhere. But I got over it, because at that point in my life, there was no way my house was going to be tidy. I was a hot mess. I had to let things go. I was forced to show up imperfectly. And guess what? The sky didn't fall. No one burst into flames. My mother-in-law didn't disown me.

I even started bringing an "Eh, good enough" mindset to Latched Mama. I was the face and body of the brand, and I noticed that the more I leaned into imperfection publicly, the more responses and engagement we would get from the Latched Mama community. A photo of me shipping orders in my pj's with a baby on my back would get twice as many likes as a shot of me in neatly coiffed hair and makeup. I think moms responded to the realness of the photographs where my hair was pulled back haphazardly in a pony. There was something so freeing about being able to put a messy version of myself into the world. I wished I had found that something earlier so I could have gone to Kim's parties without worrying whether people would think I sucked as a mom because Nathan had colic.

My perfectionism addiction is a work of constant recovery. There are moments when I wished my kids looked more put together and that there wasn't clutter on every flat surface of my house and that our silverware matched, and I am tempted to buckle down and put in the work to clean things up. But then I ask myself, *Does it matter?* If guests who come over for dinner are upset that their forks don't match mine or that my kids' shorts are clean but stained (very different from dirty and stained), I don't want to be friends with them anyway.

The people I feel closest to these days are those who are comfortable with chaos. My friend Lindi, now the creative director at Latched Mama, and I have twelve kids between us (six each). We start nearly every day exchanging stories of our fails from the previous night—how one of our kids excused himself from dinner to "use the bathroom" but instead snuck into the pantry to make a peanut butter sandwich so he didn't have to eat the stir fry we'd made. Or how my dog, who is basically the size of a miniature horse, finds every mud puddle he can and then runs his wet dirty body across the light gray family-room wall before he flops onto the floor. Or how there are so many severed dolls' heads in our sandbox that it looks like I'm raising a family of Dexters. Those shared moments when we are able to say, "Get this . . ." and then laugh at ourselves and with each other sustain me much more than a spotless kitchen does.

It is liberating to let go of the need to have it together 24-7. I take pictures of my kids all the time now. In half of them, they are crying. It's all right. It doesn't mean I'm a bad mom. It just means I *am* a mom.

The truth is, we are all innately worthy of connection. You don't need to be whatever the mom equivalent of valedictorian might be to deserve respect and kindness from other people. You deserve respect and kindness simply by existing. That sounds laughable, doesn't it? See that? Exactly that reaction speaks to how deeply we are convinced that we need to achieve to belong. That we must hide our flaws in order to increase the chances that we'll be accepted. The result is a terrible case of perfectionism—one that only increases the sense of isolation.

The only way to disarm this way of thinking is to let go of the idea that we need to be perfect in order to connect with other people. After plenty of stumbles, I have learned that it is only when two people show up, ready and willing to reveal their imperfect selves, that true connection happens.

So, friends, I'm asking you to allow yourself to be imperfect in front of other moms and in front your children. Allow yourself to be imperfect *for the sake* of other moms and your children. Let's metaphorically raise our middle fingers at a society that tells us we need to be perfect to be loved. Let's show them we will not perform for them. We will simply be our full, imperfect selves *for us*.

Build Your Village

Below are a few ways to battle mom impostor syndrome.

- *Dare not to compare.* Dr. Douglas has a brilliant solution to the comparison conundrum. She suggests that moms try a mindfulness exercise that reflects "values-based living,"[5] a mindset in which we let what is most important to us guide us internally instead of being ruled by external pressure. It works like this: when you catch yourself in a tailspin of comparison because, say, your neighbor drives by in her new Odyssey and you are still driving a 2013 Corolla, ask yourself, What's really important here? Do I value having a fancy car? Or am I letting a minivan symbolize being a good mom? If what I really want is to be a good mom, not just look like one, what is the next small step I can take to connect to my values? Maybe it's looking down at your kid and making eye contact and giving him a big smile. Maybe it's taking ten seconds to notice something in the natural world. Maybe it's sending a "How's it going?" text to your best friend. When you zero in on what matters to you instead of the way other people are perceiving you, you jolt yourself out of the comparison mindset.

  So swap out the emptiness of comparison for the fullness of living your values. Embrace what you already have that makes *your* life meaningful and worthwhile. Comparison pulls you out of the moment, out of your own life, whereas a values check is about taking the next best step into your current moment.

- *Go easy on yourself.* Our mom perfectionism is rooted in love. We try our best because we want what's best for our children. The reason you are up at 4:00 a.m. researching ice teethers is because you love your kid. This obsessive need has biological roots. Dr. Douglas explains that for our ancient ancestors, a small decision such as "Should I eat this white berry or that black one?" had life-and-death consequences. It's hard to override our primal brain's obsession with getting it right, even though the stakes in choosing between the Graco and the UPPAbaby are considerably lower.[6] So gaze upon your crazy with compassionate eyes. When you catch yourself succumbing to perfectionism, note with kindness that you're doing your best, then adjust course. Gently remind yourself that most of the time, that perfectionistic behavior moves you away from connecting with your child and other people and adjust course.

- *Tweak your perfectionism dosage.* Part of being compassionate about your perfectionism is allowing yourself to give in to temptation occasionally. You don't have to quit cold turkey. If you are bone-tired from breastfeeding four hundred times a night, there is no shame in taking a breather by scrolling around on the internet for a few minutes, gazing longingly at deluxe breastfeeding pillows. But if you are spending sixteen hours a day listening to every single episode of the trendiest parenting-expert podcast, you may want to tweak your dosage. Anything can be toxic if you have too much of it. Even water. (Seriously, did you know you can actually drink too much water?)

PART II

Get Out There and Find Your Village

Chapter 5

The Three *E*'s of Engineering Connection

ISOLATION MINDSET: My life just isn't designed for meeting new people. It's hopeless.

VILLAGE MINDSET: If am conscious about my life choices—big and small—I can create opportunities to connect.

*I*n 2020, after my miscarriage, I felt totally, utterly alone. But after a few years of consciously working to build my village, I gained some insight into why I'd ended up so isolated in the first place. Looking back, I can see that nearly everything about my life at the time formed an obstacle to creating community. It was as if my worst enemy had designed my life to undermine my prospects for connection. She had tented her hands, super-villain style, and set me up for devastating loneliness by

- making me a perfectionist who refused to reveal her vulnerability;
- moving me to a home far away from other people;
- allowing me to treat my cell phone as my best friend;
- convincing me that if I wasn't momming hard at all times—to the exclusion of all other activities—I wasn't good enough; and
- fooling me into thinking that the walls I had built around myself were protecting me whereas in reality they were cutting me off from vital connection.

The irony is, I now see, that my worst enemy was *me*. I had done all this to myself.

In self-compassionate moments, however, I can acknowledge that my isolation wasn't *totally* my fault. I was just following the lead of the world around me. These days, many of us live the way I had been living: we make choices that prioritize convenience and privacy over community. For me, that meant choosing my beautiful, private property over my old neighborhood, peopled by families with kids. It meant that I drove everywhere. I ordered everything. I wasn't taking my kids to the farmers market, where I'd run into other moms; I was buckling them into the car so I could drive to Target and have someone load my online order into the trunk. It'd be easy to tell you that COVID was to blame for my isolation, but the truth is that I had been behaving this way for years.

Does this sound familiar? It can be sobering to pull back and realize just how many of our choices stymie connection. The good news is that you can reverse-engineer those choices. You're not powerless. You're not stuck. You're not doomed. You can stop your own personal supervillain from undermining your connections. How can you do this? By structuring your life to include what I like to think of as the three *e*'s of connection—encounters, engagement, and exposure.

ENCOUNTERS:
GET YOURSELF AROUND
SOME OTHER PEOPLE

In many ways, the farm is exactly what I hoped it would be—a gorgeous, spirit-elevating place where the daily tasks of motherhood are less complicated than they were in the suburbs. I can raise my kids the way I want to raise them without being subject to anyone's judgment. If we want to have a forest day when no formal schooling gets done, we put on our hiking shoes and head out into the woods. If one of my kids wants to wear an owl mask to lunch, there is no one to tell him he's weird. There is so much freedom in our bubble, but I hadn't anticipated how much harder it would be to maintain connections, let alone make new ones, simply because I was physically distant from other people.

At first, it was easy to ignore the trade-offs we had made. But when summer rolled around, I got a big fat reminder of what we were missing. The kids decided to join the summer swim team at our old pool—the one at which I'd spent every sun- and rain-filled summer day as a kid—even though it is a thirty-five-minute drive away. I'd pack the car full of kids and goggles and towels, and we'd make the trek. While the kids did their sets, I'd sit on a plastic chair in my cover-up and chat with other moms. There were dozens of other families there catching up on the latest news—whose kid was anchoring the relay, when the new Walmart was going to open, which kids were starting to flirt with one another—it was like the town squares of old, and even though it was seven hundred degrees and required endless snack packing and sunscreen application, I was relaxed and happy. *This* was what I had been missing.

The gorgeous weeping willows, the high dive, and the snack bar are all gone, but spending time poolside surrounded by friendly faces took me back to my own childhood. I grew up in a neighborhood in Virginia that won an award for best planned community in America. It had fifteen miles of winding trails that connected all the houses, and after school I spent time biking on them to meet up with whichever kids had finished their homework already. During the summers, everyone gathered at the community pool to make friendship bracelets and eat pizza from the snack bar. I hung out with whoever was around, whether they were the jocks or the readers or the band kids—in the summer it didn't matter. Your people were the people around you. There was no need to send fifty text messages to arrange a

meetup because everyone was just there. I wished I had something like that as an adult. Living on the farm, I could still invite
friends over for a wine night, or I could join a book club, but it
was much harder to make those things happen.

That summer after we'd moved to the farm, I decided that
my address did not have to be my destiny. And so I began to
push myself, every day, to make room for more chance encounters in my life. It took work. The internet has made it easy to get
every single thing you need without leaving the comfort of your
couch. This was a lifesaving blessing during COVID, but the more
we have gotten into the habit of living this way, the more it has
become a massive barrier to connection. I've been putting on my
sneakers, doing the small thing that will put me in front of other
people. Even if I only exchange a silent smile with a stranger, it
takes the edge off my feelings of loneliness. It seems so obvious,
but it's easy to forget: we can't connect if there's no one around to
connect with. That's why the first step toward decreasing isolation
is to increase the number of people we encounter.

The changes I have made may seem small, and it takes effort
to do these things, but the upside is enormous. I choose to go to
a teller at the bank so I have to walk through a crowd of people
to make my deposits instead of using the ATM. Instead of going
through the drive-through for burgers, I bring the family inside
Chick-fil-A. A few times a week, I try to exercise around other
people by going to the gym or the pool occasionally instead of
just walking by myself. I take the dogs to hike on well-populated
trails instead of letting them out in the yard. Simply being around
other people who are also in the act of living and, more specifically, parenting—wiping faces, unsticking fruit chews from shirts,
going along on trips to the bathroom—reminds me that I am not
alone even when I am by myself.

You can do it, too. Challenge yourself to increase the number of people you encounter each day. Below are some easy ways to start.

Shop IRL. I know how tempting it is to worship at the altar of Amazon, Uber Eats, and Whole Foods delivery. Online shopping is an incredible time-saver. But it also keeps you indoors and away from other people. Whenever your schedule allows, buy your toothpaste in person. Pick up your takeout. Choose a book at a bookstore instead of at BN.com. Even if the only person you speak to is the person swiping your credit card, you have exposed yourself to the possibility of connection.

Get out of your car. Remember that old Sesame Street song "People in Your Neighborhood"? The lyrics cheerfully remind us that "They're the people that you meet / When you're walking down the street." Note that the lyrics don't mention anything about driving down the street. You can't say hi to your letter carrier if you're in your car. Cars are metal bubbles that keep us away from one another. It is so comfortable—and quick—to drive to pick up your morning coffee, but you miss the chance to run into the people in your neighborhood. Could you get your steps in walking to a café instead? Or if it's too far to walk, could you park and then simply walk inside to place your order instead of doing the drive-through? Dog owners have a leg up here. We're already out a couple of times a day. I always feel a sense of camaraderie with my fellow leash holders.

Neighbor it up. Sometimes we treat our neighbors as if they were debt collectors and deliberately avoid them so we can maintain our peaceful existence. Actually, neighbors are the low-hanging fruit of encounters because it takes so little effort to encounter them. Sit on your porch or your stoop. Go to the block party. Attend the community board meeting. Work on your front yard. Open a lemonade stand with your kids. You don't have to host a potluck and invite everyone on your block, but a friendly exchange with a passing neighbor while you're raking leaves creates a sense of community. It also helps kids feel safe in the world, knowing that there are other adults and families looking out for them.

Work in public. Remote work can allow you to go to meetings in your pj's and have access to your fridge all day long. However, it also leads to isolation. Working from a coworking space or schlepping your laptop to a café, the park, or the library brings you in proximity to potential connection. If you're in an office environment, keep your door open. Visit the break room. If you are a SAHM, don't SAH. Get yourself to the playground, to story hour, to music class. While your kids are at school, go to a coffee shop to scroll through Instagram or balance your monthly budget.

You can calibrate your encounter meter according to your energy level and your place on the introvert-extrovert spectrum, but you need to turn the knob toward "See more people in person" if you are going to find connection.

2. ENGAGE:
CHANGE YOUR DEFAULT SETTING

Going out into the world is an excellent first step in making more connections. If you are already pushing yourself to drink your tea on your front steps instead of in your breakfast nook, kudos— you're partway there. But as we all know, you can be lonely in a stadium full of people. Encounters don't mean much unless you engage.

Like many of us, I had my default mode to set to "Please don't talk to me" for a long time. I was basically wearing that on a sign around my neck. And even though I am trying to work on expanding my village, much of the time I am still very, very guilty of putting up walls between myself and other people. One day recently, as I was rolling my cart of groceries toward my car, I acted busier than I was so I wouldn't have to talk to one of my former neighbors. As soon as I spotted her, I put my cell phone up to my ear while wrangling my cart with the other hand, nearly denting someone's Nissan in the process. All to avoid a five-minute conversation with her. And I like this woman!

I worried that if I stopped, I'd get stuck. My schedule would get all screwed up. Worse, I'd have to answer the question "How are you?" I'd either have to tell the little white lie we all tell— "Great!"—or I would be the weirdo who told her the truth: "Barely keeping it together." Both options sounded like they would take more emotional effort than I was willing to expend. Better to make grocery shopping a surgical strike—get in, get food, get out—with as little interaction as possible.

Another particularly egregious example of my antiengagement mode occurred a few years ago when I was with my kids at the park on a spring day. It was a rare moment: all the kids were absorbed in something and happy. My older boys, four and two at the time, were making sand and dirt castles as I nursed two-month-old Caroline. The sunlight was just coaxing the buds on trees open. Oxytocin flowed with every sip Caroline took. Life felt full of possibility. Then another mother sat down next to me on the bench, and the happy melody that had been playing in my head record-scratched. *No*, I thought. *Not now.*

"I love your nursing top!" she exclaimed, beaming.

"Thanks so much," I said, trying not to appear rude but also projecting move-along-now vibes. I willed her to move to the bench across from me, where she could watch the birds fly and the wind blow in the trees—silently. Instead, she asked, "Where did you get it?" So much for silent bliss. You probably guessed this, but it was a Latched Mama top. I could have told her the exact day when Lindi and I talked about the pattern. I could have described the factory where it was made, the mission of my company, and the item's profit margin and sell-through rate. But instead, I chose to lie. Simply for the sake of avoiding a conversation with another grown human.

"I don't know," I said.

It got worse, as lying normally does. She asked if she could check the tag. Reluctantly, I moved my hair out of the way, and she informed me that it was a Latched Mama top. You don't say. She told me that she had many tops by "them" and that she absolutely loved the company.

"Me, too," I said.

After a few moments of awkward silence, she muttered, "I'll let you be," and pushed her stroller away.

I'd like to think that there was a mutual understanding in that moment that motherhood is damn hard and that I just needed to be alone. But if I put myself in her position, I can see that what really went down was that I kneecapped her attempt at connection. I had half of it right. I had left the house, and I was in a public place where I could meet other moms. But I was in nowhere near the right mindset to welcome connection. I try to forgive myself for that moment, but I'm not proud of it. It's a reminder of just how hard all this is. What if I had said, "Yes, it's a Latched Mama top. That's actually my company. Holy moly, I'm tired, but it's such a beautiful day. How old is your daughter?" Maybe our exchange would have ended the same way. Or maybe it wouldn't have. The problem is that I will never know.

I'm sure I'm not the only one who has been in this situation—choosing to shut down connection before it starts because it's more comfortable to stay in my little bubble. How many times have you acted like you were on the run from the FBI simply to avoid having to talk to someone you know? Small talk gets a bad rap. We think of it as the hallmark of superficial relationships. But it serves an essential purpose. It's a verbal wave, an acknowledgment, and sometimes a gateway to finding common ground. And once we do it, we hate it less than we think. One study cited in *The Good Life* by Robert Waldinger and Marc Schulz asked people to guess whether they would enjoy talking to someone during their commute instead of working or keeping their heads down. Most people answered as I would have: "Uh, no, thank you. I'd rather do me." But once they chatted with other commuters at the insistence of the researchers, they found the experience to be much more pleasurable than they'd anticipated.[1]

Think about the last time you had to talk to someone you hadn't planned to talk to. How bad was it? Not terrible, right? Maybe it wasn't the most scintillating conversation you've ever had. Maybe you just bemoaned how expensive blueberries had gotten or made a joke (that was actually not a joke) about the fact that you hadn't showered in days. But how did you feel afterward?

As long as the exchange didn't go on for too long, I'm guessing you felt a little lighter. Even though I'm an introvert, a few minutes of a pleasant or even neutral exchange usually gives me a momentary boost.

Take Off Your Scuba Suit

So many of us go through life with barriers around us that keep anything unwanted from creeping in. These barriers are like a scuba suit—close to the skin, thick, and protective. We send the message, "I'm doing something here. Don't bother me. I'm a fully functioning entity with my own life-support system that I carry around on my back. All good. Go about your business." In the world, this suit looks like the omnipresent headphones we put on as we run errands or the sleep mask we wear on airplanes or the phones we get lost in anytime we wait for anything ever. We avoid situations where we might get snagged by a social encounter, preferring instead to slip unfettered through the world.

When I took that fake phone call to avoid my neighbor, and when I lied to that Latched Mama fan, I was making an intentional choice to shut down connection. But with so many of my other habits, I realize that I am cutting off connection before I even have a chance to make a choice about it.

In 2023, I witnessed an interaction between two moms that made a big impression on me. I saw so much of myself in that moment, especially my tendency to automatically repel connection.

I was in Starbucks (again), drinking my coffee, when a comfortably dressed mom in a high ponytail walked in with her daughter, who I would guess was around three years old. The kid was cranky. Her face was blotchy, and she was whining like crazy for a cake pop. The mom looked like she was over it. I swear I could see the exact moment she caved and decided that three minutes of peace was worth the outrageous price for a treat. I've been there, sister.

As they were carrying their order out of the store, the mom noticed someone she knew at a table behind me. "Dora!" she said brightly, but Dora had on noise-canceling headphones, and her eyes were locked on her laptop. Ponytail mom tried again, letting go of her daughter's hand to wave in order to get Dora's attention. It worked. Dora tinkered with her laptop for a second, obviously pausing whatever she'd been listening to as she worked, and took off her headphones, but in the time it took for her to detach from her machine, the three-year-old had made a beeline for the door. The mom called over her shoulder, "We should catch up sometime!" as she chased her kiddo.

I saw my MO reflected in that interaction. I saw myself bringing my laptop with me everywhere I go, hiding in my car during the kids' swim practice, and listening to a podcast when I go for a walk. I've missed many opportunities for village connection because of these habits, which are so much a part of my routine that they are like breathing.

Contrast that moment in Starbucks with what I saw a few minutes later. I dropped my empty cup in the trash and headed back to my car. When I turned the corner, ponytail mom was standing next to a woman with a dog, laughing as her daughter tried to offer it a bite of her cake pop. The little girl looked delighted, and the mom looked like a plant that had just been watered. The two women kept their charges in sight, but there was nothing keeping them from sharing the moment with each other. They looked . . . happy.

Maybe that mom was secretly annoyed to have to talk to the dog walker and they were just faking their laughter. Maybe the little girl started begging for a dog the moment they said goodbye to the dog walker, but in that moment, it sure looked like a serendipitous encounter had turned things around for ponytail mom in a way a cake pop couldn't. Ever since I witnessed that interaction in Starbucks, I've been working to switch my default setting from merely Open to Engage. I don't always succeed, but occasionally I push myself to experience a little friction, and it results in an energizing spark.

On another occasion, I was in a crap mood. I hadn't slept well the night before. I'd gone into work even though I could tell I was coming down with something. Every time I moved my head, it sounded like I was under water. *Whoosh, whoosh, whoosh.* I didn't know what was wrong. All I wanted to do was shut my office door and power through to the end of the day, when I could go home and beg Eric to do kid duty so I could put on a sleep mask and go dark. When I got a call from our warehouse, I could barely hear what our manager was saying through my stupid clogged ears. I was tempted to just send an email to ask her to clarify, but, with my new mindset, I decided to walk over there to see what they needed for myself.

I opened the door to find some of my employees packing our newest shirts into boxes. I explained that I'd come in person because I'd suddenly turned into Jacques Cousteau. One of my employees had an otoscope in her backpack. (Why? I don't know. She's just really prepared.) We joked around as they tried to solve my problem with peroxide and silly jumping exercises. Pretty soon, we were all laughing hysterically. I felt very taken care of. By the time I got back to my office, everything still sounded funny, but I felt a thousand times better. It was a great lesson in just showing up. I still went home and got straight into bed that night, but those twenty minutes of engaging with other human beings had turned what would have otherwise been an awful day into a not-so-bad one.

It has been a process, but I'm learning to peel off my scuba gear and move through the world as if I'd put on a wool sweater. It's not as protective. In fact, it's itchy and kind of a pain to take care of. It catches on things and picks up odors, but it also breathes and keeps me warm. In wool sweater mode, I leave my AirPods and my phone in my bag when I run errands or go for a walk. I take the time to ask, "How's David doing?" as I pass a neighbor in the parking lot. I make eye contact and say, "Thanks, Liz," to the barista who hands me my coffee in the morning. I smile when I hold the door for the next customer at CVS. And those microinteractions add up over the course of a day, helping fill my social cup.

Give Yourself Permission to Start Small

When we talk about engineering connection, we're not talking about taking on a project the size of the Brooklyn Bridge. A major overhaul is too daunting to undertake when you are already struggling to get by. Start with a nice little footbridge, like a single log knocked down over a creek, that will bring you a bit closer to the people who may someday make up your village.

We can get freaked out by the prospect of engaging. We think we're going to have to go from zero to sixty. In my darkest moments after my miscarriage, I was not in an emotional place where I could go out and find a group of vivacious, supportive women with whom I could share my deepest insecurities. My intimacy muscle was shriveled up like an old tomato. If I had tried to talk to someone new about my feelings, I would have exploded into a messy blob. Real connection and vulnerability are things to build up to, not tackle on your first try. Chances are that mom in the park didn't want to go deep on my latest therapy session. She probably just wanted to share a moment of commiseration about how hard it is to find good nursing clothes.

This is why the first types of connections you should work on cultivating when you start to build a village are weak connections. Weak connections are the people in your life whom you rely on for an everyday feeling of belonging—not for deep emotional support. They are the people you wave to from across the street; the mom you smile at during drop-off each morning, even if you don't necessarily know her name; the FedEx driver who comes to your house an embarrassing number of times each week. You may not ever form the kind of connections with these people that expose your tender, vulnerable heart, but not every connection needs to be soul-baring. There is also a place for casual, kind interactions. They can be soul-healing. These moments of microconnection create weblike strength, a thousand delicate strands that weave together to make one helluva net.

The brilliant thing about weak connections is how easy they are to form. All the emotional effort required to make a truly lasting friend? Not necessary! All it takes is a willingness to remove some of the barriers we've mindlessly erected in modern society and surround yourself with a network of familiar faces who make you feel welcome.

One of my first exposures to the magic of weak connections was at a Burn Boot Camp here in Richmond. Lindi and I joined together after my fifth baby was born, and we went religiously for months. Over the weeks, I got to know Gabby, the head trainer. She met with each of us monthly to check in on our nutrition, our bodies, and our overall happiness with the gym. Somewhere, in between the smiles and hearing her tell me, "Melissa, you got this," connection was built. My trainer is not going to be my best friend, but if I have a ten-second interaction with her at the beginning of the class, that's another drop in my bucket. That's one more person who sees me. When she would hold the door for me on the way out, I felt just that much more seen, protected, and taken care of.

In the past, I would have labeled my connection with a fitness professional "fake" or "manufactured." But when Gabby's dad was diagnosed with a terminal pulmonary disease, we sat on the soft floor and cried together. There was nothing fake about any of it.

EXPOSURE:
THE ALCHEMY OF PROXIMITY

How do you turn weak connections into solid bonds? If you want to engineer the possibility of growing a relationship from a casual connection into something substantial, you need exposure.

Research shows that the more exposure we have to something, the more we tend to like it. Known in psychology as the propinquity effect, this tendency explains why you grow fond of someone you spend time with even if, on paper, you wouldn't necessarily have chosen that person as a friend. The more time you spend with someone, the more likely it is you'll connect.[2] What we've experienced as safe in the past makes us comfortable in the future. If something hasn't bitten our head off or tried to poison us, our brains begin to recognize it as friend, not foe.

We have more exposure to things and people when they're physically close to us. Dr. Jen Douglas tells her clients who are struggling with isolation to look around their neighborhoods for potential connections. "You want that level of proximity," she says. "Proximity leads to frequency. That's why everyone becomes friends with the people they live with in college."[3]

You can also create proximity and frequent interactions by establishing a consistent routine, like going to the same mommy and me class each week, stopping by the same coffee shop in the morning that always seems to have strollers parked out front.

A great way to build a village is to start with the people who are already in your life. They go to your church, synagogue, or mosque; they work in your office; they live next door to you, go to your dog park, and are the parents of your children's friends. You might be asking, "Is Melissa telling me that I'm supposed to make someone part of my village simply because we see each other at preschool pickup?" The short answer is yes. Building connections takes time. Studies show that it takes adults an average of ninety-four hours to turn an acquaintance into a casual friend and an additional 164 hours to go from casual friend to real friend.[4] The easier it is to hang out with someone, the more likely you are to do it, so look for people who are sprinkled throughout your daily life and might offer opportunities for connection. Not everyone will become a member of your inner circle, but the raw material for village building might be closer than you think.

I don't know that my path would have crossed with Melanie's, for example, if our kids weren't on the same swim team. She stays home with her kids while her husband works his solid government job. I run a company. She has one set of twins Nathan's age whom she worked really, really hard to conceive during a tough fertility struggle. I've had six kids without too much turmoil. Melanie's family lives in a modest house on a cul-de-sac. I live on a sprawling farm. Her boys go to public school. We homeschool. The only thing we really have in common is that our kids go to the pool together.

We became friends entirely by accident. Our relationship started out slowly. We mostly talked about our kids' favorite strokes and which protein bars provide the most energy. Gradually, over the course of hours and hours sitting next to each other, I noticed how warm and open she is. She has a smile for everyone, and she makes eye contact with every parent who arrives with a swimmer. Our relationship could have remained a weak connection, but by virtue of the fact that we spend so much time together, she has become an important part of my village. I count on seeing her during practices, and I'm always disappointed when she's not there.

I don't know how she does it, but she seems to have limitless energy for checking in on people. She'll text me just to say, "Hey, I know it's the holiday season. I hope you're hanging in there. What can I do? Can I bring over dinner?" She cheers for my kids at all their events. She'll remember if one of my kids has a fever, and when she sees me, her first question will be if it has broken yet. None of these things in isolation is an especially big deal, but they add up. As lazy as it sounds, it's been wonderful to make a friend without having to try that hard.

The first connections you make in building your village are the hardest, but the good news is you've started a virtuous cycle. If you are at a loss for where to start, just remember your three e's—encounters, engagement, and exposure. Connecting makes you feel better about yourself because it affirms that you are a person worthy of connection (of course you are!), which calms that primal panic in your brain telling you that you'll be left alone on the savannah for the hyenas. You're able to see yourself reflected in others' eyes, reminding you that you are fun and funny and worthy of connection, which empowers you to get out there and connect some more.

Build Your Village

Below are some ways you can work on the three *e*'s of connection.

- *Make eye contact and smile.* Every woman knows the rage that rises up when a man tells us to "Smile, darlin'." This is different. You're not smiling to massage someone's ego. You're smiling to say, "I see you; you are not alone." There is nothing that thrills me more than a show-your-teeth smile from a woman I don't know. It's like a secret handshake that says, "I got you, girl." If you only have one smile in you to share with a stranger, make that stranger another mom.

- *Plan for serendipity.* Instead of bolting like the Road Runner when you leave an event, linger for a few minutes and talk to other stragglers. Ask what they thought of the practice or the class or whatever just took place. Or when you're on your way there, try to coax your crew out the door five minutes early so you can chat before the event. Let the serendipitous thing happen.

- *Make small talk.* Seriously. At the grocery store when you are checking out, talk to your cashier. It usually takes just a few minutes to ring you up. You're standing there anyway— why not ask if she's tried the frozen samosas you have in your cart?

- *Give yourself a free get-out-of-connection pass.* Go easy. Some days, you're not going to feel like putting in the effort for the three *e*'s, and that's okay. Gather your resources and try again tomorrow (or next week or next month).

- *Go back in time.* As an experiment, spend a day acting like it's 1994, before you could order your dental floss from

Amazon and stream your movies on Netflix. Challenge yourself to live this way for the entire week, then tally up the number of people you encountered and engaged with whom you wouldn't have met if you'd been attached to a device.

Chapter 6

Could You Be a Joiner?

ISOLATION MINDSET: I'm not a joiner, and groups give me hives. I have everything I need in the comfort of my home.

VILLAGE MINDSET: Joining a group is an easy way to find a sense of belonging and support.

I am insanely, ridiculously, absurdly jealous of my old college friend's soccer team. It's not just because Bianca gets to miss her kids' bedtime routine twice a week for practice. The main reason I'm jealous is that she became a member of a ready-made village just by signing up.

Before Bianca moved from Minneapolis to Pittsburgh, where her husband, Peter, was transferred for his job, she would have described herself as a social person with a large group of friends. However, after two years of settling in, she still hadn't found her people, and she started to wonder if something was wrong.

Both Bianca's boys were soccer players, and watching them play travel soccer with a team called Dynamo was one of her favorite activities. She didn't miss a single game, even the ones that were an hour's drive away and took place at 8:00 a.m. on a Saturday. She stayed for every practice, watching the boys run drills as she walked in circles around the track. She had become something she'd never anticipated becoming: a soccer mom. For her birthday, Peter bought her a heated vest she could wear during chilly games and an enormous sports umbrella to protect her from sun and rain. The kids bought her a sweatshirt that said SOC-CER IS MY FAVORITE SEASON, which she wore with pride.

After practice one day, as her older son was trying to locate his water bottle, one of the other moms surprised Bianca by asking if she'd ever considered joining the Dynamoms. *The what?* Turns out there was a group of adult women who were learning to play soccer at the same field where the kids practiced. Bianca's imme-diate reaction was to pass politely. She'd played basketball in high school, but soccer? That would require her to use her feet, and her feet were stupid and clumsy, so she said no, thank you. But for the following few days, she couldn't get the idea out of her head. She'd always been sporty and had worked hard to incorporate exercise into her daily routine, but during COVID, she hadn't felt safe going to the gym, so her workouts had tapered off, which left her feeling kinda blah.

She did need more exercise, and she *was* always encouraging the kids to try new things. What kind of example would she be setting if she never tried anything new herself? So she bought herself some shin guards and cleats and showed up at the weekly clinic the Dynamoms offered.

The experience at the first practice was exactly as physically humbling as she'd feared. She couldn't control the ball at all. At one point, she made contact with the ball, and it nailed another woman in the head so hard that she had to leave the field. Bianca felt terrible—and totally humiliated. Worse, the others already seemed to know one another and had established friend groups on the team. At the very least, they knew each other's name. She couldn't believe she'd put herself in a situation in which she was having to go up to a group of strangers, stick out her hand, and say, "Hi—I'm Bianca." She might usually have assumed that everyone was whispering among themselves about this new player who sucked so bad, but as the hour went by, she realized that all she heard from these women was encouragement. No one gave her a hard time for not knowing what she was doing. Everyone was supportive, almost laughably so, racing to grab errant balls she'd kicked and passing them right back to her with a smile and an understanding "Unlucky!" By the end of the session, she felt accepted enough to want to come back for the next practice.

Week after week, the welcoming vibe continued. The most common words on the pitch were "Good idea!" Bianca noticed that some of the moms stuck around after the clinic for a beer on the bleachers, but she wasn't quite ready to make the leap from soccer to socializing.

Gradually, however, invitations to join other activities rolled in via the group email chain. There were happy hours, birthday gatherings, book clubs, and meetups at dance parties. Even though she wasn't one of the core members of the group who faithfully attended the Friday happy hours, she made a point of going to some of the one-off events—an art opening for a sculptor on the team, a concert featuring a player who was in a band. It began to transform her life in Pittsburgh. She often ran into familiar faces at events. Knowing she'd likely run into a Dynamom wherever she went made her more open to trying new experiences. It was as if she'd joined a grown-up sorority where no one cared what you looked like and everyone could name three members of the US Women's National Team.

A few months in, the group announced registration for an overnight soccer camp, which would involve four days of coached play at a nearby YMCA camp. As much as she'd grown to love the group, Bianca was on the fence about signing up. Three nights away from the kids was a big ask of Peter. But she was enjoying being part of a team so much that she cleared it with him and decided to attend.

Once she got there, she realized that when you put forty moms in charge of organizing an event, shit gets done, and it gets done well. One of the moms, who owned a bakery, brought incredible pastries for enjoying after every meal, each of which was catered. Someone had organized the cabins by sleep habits— night owls in one cabin, early birds in another. The Dynamoms had handled every aspect of the logistics, from schlepping soccer nets in the trunks of their cars to hiring a yoga instructor to help with sore muscles after games. At future camps, Bianca would be one of the people who pitched in to organize things, but during that first camp, she let the days unfold joyfully in front of her. She couldn't remember the last time she had felt so cared for or welcomed. She could bring her bowl of oatmeal to any seat at breakfast and would be greeted with smiles from her fellow Dynamoms. At the end of each day, everyone gathered around a campfire to dance and rage about the patriarchy. A blissful sense of belonging enveloped her. *This* is what she had been missing since she moved.

The Dynamoms community gave so much to its members beyond companionship. The team shared a Google Doc with recommendations for babysitters, doctors, electricians, and plumbers. When one of the moms needed kids to participate in her neuroscience study, she asked for volunteers and quickly had enough for her cohort. But for Bianca, the moment that epitomized the way the group supported one another off the pitch came when one of the players posted a message to the Dynamoms' private Facebook group sharing the news that after her divorce that fall, she was finally moving out of the house she'd shared with her ex-husband. She was hoping to find three or four people to help her pack and move into her new apartment.

She sent out the note on a Friday, and on Saturday morning, fifteen women appeared at her door. One team of women tackled the bathroom, another emptied the closet of coats, a third worked on wrapping glassware in the kitchen. A Dynamom who couldn't make it that morning sent Swedish meatballs to her teammate's new house for the first meal that the moms would share there that evening. Bianca made herself a plate and looked around at this sisterhood in action. She was filled with gratitude. She'd signed up for fitness, but she'd found a family.

JOINING A GROUP IS LESS
HORRIBLE THAN YOU THINK

I know some of you will read about Bianca's experience with the Dynamoms and think, "That is my literal nightmare. I would rather gargle battery acid than be forced to interact with a group of strangers, let alone play sports with them." Don't worry. I feel you, and I promise that you don't have to wear a sports bra—or do anything else that is wildly out of your comfort zone—to find a village. There are many ways to build your village that don't involve embarrassing yourself in front of total strangers. Joining is not exclusively for athletes, extroverts, and former sorority sisters.

When it comes to stepping out of your comfort zone, there are various levels of tolerance. Your position on the introvert-extrovert spectrum is at least partially innate. Even my five-year-old recoils every time the dog in Go, Dog, Go! asks the other dogs if they like her hat. "Mom, that's sooo cringe," she says.

We need to keep in mind that our ability to get out there and connect also changes with the season of life we're in. Making new friends and building a village, especially after times of solitude, can be anxiety-provoking and even paralyzing. The kind of connection you require is not a constant. It morphs as you enter each new stage. What you need as a mom to a newborn will likely be different from what you need once your kids are teenagers. In fact, what you need might vary from day to day. Sometimes the compassionate thing to do is honor your need for space. If you force yourself to go to a party where you will have to pretend to enjoy yourself when all you can think about is your leaking nipples and how soon you can get back in your bed, it's going to backfire.

As moms, we are not only trying to relearn connection, we may also be relearning who we are, and as a result, reaching out to other people for connection can feel impossibly hard. You need to work to find a balance. While it is important to push yourself, it's also important to honor that little voice inside that might be telling you when it's too much. For me, and for many of the women I've talked to, that ideal balance lies in starting with the safe options, having the tenacity to keep going, and then slowly pushing yourself further as you get more comfortable with the new.

Joining a group is a sneaky shortcut to connection. The great thing about groups is that they are a perfect soft landing for people—even introverts—who are trying to find a village. Below are some of the reasons why.

1. *Groups take the pressure off.* I am very wary of asking moms to make their lives more complicated. That's why, if you're having a hard time finding a village, I recommend joining a group. When you join an existing organization, all you have to do is show up. You don't have to wrangle schedules or persuade people to come or make a shopping list for the snacks you're going to serve. Most of the behind-the-scenes work—the work that, let's face it, moms usually do—has already been done, freeing you to focus on connection.

2. *Groups have purpose.* Priya Parker, founder of Thrive Labs, an organization that helps groups of people from CEOs to politicians to PTOs gather effectively, wrote a wonderful book called *The Art of Gathering*. She points out that when we get together with other people and have a meh

time, it's usually because there is no intention behind the gathering other than "gather." Her research and work show that defining an intention for being together transforms a roomful of people into a meaningful gathering. When you have a shared purpose, connection follows.[1]

When you join something, whether it's a neighborhood watch or a *Game of Thrones* viewing club, you know why you're there. Parker would push harder and suggest that whenever your group meets, you should have a particular purpose for that particular gathering, whether it's looking for ways to improve visibility on street corners or coming up with an alternative finale that will satisfy fans. But I want to set the bar a little lower. I think simply showing up at a group event and opening yourself to connection with other people is purpose enough. Plus, when you join a group that gathers for a particular reason, you're never at a loss for things to talk about. You have a default topic of conversation, one you know everyone is interested in.

3. *Group activities are (usually) scheduled.* You are less likely to blow off something that is regularly scheduled than something you have to remember to plan. You can put off a drink with a friend indefinitely, because there will never be a perfect time. But if your regular pickleball game takes place on Saturdays at 9:00 a.m., you know you have to show up or risk disappointing your pals. When you make it automatic—third Thursday of every month is book club—you decrease your opportunity to make excuses.

One of my favorite pieces of parenting advice I got when I first became a mom was "Defer to the higher authority." This became a technique I'd use to defuse fights. Instead of telling a toddler that I needed him to go to bed or that he needed to put on his shoes, I would say, "The clock says it's time for bed" or "The restaurant's dress code says you have to wear shoes." It wasn't a cure-all—it maybe cut down on arguments by 20 percent, but even that was a welcome improvement. We can use the same technique on ourselves when we schedule a group activity. Instead of saying, "I have to go connect with some moms," we can tell ourselves, "It's book club night."

4. *Group activities are not a referendum on you.* When you invite someone to hang out one-on-one, there's a social risk involved. If that person says no, even with a great reason, it's nearly impossible not to feel hurt. But when an event has been put together by an organization, it depersonalizes the RSVP. "Kathy is too busy for trivia night" sits easier than "Kathy can't come to my dinner party; she must hate me." Maybe someday we'll all be up to our eyeballs in self-confidence and we won't worry about whether people like us enough to accept us, but until then, joining a group is a great way to find instant acceptance. You joined! You're already accepted. The thing on the table for not liking or liking is the activity, and guess what—you and everyone else there have already decided on "like."

5. *Groups create belonging in the wider community.* When you join a group, the sense of belonging isn't limited to the gatherings themselves. It spills out into the rest of your life when you run into people from your group at Trader Joe's or the movies.

DRAFT OFF A PACK LEADER

Even if you're convinced that joining a group is a good idea in theory, it can be tough to take that first step and show up. To ease your way in, I suggest you draft off a pack leader.

The best way I can explain the concept of drafting is to use an example involving a famous bike race—the Tour de France. The first time I watched the event on television, I was confused. Why were the racers biking in a line like that? Wasn't it a race? Shouldn't they have all been trying to edge one another out? My sister had to explain the concept of drafting to me. When racers draft, the lead cyclist takes the brunt of the drag from the wind. He pushes air out of the way for the benefit of the rider behind him, who experiences less drag and even gets sort of sucked forward by the vortex created by displaced air. The second rider doesn't have to expend as much energy because he's following the leader.*

Connecting with a group can work the same way. If you're feeling draggy about joining an activity or organization, find a leader and follow her. You probably know a natural pack leader. She's almost always the "class parent." She's the one who sends the text saying, "Who wants to go to the puppet show at the library today?" Or "You should totally meet my friend Amy; she lives right near you. Here's her number." Pack leaders are hubs that connect disparate people into a cohesive unit.

If you are a pack leader, thank you for your service, and keep up the good work. You might even want to take your turn behind another leader now and then. Maybe you would enjoy taking a break and letting someone else coerce the neighbors into

---

* I learned from a cycling friend that the rider whose role it is to take on this job is called a *domestique*, but to me that sounds like "domestic worker," which is not the vibe I'm going for here, so I prefer "pack leader."

participating in the block party. Sometimes, you can just bring your cheese plate and hope no one gets injured in the bouncy castle. But if, like me, you are not at all a pack leader, I suggest you find one who can hold your hand as you take baby steps toward building a village.

Maggie, a stay-at-home mom to a four-year-old boy named Weston, is a born pack leader. She is bubbly and energetic, and she gets a thrill from researching activities, so she's the first to know when there's a free music class or a new exhibition at the children's museum. Katie, however, is a drafter. She enjoys being around other people, especially when she's taking care of her three-year-old, Tyler, and his little sister, Nina, on the days she's not working—but it'd be too much pressure for her to be the social glue in a group. *What if people don't like one another? What if I have to spend all my energy making sure everyone is having a good time?* So she's never the one to suggest bringing people together. Let's see how these two personalities found each other.

In her LA neighborhood, Maggie decided to put her passion for being around people to work, and she assembled a crew called the Playground Adventure Group. It's not fancy. It doesn't have an agenda. It's just a loose affiliation of parents whose kids play at one particular playground in Silver Lake. When Weston was around two years old, Maggie started taking him to this playground regularly. There she chatted up the parents she encountered—including Katie—grabbed a bunch of phone numbers, and started a WhatsApp group. Instead of just turning up at the playground haphazardly, she'd shoot out a message saying, "Weston and I are headed over at three o'clock. Who's in?" and a handful of families would meet up. Katie relished getting the messages. Being part of the group was the kick in the pants she needed to keep her from succumbing to routine and staying indoors all day. Every time the group got together, the parents were able to enjoy one another as the kids occupied themselves on the equipment.

One day, Maggie suggested a beach excursion via WhatsApp, and Katie decided to go along. She was glad she did. Going to the beach with a pack of fellow parents was so much better than going to the beach as the sole adult in charge of Tyler and Nina. Having extra eyes to track little bodies in the surf and sun collectively lightened the load for all the parents who attended. If one of the parents spied a kid wandering off, she would be quick to grab a tiny hand and lead that kiddo back to the group.

For Maggie, parenting in a pack feels natural. Like me, she grew up in the suburbs, where there was a communal feel to the neighborhood. Kids ran through everyone's backyard, and neighbors reported back if a kid got out of line. There were always adults around keeping communal watch. She remembered that in middle school, whenever she missed the bus after her parents had left for work, she'd just knock on a neighbor's door and ask, "Can you please drive me to school?" and that adult would dash her over. That's the mentality that emerged in the Playground Adventure Group—everyone looks out for everyone else's kids as well as their own.

Although Katie didn't start the group, and although she rarely uses WhatsApp to suggest an activity of her own, she's been able to benefit from drafting behind Maggie's pack leader position. Her ride has been better—both easier and more enjoyable—because she's doing it as part of a pack.

START YOUR OWN THING

If the idea of joining a group of strangers, even by riding behind a pack leader, sets your teeth on edge, there is another way to round up the beginning of a village: start your own group. Before you object that starting a group from scratch sounds even harder than joining something already established, keep in mind that the group you start doesn't have to be a large, structured group. There's no need to establish rules, regulations, or a secret hand-shake. It could just be an informal conglomeration of people you think might get along, especially if you have an interest in common. You can gather as frequently or infrequently as you like, online or in person. Starting your own group will require *a bit* more up-front effort, but it doesn't have to make you break a sweat. One of the best ways to ease into starting your own group is to do it with people you already know.

Ellie is a perfect example of someone who started a group that turned into an essential part of her village.

Ellie knew other people in Portland who had made friends at the local YMCA or through their churches, but she wasn't especially athletic, and she preferred to reserve church for spir-itual activities, not social ones. Instead, the environment where she felt most natural connecting with other parents was her kid's school—at least initially. Her son, Ben, sailed through his first cou-ple of years of preschool and kindergarten. He was vivacious and talkative, and she loved having his friends over for playdates on the weekends so she could chat with the other parents. But once Ben entered first grade, something shifted. Ben wasn't picking up reading as quickly as his classmates were, and Ellie could tell it bothered him. His teacher reported that he had been acting out in class: getting up, running around the room, and interrupting. He simply couldn't keep focused.

Ellie wanted to talk about Ben's behavior with other par-ents, but she felt protective of him, and, if she was honest, the whole thing made her self-conscious. The school was full of little achievers. Other parents were already deeply invested in where they would send their kids to college. Many of Ben's classmates spent their weekends at chess tournaments and fencing lessons to give them an edge in their years-in-the-future college applications. Ellie could barely keep Ben interested in attending first grade, let alone think ahead to the future. He was a creative, interesting kid, and she adored him. She was so proud of him every time he managed to get through his morning routine, but she felt like an idiot crowing about that when other parents were humblebragging about the fact that Suzie barely left the house over the long weekend because she was hell-bent on finishing three Harry Potters. When Ellie did mention that Ben was struggling, other parents dismissed her concerns with "Oh, he'll catch up. Just wait." But her maternal instincts told her it wouldn't be that easy.

Eventually, Ellie met with Ben's teacher, who suggested she should have him evaluated for ADHD. The evaluation confirmed the diagnosis. It made so much sense. That was why Ben was struggling to keep still. He wasn't a bad kid; he just had different needs. Ellie had grown up in a household where the attitude was that asking for things like accommodations in the classroom was a form of weakness. She didn't share that belief, but she was at a loss for how to help her son.

She knew she wasn't the only mom out there with a kid whose brain worked differently, but she felt very alone among her peers. Surely she had to know *someone* who had a kid with learning difficulties. That's when she remembered her former coworker, Julie.

The previous summer, when Ellie's family had gone on vacation to Seattle, she had met up for coffee with Julie, who had moved there from Portland a few years before, after switching jobs. They were catching up on office gossip when Julie mentioned in passing that her daughter had dyslexia. The fact barely registered with

Ellie at the time, but now it suggested an opportunity. Maybe Julie would be someone she could talk to about Ben's struggles. She also recalled that over Thanksgiving, her cousin Laura had said something about her nine-year-old, Andy, needing a special coach to help him stay organized. She called Julie and Laura individually and asked if they'd be interested in starting up a small moms group online to talk about their kids' struggles. They both leaped at the idea. The three moms decided they'd meet once a month on Zoom to download their difficulties and sympathize with one another without fear of being judged.

I like to think of what Ellie did as the friend equivalent of "shopping your closet" when you need a wardrobe refresh. You know—the advice women's magazines give you when you want to start a fashion revamp: look carefully at what you already own. You don't necessarily have to go out and find new people; you just need to look at the ones you know with fresh eyes.

During the first Zoom, Ellie felt like she was exhaling a long-held breath. She didn't need to put up a front or wear a brave face for these women. She didn't need to pretend that Ben was thriving at school. She could speak freely. She also felt reassured by their openness about the hardships their own kids were dealing with. Julie shared the names of the programs she'd found helpful for kids with dyslexia, and Laura was sympathetic when Ellie described feeling like she was somehow failing as a mom because Ben had trouble paying attention in class. Ellie started cataloging moments to save up and share with Julie and Laura each month. The three moms not only held one another up during the hard parts, they also celebrated the small triumphs— a homework assignment turned in on time, a ten-count of eye contact, a "Thanks, Mom" in response to help with a tricky problem. Even though she didn't see Julie and Laura in person, just knowing she could rely on their support helped Ellie feel less alone in her daily life as a mom.

GROUP THERAPY

Isolation can create insecurity, making us worry when we join a group that we're going to be the only one there who is lonely and looking for friends. But we *all* crave connection, just as a plant craves sunlight. I was reminded of the fact that I am not alone in seeking connection when I joined a group myself.

During a recent school break, when my kids' homeschool teacher was on vacation, I had two full weeks with the kids at home—the kind of thing I thought I would absolutely live for when I decided to become a mom. Two weeks to be able to focus on our little family. What could be better? You probably won't be shocked to hear that within a few days, I was drowning. Too many demands. Too much unstructured time. Too much to manage with no space to recharge. I was basically acting like a cruise director, making meals, breaking up fights, and suggesting enriching activities—*Who likes Lego?!*—while still trying to manage my business from home. Any emotional stability I'd had going into the break evaporated within a few short days. I tried moving my body and paying attention to what I was eating. I even squeezed in a little FaceTime with friends, but nothing was working to center me. I was in a funk. Worse than a funk. Fury and exhaustion were having a cage match in my brain. My social cup was empty, and my system was on the verge of shutting down.

If it hadn't been for my work on this book, I might have thought what I needed was a massage or a nice bottle of red wine. But since I'd been experimenting with the power of villagehood, I knew that massage and wine would make me feel better for a few hours at most (and let's be honest—I'd probably feel pretty bad the next day after the wine). I needed something that would do more to sustain me through difficult periods when they arose. I suspected I needed more connection to see me safely to the other side of this emotional torrent.

I called Lindi to confirm that we were going to be able to go for a walk the week the break ended, and she agreed. My blood pressure dropped at the mere thought of being able to bond with her as we strolled. At the same time, however, I realized that while I cherished Lindi, it was probably unfair to her to make her my sole source of emotional support besides Eric. Was it time to expand my village? Was I ready for that? I took stock. While I was gassed at the moment, I had built up enough belief in the power of connection and witnessed its benefits to suspect that I could take the next step. But where would I even find people to bring into my circle?

I made the best of the remaining week and promised myself that I would double down on finding more opportunities for connection the moment we got the kids back on their regular schedule.

The seemingly endless break was finally over, and less than an hour after the kids' teacher arrived at the farm to take over, I took a leap that shocked even me: I signed up for a Masters swim team. I'd been a competitive swimmer in my younger days, and my big kids were all on a team, but I'd never made time as an adult to get back into the pool. I craved more connection and more time for myself, and joining the team would provide both. I figured that the worst thing that could happen would be that I'd improve my cardio. When I told Eric, he raised his eyebrows at me. "Seriously?"

I acted more certain that this was a good idea than I felt. I didn't even know what size swimsuit I wore anymore. I ordered one online using the sizing chart, and when it came, I tried it on. It covered maybe a third of my butt. Hmm. Maybe that was a sign I shouldn't go. But I was just making excuses. The following Monday, I packed a pair of the kids' goggles in my bag, dug up a swim cap I thought might fit, and went to my first swim practice in more than two decades. Years before, I never would have dreamed of setting my alarm and trading precious sleep for an hour with strangers. But with a village mindset, I had a hunch that this kind of connection was the answer to my struggles.

Jittery doesn't even begin to describe how I felt as I fumbled with my locker before practice. I gave myself an internal pep talk: "Melissa, you run a freaking company. You put videos of yourself on the internet for millions of people to see. You have been interviewed by news journalists at national publications." But none of that made me feel any less terrified. I was sure I was about to walk into a pool where I would encounter Olympic-level swimmers who would be annoyed with me for being so poky and out of shape. What was I doing? I knew I wasn't going to drown, but was I going to be humiliated?

I forced myself to leave the locker room and head out onto the deck, where I tugged my suit as far over my rear as I could and slipped into a lane where a handful of women and one man were warming up. I plunged under water right away so I wouldn't have to talk to anyone. I knew my voice would be all wavery if I tried to speak. After a couple of laps, I was exhausted but a little calmer.

At the very least, I felt I'd made a good choice. Joining a Masters team was perfect for me. It was a coached program, so I just had to follow directions. Each time I hit the wall, I knew what I was supposed to do next. But I also knew I wasn't there just for fitness or a meditative dip. Finally, between sets, I said a quiet hello to the woman I was sharing a lane with. Turns out Sylvia was a wine distributor who had a ten-year-old and a twelve-year-old and was just getting back into swimming herself. Ah, sister. We did the whole practice at around the same pace, having get-to-know-you chats during breaks (always a little weird in a bathing suit).

When it was over, I floated through the rest of the day. The exercise had gotten my blood going, and the chatting made me feel like a person again. I promised myself that I would go for at least two months—long enough for it to become a habit. By then, my body would have physically adjusted to the new movement and exercise and I could assess how I was feeling emotionally. Within two weeks, I realized that it was one of the best decisions I had ever made.

One day, Nathan was having a really hard morning as I was getting ready to leave for swim. When he gets physically hurt, his brain short-circuits, and he can't calm himself. So when he stubbed his toe, he freaked out, at which point his brother started calling him names. Level-three crisis in the Wirt home. So many of my instincts were pulling me into the vortex, telling me that I would be a bad mom if I went to swim practice instead of staying home to soothe Nathan. But Eric was there; he had it. I could trust him. I gave Nathan a hug and told him, "I'm so sorry about your toe, buddy. I hope it feels better soon." Then I picked up my swim bag and headed for the door. The crisis was over by the time I came home, and I was able to be fully present for the rest of the day.

As time went by, I began to see the benefits of my time in the pool. I could feel my whole system regulating. The little things that used to piss me off in the mornings—the spilled coffee grounds; not being able to find my bleeping phone—didn't get me as worked up anymore.

Once I got rolling, it was so much easier to keep rolling. The inertia I felt was easier to overcome because I knew Sylvia was going to be there waiting for me, and I didn't want to feel like a jerk by standing her up. It worked both ways. There were days where I was the gung-ho one, texting "See you in ten?" The good feelings we got from hanging out with each other created a virtuous cycle.

I eventually struck up a rapport with another one of the women, Elaine, who worked in HR for Capital One. She had a three-year-old and a one-year-old at home. I told her one Friday about an issue I was having at my company, and she gave me excellent advice from an HR perspective. The following week, she asked how the situation was going. She told me she had just switched roles at Capital One herself. She used to have a boss who was a mom, but her new boss was childfree and she felt dismissed by her. We talked through ways she could advocate for herself in the office, going deep on what she needed as a mom in the workplace. It felt amazing to connect with her.

Before long, Elaine, Sylvia, and I became a trio. We confessed how scary it had been for us to start swimming again. We'd *all* worried that the others would judge us for our rusty strokes and lumpy bodies. But once we'd joined, we found so much comfort in the fact that we were all out-of-shape moms just looking for connection. That drove home for me how common it is among mothers to be searching for what the three of us had found during those early mornings in the pool. Other people are looking for connection every bit as hard as you are. You're doing a service by offering your own gifts to others.

Months after I joined, Elaine, Sylvia, and I walked through the parking lot after practice. It was snowing lightly, but we were still riding our endorphin high, so our coats hung open. We were all moms, with a fifteen-year age spread among us. We had navigated several months of early morning swims together. We had talked about our kids' sleep schedules, ear infections, learning struggles, and had even lived vicariously through Taylor and Travis's love story. As the three of us stood by our cars, Sylvia turned to us.

"This has changed my life. You all have changed my life," she said, tears in her eyes. "Same," Elaine and I said in tandem.

We noticed our twenty-four-year-old coach walking in the opposite direction to his car. Sylvia looked over at him walking up the hill, then looked back over at us. "Do you think he knows?" she asked.

"He has no idea," Elaine answered back.

I still go to practice every morning. I haven't missed a day. I put my phone away, and I swim my little heart out. I'm in better shape than I have been since before I had kids, and that feels terrific. But mostly, I feel lottery-winner-level lucky to have plunged into a welcoming place where connection comes easily. Of course it wasn't luck. It was the fact that the need for a village is written in our DNA. You don't have to join a Masters swim team or even a book club, but if you can find a group to join, you'll have yourself a starter village.

Build Your Village

If you're up to the challenge of being a joiner, below are some ways to get started.

- *Identify the leader in your pack.* You know the type. She's always texting you to ask whether you want to join her at the local bookstore for story time or if you and your family want to go camping over the weekend. This person is a blessing, a gift, a catalyst for connection. Make a list of the people in your life who pull other people into their orbits. Next time someone on that list asks you to do something, allow yourself to go with the flow. Let her do the planning for you. Tag along. You don't need to volunteer to slice apples for the whole crew—just enjoy the ride.
- *Join an existing group.* What activities interest you? Maybe you have always enjoyed cooking or speaking Italian or you're curious about investing in crypto. Hop online and find a club or organization that aligns with your interests.

  Mothers are sponges for connection, and that fact is not lost on our capitalist society. There are many places that bring our demographic together and offer community. Ask your pediatrician for a referral to a mothers' group or check out the bulletin boards at Mommy and Me classes.

  Below are a few suggestions for places where you might find connection.

- A house of worship
- A coworking space
- A book club
- A birding club
- A bridge club
- A knitting group
- Dance classes
- Yoga classes
- One of those groups that meets in a café to read in silence together (this exists!)

- A class at your local community college
- A meditation group
- A volunteer group
- A walking club
- A group text with a few mom friends

If you are feeling shy about showing up to a new activity alone, maybe invite a friend to go with you, buddy system–style.

- *Join something virtually.* If the idea of showing up regularly in person for a group activity is too much, try this easier step: look for a "buy nothing" group on Facebook. There are usually dozens of moms on there looking for free stuff or hoping to pass things along to a good home. Find something to give away or choose something to accept, then start a conversation with the mom when you make the exchange. This is a great low-effort first point of contact.

  Even easier: find an online group of moms whose attitudes you like. Maybe you're looking for people who are irreverent or sincere or who are at the same stage of parenting as you are. Read the comments and participate in the conversation online.

- *Start your own thing.* If you can't find an existing organization that makes your heart sing, start your own. You don't need to host a twenty-person yoga class in your home, but maybe you can invite two friends over for an online yoga class on Saturday mornings. Or ask a friend to cowork at your house every Monday. Or arrange for a ten-minute phone call with another mom one morning a week on your way into work. Or exchange monthly emails with an old friend about the hardest parts of being a mom. Give your activity a name and a purpose, make it regular, and then watch your village grow.

Chapter 7

Operation Mom Friends

ISOLATION MINDSET: I have plenty of friends. I'm certainly not at a place in life where I want to meet anyone new.

VILLAGE MINDSET: Now that I'm a mom, other mothers provide a type of connection and support I can't find elsewhere.

*M*eeting Lorrie in college had been a godsend for Taryn. Taryn hadn't been one to go to rowdy fraternity parties. She was more interested in watching the improv comedy troupe on campus and socializing in small groups. She met Lorrie, a wry econ major, in the ceramics studio where Taryn had a campus job. Lorrie would come in to unwind at the end of the day by throwing simple bowls on the wheel. The two struck up a conversation while elbow deep in clay. From their first night together in the studio, their talks felt like a tennis match, volleying subjects from Proust to *Bachelor in Paradise* back and forth. It was joy for Taryn to find someone to banter with. They eventually started hanging out outside the studio, studying together at the big wooden tables in the library and then heading back to Lorrie's dorm room to watch reruns on her laptop. They stayed up late talking about their good dates, their bad dates, their professors, whether it was still okay to laugh at the jokes on *30 Rock*, and their futures. With their eyes fluttering closed, they talked until sleep overtook them.

After graduation, they both moved to Portland, Maine, and found their first jobs. They shared a comfortable apartment where they cooked dinner together nearly every night while downloading everything that had happened at work—Taryn was an admin at a dental practice, and Lorrie was a marketing assistant at a real estate company. They relaxed by bingeing on TV series and dissecting the shows' plotlines. Sometimes they joked that they didn't need romantic partners because they had each other. But eventually, each of them did fall in love with great partners—Taryn with

Patti, an IT technician, and Lorrie with John, a former track star who was working in retail.

Two years after Taryn and Lorrie had signed their lease, they moved out of their cozy two-bedroom and in with their respective partners. As they schlepped heavy boxes of dishes and even heavier boxes of books to their separate moving trucks, Taryn picked up a Liz Lemon mug and put it in Lorrie's pile, which made Lorrie sob as if someone had just killed her cat. John gently reminded the friends that their new apartments were only a five-minute drive apart.

For a while, they were religious about having a weekly girls' night. Same bar, same drinks, same friendship. They laughed about their partners' annoying habits and their own elaborate bedtime routines involving many, many lotions. Their conversations stayed as intense as ever and continued over text throughout the day. Friendship status: solid.

Then one girls' night, Taryn ordered a virgin piña colada. "What—are you pregnant or something?" Lorrie asked sarcastically. No one in their friend group had made the leap to motherhood yet. Taryn's silence said everything. Lorrie jumped off her stool and hugged Taryn tight. She was so excited that she bought drinks for everyone in the bar (which, fortunately for her, was just a handful of people in the predinner hour). "You are going to be the best mom. Seriously, that is one lucky kiddo," she said, grinning.

This meant the world to Taryn, since she had lost her mother when she was only two years old and had always secretly wondered if she'd have what it takes to be a mom, given that she barely remembered her own. Over the previous few months, as Taryn and Patti searched for an egg donor and went through the process of artificial insemination, it had been hard for Taryn to keep it all secret from Lorrie. But Patti was superstitious, and she'd been insistent that they keep their attempts to get pregnant private until they had their twenty-week ultrasound and heard the baby's heartbeat. Taryn was so happy to be able to share the news with her friend at last.

Lorrie assigned herself the role of Taryn's wingwoman during her pregnancy. Before Taryn was ready to share the news widely, whenever they went out with friends, Lorrie helped cover for her friend by discreetly switching her half-drunk beer for Taryn's untouched one. Since Patti had no interest in home decor, it was Lorrie who helped Taryn pick out cute little owl sheets and a small rug for the corner of the bedroom where the baby would sleep.

When Ramona was born, Lorrie was the first person other than Patti in the room. She got there before even Taryn's dad, who was still en route from Boston when Ramona crowned. Lorrie gave Ramona her first stuffie, a soft owl with giant eyes they called Big Eyes. Over the course of the next few weeks, Taryn wanted so much to talk to her friend about what she was feeling (exhausted, mostly, but also happy), but Ramona beckoned. Each time Lorrie dropped by after work, Taryn said a quick hello and then promised she'd call her later that night, but by nighttime, she was too pooped to dial.

Finally, at the six-week mark, Ramona was taking a bottle, and Taryn was managing to pump enough milk to persuade Patti to stay home with the baby while she met Lorrie for a catch-up. The two friends clutched each other as if one of them had just come back from a long voyage at sea. After asking quickly about Ramona, Lorrie launched into a rant about the final season of *Lost*, which she had just rewatched. Taryn tried not to show how lost she herself felt. She hadn't so much as turned on the TV for weeks.

Her mind was not on the Island. It was on her new body and her new baby and her new life. She had trouble concentrating on what Lorrie was saying. When Lorrie finished, she apologized. "I haven't seen *Lost* in ages."

Taryn got out her phone to show Lorrie pictures of Ramona with Big Eyes and told her that her boobs were feeling like over-inflated basketballs. She described how insanely cute it was when Ramona tried to reach for something but didn't yet have the motor skills to grab it. She even worked up the courage to confess that it was harder than she'd thought to figure out how to meet Ramona's needs. She'd expected it to "come naturally," but nothing about it felt natural. It felt awkward and clumsy, and she was full of insecurity that she was doing every single thing wrong. This was the kind of secret she'd always shared with Lorrie, and she yearned for her friend's soothing, empathetic take.

But as she talked, she got a weird feeling. Lorrie was there beside her, but she wasn't really engaging. This was a woman who had once listened with rapt attention to a play-by-play of how Taryn had gotten a splinter in her elbow. How come she didn't seem interested in the biggest thing that had ever happened to Taryn? At the end of the night, the two friends promised to get back on their regular hang-out schedule, but for the first time since they'd met, Taryn wasn't entirely enthusiastic about the prospect.

Taryn nursed the hurt of Lorrie's not showing much interest in Ramona. She thought maybe they just needed to get their sea legs, but the next time they hung out, it was the same thing. Lorrie wanted to keep talking about things they had always talked about, and Taryn just didn't have the energy.

Between hang-outs, she sent Lorrie texts about how well Ramona was gaining weight and pictures showing her doing tummy time. Silence. It was heartbreaking to Taryn not to have Lorrie's reactions. Was it possible that she was losing her friend? To a lesser extent, the same dynamic played out with her other friends. She could almost hear their "polite applause" anytime she shared anything about Ramona. She worried that she no longer fit in with her friends.

Taryn's experience is a familiar one for many of us. As Dr. Jen Douglas points out, the friend groups we have premotherhood, whether they are from school or work or as far back as childhood, have a rhythm to them that gets established over the years. There's a dynamic you fall into—a certain way of talking or a certain subject you return to again and again. Maybe you talk about dating or you talk about work or you talk about movies or books—then you have a baby, and your life is taken up by taking care of this thing, and for you, the focus and the rhythm changes. Suddenly, unless others in your group also have children, you are out of step with your people.[1]

If most of our established connections are with people who don't have kids, it can leave a big gap in our ability to connect. That isolation can be terrifying, but you can calm that fear if you find people who make you feel like you belong. Translation: you need to increase the number of moms you hang out with.

As Taryn was despairing about feeling unseen and unheard by her friends, Patti reminded her that, a few years earlier, when Lorrie decided to run a marathon, it was all Lorrie wanted to talk about. Taryn had wished her friend well, but she was not a runner herself, and she just couldn't bring herself to care about training regimens and off days. She hadn't stopped caring about Lorrie—she just wasn't especially interested in that part of her life. The reminder was a good recalibration. She understood that Lorrie's zoning out when she talked about Ramona didn't mean that Lorrie loved Taryn any less. It's just that Lorrie didn't have a genuine interest in the details. Taryn didn't want to cut Lorrie out of her life—far from it: she wanted to stay connected to her dear friend, but she also wanted to be able to share her experience with someone who could relate. She was going to have to make some new friends—some mom friends.

MOM FRIENDS—AN ESSENTIAL PART
OF YOUR VILLAGE

When you become a mother, it's as if you suddenly speak a new language. You need to practice it with other people who speak it, too. There are certain aspects of motherhood that can only be fully understood if you have experienced them. They range from the small moments, such as the frustration of trying to get your baby to latch, to much more serious moments—like the desperation you feel when your child is being bullied or the anguish of having a child who is seriously ill.

Consider the following scenarios. Does any of them feel familiar?

- You're at the office holiday party, and it's past your bedtime—not to mention the kids' bedtime—and you are ready to head home, but your childfree coworkers keep urging you to stay for just one more drink. After all, it's the holidays!
- You're at work when school calls to tell you that your child has come down with a fever. You knew you were pushing it when you sent her in that morning with a runny nose. The guilt hits: *What kind of mother am I, anyway?* As you gather your things, you could swear

the twentysomethings in the room are rolling their eyes at one another as if to say, "Guess we're stuck picking up the slack for Mom *again.*"

- You're grocery shopping, and your toddler is having a class 5 meltdown. He throws every item in your cart on the floor. You could really use a hand—not that anyone is offering one. Countless people walk by, stepping around you as if you were a rabid dog.

Individually, these events may sound like minor blips in the day of an average parent. We've all been there, and we usually recover from them quickly. However, if we don't have anyone to share them with, the slow accumulation of moments like these can make us feel disconnected and unseen, adding up to a pervasive sense that we are alone in our struggles.

If you're looking for support for your new exercise regimen, you can turn to your fitness-obsessed friends and go to town designing the perfect Tabata workout together. If you want someone to go to the ballet with, find your most cultured buddy. But if you're looking for a supportive group to help you navigate the wilds of motherhood, you want other moms by your side. No one is going to understand the meaning of "bone-tired" like another mom. No one is going to understand the truth of the cliché that your heart now lives outside your body. No one is going to understand why it took you forty-five minutes to get out the door because you needed to find the *red* sweater.

Back when I was experiencing the identity crisis of becoming a new mom, I was overwhelmed by all the new feelings that washed over me. Before becoming a mother, I could watch the news and hear about a child who'd been affected by something horrible like a flood or a car accident and think, *Whew—that's terrible.* But after I became a mother, it took a lot less to move me to tears. Show me a commercial where the parents failed to notice when a little girl drops her ice cream, and I'm absolutely gutted. Hearing about an actual tragedy? Forget it. I could spiral for hours. I had no idea what was going on with me. Where was the strong, stoic Melissa I knew myself to be? Were other moms going through the same thing?

To make matters worse, I doubted my ability to make decisions about what was best for new baby Nathan. Should I put him on a sleep schedule or tune in to his signals? Should we cosleep or were we going to roll over on him in the middle of the night? Was I damning him to live on a planet choked with plastic by using disposable diapers? Every decision took on outsize importance. Was anyone else feeling this way?

If only I'd had the wisdom to reach out to other moms for support, I would have saved myself a lot of pain and insecurity, because, as I now know, I was far from alone.

THERE'S NOTHING LIKE MOM FRIENDS

After talking to Patti, Taryn resolved to try to find a way to meet some moms. She saw flyers at the pediatrician's office for moms' groups, but there was no way she was going to show up at a coffee shop and meet with a group of total strangers. Not her style. Taryn had no interest in following the "join something" mandate. Fortunately, a neighbor named Andra came to her rescue.

Taryn had occasionally seen Andra in Saturday morning yoga classes before they had kids. Once they both got pregnant and started showing, they engaged in "When are you due?" conversations as they were rolling up their mats, but it had never gone deeper than that. Andra had always struck Taryn as perfectly nice, but she wasn't sure they had a shared sense of humor, so she'd been content to leave their relationship at a friendly distance.

Two months after Ramona was born, they ran into each other at the grocery store. They admired each other's babies. Taryn noticed Andra's giant smile as she said hi to Ramona. It made her feel kind of glowy, like someone had just admired a painting she'd done or laughed hard at a clever joke she'd made. As they were saying goodbye, Andra tossed out, "You know, I host a moms' group. Just a few neighborhood moms and their babies on Saturday mornings if you ever want to drop by." She gave Taryn her number, and Taryn saved it under "Andra Mom."

She must have started a text to Andra fifty times. Was she really going to show up at this woman's house just because they both had given birth recently? Then she remembered how it felt when Andra smiled at Ramona, and she finally typed, "About that moms' group—I'd love to come. Can you remind me when?" She didn't know if she wanted to hear back or be completely ignored. At least if Andra didn't respond, she'd have an excuse for not going. Five minutes later, Andra texted her the address and wrote, "See you Saturday."

The next Saturday, Taryn slid Ramona into a sling and headed over to Andra's house. Once she was inside, she nodded to the other guests, who were all chatting like old friends, before making a beeline for the dining room, where there was a spread of food. She took her time choosing the right butter cookie from the tin so she wouldn't reveal how out of place she felt. Finally, she made her way back to the living room, spread out a blanket on the floor, and laid Ramona on it. Andra made introductions, and Taryn felt her face flush. The four other moms who were sitting there with their babies looked perfectly nice, but what if they didn't like her? What if she said something stupid that revealed how uncertain she felt as a mom and how long it had been since she'd made a new friend?

That first meeting was awkward. She pretty much picked at her cookie and fussed with Ramona's onesie while the other women traded horror stories about mastitis. They were all so *sincere*. No one made a single joke. She imagined how Lorrie would have rolled her eyes at the earnest talk about dairy sensitivity if she had been in the room. Taryn practically flew out of the house when things wrapped up, wondering if she'd ever come back. She took a deep look inside herself as she walked home. Why did sitting there make her feel itchy? Had it actually been unpleasant? Or was she just uncomfortable trying something new? If she was honest with herself, she really *was* interested in what they had to say. They were talking about topics that consumed her days. That night, when she was tempted to go to bed without pumping, she remembered that Andra had described mastitis as being worse than the flu, and she got back out of bed to hook herself up to the machine. She decided she'd give the moms' group another go.

The following week, she waited for an opening to enter the discussion like a kid trying to decide when to jump into double Dutch. When the women started talking about breast pumps, she found her moment: she told everyone that it always sounded to her like her pump was chanting, "ass-hole, ass-hole." A few people laughed, and she felt a huge sense of relief. She'd broken the seal. After that, she felt a little more engaged each week and started nodding along and saying "I know exactly what you mean" as the women shared tales from the trenches.

She joined a group text with the other moms, which quickly became a lifeline for her as she navigated new motherhood. When Ramona left a diaper a color that didn't seem like it could have come from nature, she asked the group if they'd ever seen anything like it. Two other moms chimed in immediately and said their little ones had done the same thing. That was a relief. At one meeting, she even confessed that once, when she was extremely sleep-deprived, she got so frustrated when Ramona wouldn't stop crying that she shouted at her sweet little baby, "Shut up!" Her cheeks burned as she said it, but when Andra and the others immediately raised their hands, saying, "I've done that!" she felt a million times better.

These feelings of solidarity with women who were in the mommy trenches were almost physical. The only way to describe it was "grounding." They were the first people she told when she was panicking about going back to work while still nursing, and they coached her through how to ask for a place in the office fridge for her breast milk. When she needed to take her car to get inspected, Andra volunteered to watch Ramona for an hour. She texted the moms in her group when Ramona first laughed and was gratified to get a series of smiley emojis in response. And the moms were the first people she reached out to when she had an awkward inter-action with Lorrie. They'd all been there with certain friends and family members who weren't tuned in to the motherhood journey.

I love Taryn's mom group story because it perfectly embod-ies the distinct benefits of social contact that psychologist Susan Pinker points to in her book *The Village Effect*.[2]

> *Timely information.* Mom friends offer important informa-
> tion and advice: in Taryn's case, this took the form of
> warnings about mastitis.
> *Material assistance.* Mom friends offer logistical help, such
> as babysitting.
> *Improved mental and physical health.* Perhaps most impor-
> tant, on top of the physiological benefits of connection

I mentioned in chapter 1, mom friends offer a sense of belonging like the feeling Taryn enjoyed when they welcomed her into their group, and emotional support like the compassion they offered when she expressed vulnerability.

What gives moms these superpowers when we get together? What allows for connection on so many different levels? It comes down to a concept social scientists refer to as "shared reality."

SHARED REALITY:
THE CURE FOR GASLIGHTING

Shared reality results when a group of people undergo the process of "making sense of the world together,"[3] and it is a crucial element of forming a meaningful connection with other people. Making sense of the world—understanding what is true and determining how to behave accordingly—is a tall order. It's nearly impossible to do it by yourself. By the time most of us become mothers, we've already said goodbye to many of the systems that helped us understand the world and make choices—formal education, team sports, daily contact with our parents. Some of us have moved away from the cities and hometowns where we had community or extended family. On top of that, many of us these days have parted ways with organized religion. We're left to figure out how to be in this new world of motherhood all on our own— a task that becomes exponentially harder once we have to impart that worldview to the new little people we've just welcomed into the family. It's too much for one person.

It is much less daunting to make sense of our experiences alongside other people. Having access to other people's perspectives helps us calibrate our own. Looking to others to affirm our experiences is a natural instinct. We do it from our earliest days. A toddler will look to her parent to confirm that she is interpreting a situation correctly—this is hot; this is soft; this is scary. Toddlers have their own reactions, sure, but they don't fully solidify until the people around them agree that yes, that is hot or soft or scary. We are reassured when someone else's view lines up with our own.

You may not become besties with another woman simply because she also happens to have children. However, regardless of whether we live in Tulsa or Tokyo, whether we have a two-year-old or a ten-year-old, or whether we vote red or blue or not at all, we're all raising human beings. There are certain things that every mother is going to encounter. Every mom has probably had a kid with an ear infection or has had to struggle with sleep issues or discipline or whether the kid was ever going to go to the bathroom alone. You can start a conversation about any of those things and suddenly have a moment of connection. We often find common ground when it comes to wanting what's best for our kids. Members of your village might have ended up in a different place when it comes to child-rearing philosophy, but their understanding of what matters, what the issues *are*, will likely line up with yours. For example, although I might be a "breast is best for my kid" mama and you might swear by formula, both of us are linked by the fundamental need to feed our babies the best way we can. There's a common sense of shared purpose and perspective. That shared perspective creates shared reality.

Think back to high school when you met that one other kid who loved the same obscure band as you did, and you felt a connection. It's as if finding someone who likes what you do is a confirmation that the way you're interpreting the world makes sense. It verifies that you're not mistaken about your take on the world.[4]

A friend of mine had a moment of shared reality on Mother's Day when she talked her kids into going for a walk. She was eager for some bonding in nature, but after around fifteen minutes, the kids complained that they were tired. She was feeling down about the whole endeavor when she ran into another mom she knew—whose daughter was having a full-on meltdown in the woods. She *knew* that mom was having the same disappointing experience she was. "Happy freaking Mother's Day!" she said brightly, and the two of them laughed knowingly together. When they acknowledged the shared experience of the gap between their hopes and reality, the bond that crackled between them brightened my friend's mood.

I think of moms who form bonds over their shared concerns as being like soldiers who have been deployed in a war zone: they have an instant understanding of one another's experience. Or maybe, less dramatically, they're like people who went to the same summer camp: they immediately know they shared a formative experience, which provides kinship.

The reason it feels so comfortable to connect with other moms is that *we get it*. Another mom might catch your eye in Target when your kid goes boneless as you say no to buying yet another Squishmallow. They might shoot you a smile of understanding when your tween daughter walks ten steps ahead of you because God forbid she should acknowledge that you are her mother. Your nonmom friends might bring over a casserole when your baby is two weeks old, but chances are, they are not the ones who will volunteer to come over in week 12 to hold your baby while you shower. Only another mom knows how clutch that is.

UNDERSTANDING IS OUR SUPERPOWER

When we tap into the deep understanding of our shared reality as mothers, it can become a superpower that produces real joy. I've had several of those moments, and one in particular stands out.

Being a mother during the winter, when the days are dark and cold, is particularly hard for me. I find parenting outside much easier than parenting inside, so when nature's playground is taken away from my bag of parenting tricks, I go a little stir-crazy. On this occasion, I had made it through the first five months of Benjamin's life and the dreariest part of the year. It was finally March. I had four kids under the age of six and a fast-growing company, but the sun was shining, my baby was sleeping-ish, and I felt much happier than I had during the winter.

One morning, after kissing the kids goodbye, I hopped in my minivan for the short drive to the office only to find lights on the dash blinking at me. Lights I had never seen before. I'm an old pro at the occasional tire-pressure or check-engine light, but these lights were different. It was something about the airbag. I deduced by reading the manual that this was worse than the check-engine light. Not good. But it was a beautiful day, the windows were down, and the music was loud. I let my good mood distract me from the blinking lights.

The next morning, after a harried night with four young kids and a case of amnesia about the warning lights in my car, I once again climbed into the van to go to work and noticed some weird dirtlike droppings on my seat.

There is something you should know about me. In the juggling game of life, I dropped the clean-car ball long ago. On any given day I could clothe and feed an entire elementary school simply with the items on the van floor. I let the kids eat in the car because how else are we going to get where we need to go (close to) on time? Things always spill; food always falls to the floor; and I spend the summer months with apple cider vinegar fruit-fly traps in the back-row cupholders. So the idea that there was noticeable dirt on my seat wasn't particularly surprising, but this particular dirt was something I had not seen before.

My brain flashed to a moment a week earlier when two-year-old Caroline with her hundred or so words was staring out the family-room window, saying over and over, "Mama. Car. Squirrel."

"Yes, baby, you're right. That's Mama's car. And look at all those squirrels in the trees." But maybe, just maybe, Caroline had been talking about seeing a squirrel *inside* the car. Maybe the dash lights were on because a squirrel had climbed into the car and eaten through the airbags. Does that even happen?

How messy a life do you have to lead for a squirrel to live in your minivan?

That night, I told Eric what I thought was happening. He was not amused. Judgment was all over his face. After insisting that I couldn't safely drive with those lights on any longer, he asked me what my next step was.

I had two options. I could bring the car to a shop and deal with the shame I felt for my messy life by myself, or I could surround myself with people who would understand. I worked the phone. Within an hour, I'd rallied some mom friends.

My friends Colleen and Lindi came over the next day, and we cleaned out the van from top to bottom. There was zero judgment, because they had been there. Or close to there. Although Lindi never had a squirrel take up residence in her car, she did tell me about the time she forgot a whole roast chicken under the third row of seats and didn't discover it for *an entire month*. We filled two trash bags with empty water bottles and floor scraps and two laundry baskets' worth of soccer socks, jackets, and missing shoes. Throughout the process, we juggled kids, ate snacks, and made jokes. *(What is a squirrel's favorite streaming service? Nut-flix.)* Finally, we started disassembling the dash. I didn't know whether to laugh or cry when I saw a bushy tail sticking out from below the radio.

We placed a catch-and-release trap on the dash, and each night I put fresh peanut butter and trail mix in the trap. There were daily updates via text to my mom crew. Everyone was invested. Eventually, I woke one morning to find our adorable yet destructive friend safely in the trap. We released him into the woods to forage for food, as nature intended. I was left with a busted minivan, which I still had to take in for repairs, but a profound appreciation for the support and love the moms in my life had shown me.

THE POWER OF "I'VE BEEN THERE"

If I had to choose the most powerful way that moms support one another, it would have to be the way we share the emotional weight of parenting.

In the Latched Mama Facebook group, it is nothing less than inspiring to witness moms assuring one another that the chaos, turmoil, and emotional upheaval they're experiencing is totally normal. The women who post are bravely putting themselves out there. They can afford to, knowing that their vulnerability will be met with compassion from other moms. When one member of the group posted about being at her wit's end with her toddler's behavior and her husband's unhelpfulness, it was clear from her tone that she was in a dark place. Dozens of moms jumped in to reassure her that she wasn't the only one who felt overwhelmed with frustration. They, too, had found themselves pulling their hair out on occasion. After a series of "I've been there" comments, one fellow Latched Mama wrote to reassure the original poster that her experience didn't mean she was broken.

How badly do we all need to hear that? We're not broken. Being a mother is *hard*. If you're struggling, it's because it *is* a struggle. No one knows that better than another mom.

Only another mom can understand how deeply insecure you might feel about every single parenting decision you make. There are *so many* decisions. So many opportunities in a single day to misstep or do it wrong. So many chances to second-guess yourself and be beset with regret and self-recrimination. Should you go back to work? If you do, should you find day care or a nanny? Public school or private? A full, stimulating schedule? Or loads of free time to encourage creativity and friendship? Should discipline be strict or compassionate? Will using a scented laundry detergent make your children infertile? The worries are endless. For many moms I know, the primary question that hovers over their days is "Am I doing this right?"

The big secret is that none of us feel one hundred percent certain that we are doing it right. When I figured that out, I felt a massive sense of connection to every mom out there. I felt the way I imagine germophobes must have felt during the early stages of the coronavirus pandemic—*Look at that: we're all worried together!* I felt more connected just knowing I wasn't the only one who wondered whether extra screen time during vacation was going to contribute to my kids' "summer slip" or if seeing me cry—or refusing to cry—would send them to therapy. These other women were doing their best, just as I was. We were imperfect, and trying to do our best, together.

One of my favorite stories about how moms can help one another combat insecurity comes from a woman named Sapna. Sapna is a business writer in Bethesda, Maryland. She is very intentional about making mom friends, possibly because of the way she grew up in India, surrounded by helpful "aunties" who were always willing to drop by with food or scold her if she stepped out of line when her mother wasn't watching. Sapna invites her cookbook club over once a month to try new recipes together. She plans camping weekends with her female friends. She has a separate group text for the moms of each of her kids' friends so she can keep up on school events and missed assignments. She truly has a village.

Sapna is also great at foraging for food—not in her refrigerator for lettuce that hasn't gone bad, the way I do, but in the actual woods with dirt and chipmunks. She makes meals from foraged fiddlehead ferns, wild raspberries, hard little apples, and, occasionally, mushrooms. She was thrilled one fall when she found a cluster of hen of the woods at the base of a tree in a nearby park. She gathered them in a paper bag, brought the mushrooms home, sautéed them with butter, and served them over pasta at lunch for her husband, Nick, and her son, Sathya, nine, and daughter, Priya, six.

An hour after they'd eaten and she'd released the kids to play outside, a friend of her son banged on the door and said, "Sathya needs you. He's sick." She rushed outside and saw that Sathya had thrown up. She figured he'd caught the stomach bug that had been going around at school, so she scooped him up, tucked him into bed, and went to check in on Priya. When she reminded Priya that she wanted her home when the streetlights came on, Priya said, "Actually, I think I'll come with you now. I don't feel so good."

Within an hour, the entire family was fighting for space in the bathroom. Sapna's heart lurched as she remembered the mushrooms. What if this wasn't a stomach bug? She'd never picked a bad mushroom before, but how confident was she that the ones she served were edible? To be safe, she packed the family into the car and went to the ER. She was glad she did. Those mushrooms hadn't been hen of the woods: they were jack-o'-lanterns, a toxic variety. The family received fluids and were monitored for food poisoning. Fortunately, they recovered quickly and fully, but Sapna was shell-shocked—and ashamed. What kind of mother poisons her children?

The next day, she woke up to find a series of text messages from her mom friends. As she scrolled through them, her heart rate slowed. Each of them had shared a story of their own "yikes" moments. Becca told Sapna that she'd unintentionally left a pot of pasta boiling on the stove when she went out—and only learned of her mistake two hours later, when her thirteen-year-old came home to find the kitchen filled with smoke. Holly wrote about the time she'd taken her second and fifth graders hiking on a trail so treacherous that she learned the next day it had been closed after a hiker had fallen and was paralyzed. Sapna didn't need to explain to her friends how ashamed she was. They just knew—and they knew what she needed to hear.

That's the power of having someone who can look you in the eyes and say, "I have been there." That's why it is so valuable to make other moms a key part of your village.

Keep the friends you had before you became a mom—cherish them. But I can promise you that you won't regret widening your circle to include mom friends. You'll be more informed. You'll have more people you can turn to for help in a pinch, and, most important, you'll feel less alone. Doesn't that sound wonderful?

Build Your Village

Below are a few suggestions for ways to get out there and find your mom friends.

- *Ease in.* Identify three women you know who have children. Make it a goal to get together this month for tea or a walk or a drink with at least one of them. Send off a quick text right now. They don't have to be close friends; they can be women you've only spoken to occasionally—neighbors, coworkers; it doesn't matter. The point is to be intentional about choosing someone who is also a mother so you can spend time in the presence of a person who shares your reality.

- *Get some mom mentors.* Arrange a monthly Zoom with two or more moms who are further down the road on their motherhood journey. People love to be asked about their lives and how they came to make certain decisions. Pay them the compliment of asking about their philosophy of motherhood and what it looks like from day to day.

- *Engage mom power.* Do a small, easy thing to create a moment of solidarity between you and another mom. Hold the door for a mom with a stroller at the airport. Distract a toddler while a mom is trying to unload her groceries onto the checkout counter in peace. Offer to carpool to swim practice. Tell a friend you noticed that she took time to personalize the favors at her kid's birthday party. A collection of easy things adds up to a communal feeling of support. Make it your mission to find one opportunity for a flash of bonding in the next week.

- *Practice solidarity.* Next time a mom friend cops to a mistake or to feeling like she blew it, take a cue from Sapna's friends and tell her about a time you've made a similar mistake. She just might do the same for you next time you're doubting yourself.

Chapter 8

She's Not
My Type

ISOLATION MINDSET: If I want to find connection, the best way to do it is to seek out people with whom I have the most in common—from our interests to our approach to parenting.

VILLAGE MINDSET: We benefit from having a wide circle that includes people whose views and interests differ from our own.

A few years into owning Latched Mama, I gathered my A team in my office to discuss plans for our holiday promotion bundle. I was exhausted from parenting my three kids under three years old, but this was a critical part of the year for the company, so I gathered my focus. My closest colleagues were there: Ann, Holly, and Amy—three women who were a core part of my village and who were also new moms. Per Latched Mama policy, they were able to bring their babies with them to work each day. The rest of the staff adored those babies, and I felt unbelievably lucky to witness the collective love for them. Watching up close as Ann, Holly, and Amy learned how to be moms was one of the great joys of my life.

That day, we were about to break for lunch when Ann picked up her giant mom bag and a can of formula rolled out. There was a long moment of silence. Have you ever seen one of those movies where a grenade rolls into the room and everyone makes eye contact as they realize a bomb is about to go off? That was the feeling in the air. Amy, Holly, and Ann all turned to me to gauge my response to that can of formula. Much as it pains me to say it now, they were right to worry. I wouldn't have *said* I was judgmental about moms who use formula; it had just been so easy for me to breastfeed. I didn't see why anyone would make another choice.

I guess I'd been pretty vocal about my "breast is best" perspective, because all my employees tensed as they prepared for me to explode. I looked at Ann. Sweet Ann. She was so dear to me, like a little sister. She had left college after getting pregnant unexpectedly, and she and baby Lukas had become an extended part of our family. After the Similac rolled across the floor, a tear slipped down Ann's cheek. She knew I thought she had been exclusively breastfeeding. It stung to see the fear in her eyes.

Looking back, I have to confess: I wanted Ann to breastfeed, just as I had. I had fooled myself into believing that the best way to find belonging was to surround myself with other moms who thought the way I did. I wanted to be a crunchy, all-natural mama. I leaned waaaaay into that identity. I was a ride-or-die natural-child-birther. I pushed *The Business of Being Born* documentary on everyone who would listen, and Mother Earth was my doula. I did cloth diapers. I avoided plastics. I was on team granola, and if you were feeding your kids chemical-laden Goldfish—or, heaven forbid, formula—you were not my people.

I was sure that there was a "right" way to parent, and my parenting rules governed my days and my relationships. They also shrank my circle drastically. I didn't have space in my life or my heart for moms who followed different recipes for parenting "success." Their divergent choices made me question my own, and I couldn't have that. I cringe when I look back on it all. In hindsight, I recognize that my behavior stemmed from a place of insecurity. I tried to surround myself with other moms whose choices mirrored my own to reassure myself that my choices were the best.

That day, when Ann's formula rolled out of her bag and I saw her terrified expression, I recognized that I had made a terrible mistake. How could this person whom I admired so much have felt like she was disappointing me—just for supplementing? Why had she felt like she had to hide this from me? One of my closest people was not fully herself around me because I'd been so judgmental.

In that moment, instead of owning up to my mistake, I choked. I helped Ann pick up the can and handed it back to her. I should have told her that I didn't give a hoot how she fed Lukas, but for some reason, I didn't. I wish that I had let her know that I cared about her and her family, not about her choices, which were her business. I missed that moment of connection, and something shifted in our relationship after that. We saw less of each other, and when we did interact, I could tell she was walking on eggshells.

As I've started paying more attention to the ways we connect (or don't connect) with other people, I've noticed that I'm not the only one who slips into this familiar pattern when searching for community in motherhood. We fall for the false belief that we can only connect with people who are like us—people who come from the same background, share the same political views, or follow the same parenting approach. We are so entrenched in our obsession with sameness that we rule out connecting with people who are even slightly different from us.

I get it. Really, I do. There are days when all I want in the world is a girl squad made up of women I can freely swear in front of and who will feed my kids the exact same snacks at their homes that I would serve at mine. Familiarity puts us at ease. When we interact with people who agree with us on most issues—from religious beliefs to fashion choices—we don't have to worry about offending anyone. We don't have to work to make sure other people understand us. Conversations unfold without anyone setting off a land mine.

It's very tempting to wrap myself in the safety of like-minded people. As the head of Latched Mama, I talk about my family and my beliefs online, with the media, and on my podcast. Trying to walk the line between being authentic and cautiously protecting myself from haters sometimes gives me vertigo. I often second-guess what I'm about to say because I can hear the approaching thunder of clapbacks. It makes me want to bunker down with friends who are just like me.

Our culture seems to work as a sorting machine. We gather online and in person with people who laugh at the same jokes, subscribe to the same magazines, know the same people, send their kids to the same kind of schools, and have the same level of education. In a twisted paradox, we crave belonging, so we seek out people with whom we think we will have the best chance of being accepted—people who are most like us, who make the same choices. But when we focus on connecting only with people who mirror our values, we cut ourselves off from untold potential connection. The more we look for people who are like us, the narrower the identity we have that allows us to feel a sense of belonging.

~

A few months after the can of formula fell out of Ann's bag, I still hadn't learned this lesson. I had been asked to lead a home-birth circle after the woman who usually led the group got sick, and I was truly flattered. I'd been part of this circle myself in the months leading up to Nathan's birth and had kept in touch with the instructor. I knew a thing or two about home birth. Four of the five kids I had at the time had been born at home (five if you count Nathan's back-seat-of-the-car arrival). I was eager to share my experiences with the group. Plus, what better opportunity to connect with a bunch of crunchy moms and moms-to-be who were just like me?

Channeling my best yogini impression on my first day in charge, I opened the floor for discussion. The atmosphere in the room was very mellow as everyone shared her feelings and fears about home birth, sort of like a group therapy session where you talk a lot about tearing your private parts. I'm not sure I've ever been in a bigger group of hippies. I loved every second.

After a few minutes on the subject of how to tell Braxton Hicks contractions from the real deal, for some reason, people got onto the subject of paper towels. Specifically, how terrible they are. A scourge. Morally reprehensible. Anyone who uses them is essentially a climate terrorist. Uh-oh. I had around fifty rolls of Bounty in my basement. Should I fess up that I was addicted to the quicker picker upper? What if these women saw me as a tree killer and a landfill filler? I wanted their approval, so I chimed in, "Oh, yeah, they're awful." I felt ridiculous, knowing that when I went home that night, I would probably go through an entire roll during dinner prep.

I tried to steer the conversation back to the wonders of home birth, but not a minute later, someone brought up the fact that cats were decimating the squirrel population in her neighborhood, and everyone started hating on outdoor cats. We live on a farm, so we have outdoor cats who roam about the property. (In my defense, though, none of our cats has ever caught a squirrel. Squirrels are fast! A cat who can catch a squirrel would be the Usain Bolt of cats.) Needless to say, I did not admit to harboring murderers.

I wanted these women to like me, so I pretended to be a tree-hugging, indoor-cat-loving earth mama. But I left the birth circle that night with that achy emotional hangover that arrives after you show up inauthentically. Instead of getting the belonging I so craved, I was haunted by the feeling that I was unworthy of connection.

We never did buy bamboo cloths to replace our paper towels, and I still let my cats outside. I also never went back to that circle.

It sounds absurd now, but I really thought I needed to be a carbon copy of the people I wanted to connect with.

JUDGE JUDY IS A BAD FRIEND

I've seen loads of women make the same mistake I did, especially at the beginning of motherhood. We come face-to-face with somebody who's doing things differently—a mom who sleep-trains instead of cosleeping, a mom who sets a rigorous eating schedule instead of feeding on demand, a mom who has very strict ideas about how much screen time is okay—and our focus on that difference sabotages connection. We turn away from moms who make different choices from ours as opposed to standing toe-to-toe and saying, "Hey, there's a place in this relationship for the way I do it. There's a place in this relationship for the way you do it. At some point, we're going to find things to connect over, and we all need connection more than we need to agree about whether it's okay to watch seven episodes of *Bluey* in a row."

Judging other moms for their parenting is a by-product of insecurity. In my crunchy days, I tried to boost myself by putting other people down, which is not a reflection on them. It was my perfectionism telling me that I had to get it exactly right in order to be worthy of the title of mom. Now I know that other moms aren't my adversary. My adversary is the unrealistic expectation that any mom can make the "right" decision about every aspect of parenting while remaining healthy and sane.

I've been on the receiving end of judgment many times because Eric and I homeschool our children. It's hilarious to watch people's faces when I tell them that we've opted out of the traditional education system. I can see them clicking through the stereotypes of homeschoolers, trying to decide which one fits my family. I'm willing to bet you have your own assumptions about me based on our decision to homeschool. Maybe you think we're extremely religious or that we travel a lot for our jobs or that our kids have special health concerns that prevent them from being in school with other kids. None of those is the reason we homeschool.

We arrived at the choice because it was one of Eric's nonnegotiables before we got married. Neither Eric nor I felt particularly seen in school when we were kids. Eric was a decent student, but his parents' divorce right before he entered high school left him angry. He was picked on and hung out with a crew who made choices he'd rather his own kids not make. As for me, even though I had a couple of friends, I never found my place at school. Being in such a large sea of people just made me feel more alone.

We thought we'd have the best chance of showing our kids that they belonged and that they can be themselves if we taught them at home. Our motto is "Find your way and be yourself." You want to be weird, be weird. You want to be nerdy, be nerdy. It might not work for everyone, but it works for our family. It's always painful when I sense another mom mentally writing me off because we homeschool. Even though I am very confident in our choice, I can't help but feel judged, and feeling judged is an enormous barrier to connection.

It wasn't until I learned how to accept my imperfections that I was able to stop judging other people. Once I copped to my own insecurities, it was easier to find compassion for other moms. Everyone else was as insecure as I was! Not a single one of us has the perfect marriage, perfect kids, perfect life, perfect anything. Once I understood that, I stopped needing to see my reflection in the members of my village. I didn't have to be a mom who uses disposable diapers to be friends with people who do. I didn't have to rule out people who drive gas-guzzling cars because I object to the environmental impact. Their decisions weren't contagions that might infect me. They were just that—*their* decisions. I let go of my need to out-mom the next mother, to be the crunch master supreme. I learned that I did not have to demonstrate to them—and myself—how much better I was at raising a kid.

Years later, on the other side of learning to withhold judgment, I can see that those women in the birth circle didn't really care what I used to clean up spills. Or if they did, they probably cared more about the much bigger thing we had common: we could all relate to the leap of faith it took to have a baby in a nonhospital setting. I could have shared real intimacy if I had just confessed that I was a paper towel user and then moved on to connect at a deeper level. It's on that deeper level that intimacy and connection thrive.

GREATEST COMMON DENOMINATOR

Imagine for a moment that we're all at the top of a craggy mountain, and there is a winter storm coming. Dark clouds gather and threaten to dump tons of wet, heavy snow on the peak, potentially setting off an avalanche. We have to get down to the bottom before the sky unleashes its fury. Some people might ski down; others might snowboard or parasail or hike or sled or ride a toboggan or take a chairlift or commission a helicopter. If you are on a pair of rental skis, you might think helicopter people aren't your people, but we are all just trying to get down the damn mountain without getting crushed. Our common need to make it to the base safely unites us more than our method of transportation divides us. If we can meet one another in that common desire, we will be so much more connected. That's motherhood in a nutshell.

Focusing on the shared struggle allows us to look at other moms with compassion. I love Dr. Becky Kennedy's concept of the "most generous interpretation" of people's actions. She uses the term primarily in relation to children's behavior. If your daughter is being a little snot when you ask her to turn off her screen, instead of reprimanding her for her bad attitude, you try to cast her actions in the most generous light. You tell yourself that maybe the reason your daughter is pitching a fit is not because she wants to make sure you never have a single moment of peace but because she knows that as soon as she turns off her device, her mind will be free to obsess about her teacher yelling at her in school that day. When you choose the most generous interpretation, you generate compassion, which leads to connection.

It's a great perspective. What if we could do the same with other moms? What if we could offer moms the most generous interpretation of *their* actions? Maybe you'll never understand why another mom made the choice she did, but you can understand that she probably had reasons for it that made sense to her. Let's just all adopt the attitude that folks are making the best choices for their families.

Deep down, under all our differences, moms are defined by two commonalities: our incredible love for our families and our worry that we are not enough for them. That is the foundation of connection. No matter how much privilege you have, no matter how different your life looks from that of the person whom you're trying to connect with, there are baseline similarities that allow us to bond with one another, as long as we are willing to go beneath the surface. We can connect when we realize that we struggle with the same insecurities. On your worst days, when you feel disconnected or anxious, or you don't want to keep showing up, if you can drill down to the questions that make you feel the most vulnerable—*Am I enough? Are my kids going to be okay? Am I making the right decisions? Am I present enough?*—you'll find that other moms will be able to relate.

The conversations moms have in the Latched Mama Facebook group illustrate that meeting one another in the struggle can go gloriously right. One mom will say, "Oh, my gosh, my baby's not gaining weight. I'm pumping three times in the middle of the night. I'm exhausted. I have to go to all these weigh-ins, and every time they read the numbers off the scale, I feel like I'm failing. How do I keep my baby healthy?" Lots of people offer resources for feeding techniques, but the responses that get the best reaction from the original poster are the ones that let her know she's clearly doing her best. It's really hard; supplementing does not make her a failure; she's not the only one who finds it daunting to feed a newborn. We all care about our kids, and we want to make sure they're growing. That common sense of purpose is where we find the magic.

SOME OF THE BEST FRIENDS
ARE GOOD ENOUGH FRIENDS

If Lucia hadn't been able to look past another mom's differences, she would have missed out on an important opportunity for connection.

Lucia met Hanna on the sidelines of the football field. Their thirteen-year-old boys, Andres and Spencer, were on the flag football team in a suburb of Boston. Lucia was a huge Patriots fan. Her wardrobe relied heavily on old Tom Brady jerseys, and her weekend plans usually included tailgating with her friends after the boys' practice. That wasn't exactly Hanna's vibe. She was a director of a nonprofit organization whose beat-up Subaru was covered in anticapitalist bumper stickers. Frankly, Hanna had always struck Lucia as a little stuck-up, so Lucia gave her a wide berth.

One sweltering day when Lucia arrived to pick Andres up from practice, however, Andres told her that he and Spencer had made plans to stick around and toss the ball for a while longer. It was six thousand degrees. How anyone could want to spend more time outside in such hot weather was beyond Lucia. But Andres never asked for anything, and she wanted to encourage him to make friends outside of school, so she agreed.

She walked over to Hanna to confirm that it was okay with her. She had planned to slide onto the shady bleachers and spend some time scrolling on her phone, but Hanna said, "Why don't you come over to my house? It's just a couple of blocks away. We can sit in the AC while the boys throw the ball around. They can come get us when they're hungry. Or when heatstroke sets in." Lucia wasn't sure she wanted to spend any one-on-one time with Hanna, but it *was* horribly hot, so she agreed.

When they walked into the house, Lucia almost immediately wanted to leave. Hanna's home looked to her like a science museum. The biggest telescope she'd ever seen leaned against the living-room wall near the door. There were huge framed posters of the night sky on every wall, and a Lego space station dominated the dining-room table. Lucia got the picture. Hanna and her family were really into space. She'd never seen the appeal herself. Life on earth was exciting enough, and she found movies about "the final frontier" kind of a snooze. *Relax*, she had to tell herself. She hadn't been invited there to talk about quarks and black holes; she'd been invited to escape the heat while her son played with his friend. She could do this.

The AC was a huge relief. As they talked, Lucia figured out pretty quickly that her suspicion that the two women were very different was dead-on. Hanna and her husband weren't just into space—they planned their lives around astronomical events. They had attended five of the past six space shuttle launches, and they checked the internet daily for the latest images from the James Webb Space Telescope (Hanna had had to tell Lucia what that was). Okay, so Hanna wasn't a sports fan, but she was funny and welcoming, not at all the standoffish type Lucia had assumed she was. Lucia couldn't help but feel at ease. They talked about the boys' coach and where they were considering sending the boys for high school the following year.

What was interesting, Lucia thought, was that the conversation didn't turn to the usual subjects—*What do you do for work? Where did you grow up? What does your partner do?* That wasn't it at all. It was really just talking about mom stuff—*What do the boys eat? Are they texting any crushes yet? How much monitoring of their phones is okay?* An hour or so later, two sweaty boys showed up at the door, and Lucia and Hanna said goodbye.

From then on, the two moms found each other at scrimmages. They continued their conversations about concussion protocols and whether they would ever let the boys play tackle. When Spencer took a hard hit one day, Lucia texted that night to ask how he was doing, which Hanna really appreciated. They didn't become best friends, but it made Lucia happy to high-five Hanna after a great play. She was so glad she hadn't written Hanna off just because she could name every moon of Jupiter. She wasn't her type, but she was a perfect person to have in her village.

VILLAGERS WITH BENEFITS

My criteria for whom I want in my circle has shifted. The people I gravitate toward in motherhood aren't always the people I want to go out for a drink with. But they're people I trust. Before I became a mom, I'd say the top quality I was looking for in a friend was "Can she make me laugh?" Now it's "Do I trust her to show up when I need her?"

My standards don't have to be the same for the members of my village as they are for the rest of my friends. Things that used to matter to me in close friendships aren't as important to me now. What were once must-haves—*Can I wear sweatpants in front of this person? Does she love* Smallville?—have become negotiable when it comes to inviting someone to be part of my village. We don't have to like the same music or have the same definition of *spiritual*. My village includes women decades older and younger than I am, women who are die-hard organic types, and women who eat at Wendy's three times a week. I even have women in my village who think homeschooling is a surefire way to turn your kids into little weirdos.

As I've gotten to know a wide circle of women, I've noticed there are a lot of benefits to befriending people who don't vote the way I do, don't believe in the same God I do, and don't discipline their children the same way I do. Just some of these benefits include:

I have access to additional resources. Motherhood is not a straight path. You can't predict where it's going to take you. I don't know a single mom who has been prepared for everything she has to deal with on her journey. Maybe you are the first of your close friends to need an amnio. Maybe your daughter goes through puberty before her friends do. Maybe your son develops a keen interest in studying in Dubai, a place you can't even find on a map. The more people you have in your life with diverse experiences, the more likely you'll be able to call on one of them for support when you encounter something new.

I like to think of this as the LinkedIn effect. On that platform, the norm is to link up with anyone you have even the most tangential connection to—*I met you in a lobby before a movie: let's be linked!*—because you never know when you're going to need a human resources manager or a copyeditor. When you take the same approach to creating a village, chances are good that you'll have the connection when you need it.

You never know when someone in your circle will come through with a key resource or piece of information you wouldn't have had access to otherwise. Since I've started opening my circle, I have reached the point where I can go through my mental Rolodex and find someone I can turn to for advice on just about any aspect of parenting, whether it's getting a picky eater to eat or dealing with middle school friend drama or looking for a medical specialist.

I've broadened my thinking. You're going to get more out of your village if it contains a wide array of opinions, experiences, and wisdom. We learn so much from people who have experiences different from ours. If you can withhold judgment, you might be able to slip out of your feedback loop of people who agree with everything you say. You might just learn something new. Or you might come to understand your own perspective in a clearer way, having heard the other side.

I have more empathy. When I catch myself turning away from people instead of turning toward them, I think of Mother Teresa's famous saying "If we have no peace, it is because we have forgotten we belong to each other." Siloing with people just like us deepens our fear of people who are not like us. The tighter we close our circles, the harder it is to see the humanity of other moms. Come on out of the foxhole and look kindly at the sweaty human over there in the crumpled shirt who is fighting just as hard as you are to get through the day.

I'm learning to be comfortable with discomfort. We have somehow gotten the idea that life should be free of conflict, that agreement is the gold standard. The slightest difference of opinion sets off alarm bells, and we retreat. Getting comfortable with friction takes practice, but the more you do it—the more times you sit across from people, disagree with them, and still manage to enjoy your conversation—the easier it gets.

In the unending choose-your-own-adventure of motherhood, there is no way we will find a village of people who have made all the same choices we have. And thank goodness, because if we did somehow succeed in finding a tribe of perfect doppelgängers, it would result in a pretty anemic village.

Expanding the borders of your village takes work. Our modern cynical mindset assumes that people won't like us or that we won't like them unless we are so similar that we could be swapped out for one another on a reality TV show. But the very idea of a village requires that it be expansive, inclusive, and open. If our goal is a thriving community that helps us feel supported, we need to shift our mindset from winnowing away differences to welcoming them. I am by your side whether you celebrate Christmas or worship the Flying Spaghetti Monster. Can we all just agree that we should focus on what we have in common? Because, my God, we have so much in common.

Build Your Village

Below are a few ways to expand the types of people to include in your village.

- *Widen your circle.* Next time you're in a group situation—at the playground, at a party, milling around after your kid's trumpet recital—resist the urge to huddle with the two people you know already. Challenge yourself to say a couple of sentences to at least one other person. Bonus points if it's someone you've avoided in the past because you think you'll have nothing in common.
- *Open your mind.* Make a list of nonnegotiables in your relationships. Maybe you value integrity, compassion, and acting with respect for your fellow humans. Then look back on the previous year and think about people you met but dismissed as potential villagers. Did you write them off for one of those nonnegotiable reasons or...because of something else? Don't feel bad. We all do it. But when you next find yourself in a conversation with someone who has revealed something that would normally send you looking for a way out—maybe she's wearing a T-shirt with a slogan you don't like or is a decade or more away from you in age—stay in the conversation a beat longer than you are inclined to. What might you have in common? What shared concern or struggle?

If people's core values are different from yours—if they have a cutthroat win-at-all-costs attitude or say hateful things or are mean to animals—you're under no obligation to grant them village status. But otherwise, try to stick it out and see if you aren't surprised.

- *Get curious.* If you find yourself judging another mom for the way she does something, repeat to yourself, *Her choice is not a condemnation of my choice; it's simply her choice.* Then get curious about how she might have arrived there. Say to her, "I struggled with that, too. What made you decide on *x*?"

PART III

So You Think You Might Have a Village (Maybe). Now What?

Chapter 9

How to Be a Village Mom

ISOLATION MINDSET: Okay, I've got some friends, and I see them pretty regularly. That's basically a village, right?

VILLAGE MINDSET: A true village means actively supporting fellow moms in your immediate friend group and beyond.

*L*indsay's been in an accident."

The text from her friend Lindsay's husband, Kevin, pinged on Jessica's phone during her nightly drowsy Insta scroll. Jessica sat up in bed, suddenly wide awake. Her fingers felt numb as she fumbled with her phone and dialed Kevin's number. He picked up immediately and explained that Lindsay had left the house that morning as usual, on her way to work as a park ranger in upstate New York, but she never made it. A speeding Highlander had T-boned her as she was backing out of their driveway. Thank goodness their two kids—Alex, five, and Adam, seven— had already taken the bus to school that day. Lindsay had been knocked unconscious. An ambulance arrived and took her to the hospital, where the doctors found that she had bruised ribs and a serious concussion. The medical team sent her home with strict instructions for postconcussion care, including a week of bed rest and no screens.

"What can I do to help?" Jessica asked. Kevin said he had things under control at home, but he knew Lindsay was going to hate not being allowed to use her phone. Jessica laughed. That sounded like her friend. Lindsay might work in the woods, but she loved technology as much as anyone. She was always forwarding links to her friends from the National Park Service account, whose jokes were surprisingly hilarious.

When Jessica checked in with Kevin the following day, he confirmed what they both knew would be true for their beloved Lindsay: her pain was manageable, but she was very, very bored.

Jessica stepped into action. She started a group text with six other women who knew Lindsay. Jessica explained what had happened and said that Lindsay was not allowed to use any devices until she'd recovered from her concussion. She suggested that everyone in the group send a good old-fashioned handwritten letter to Lindsay containing a fun animal fact or animal-themed joke to cheer her up. Then she created a spreadsheet on which people could sign up for a one-hour slot to sit with Lindsay, read her emails, and then transcribe her responses so she'd be able to remain connected to the world. When the letters started rolling in and the first email session took place, Kevin texted Jessica to let her know that Lindsay was blown away by her friends' response. He attached a photo of a thank-you letter Lindsay had written by hand, which was so full of gratitude that it brought tears to Jessica's eyes.

SMALL BUT MIGHTY

What I love about Jessica and Lindsay's story is that it is an example of the way small individual gestures can add up to a meaningful show of collective support for a mom in need. Writing a letter takes, what, fifteen minutes? And Lindsay's friends took just an hour out of their week to do email duty. Those actions didn't demand much from her friends, but they meant the world to Lindsay. As this story illustrates, just because societal support systems have forgotten about us does not mean that we have forgotten about one another.

I recently read about a group called Hot Mess Express. The founder, Jen Hamilton, jump-started the organization when she saw a post on a listserv from a mom who was struggling with postpartum depression. The mom was asking for a recommendation for a house cleaner, hoping that a tidier space would lift her spirits. Jen and some pals did her one better—they decided to volunteer to give this woman, as Hamilton says on her website, "a fresh start." They showed up at her house with their cleaning supplies and took care of business. The project was such a success that Hamilton and her friends decided to start a movement, organizing additional help sessions on social media. Now there are chapters of Hot Mess Express in forty-one states. Volunteers do the dirty work to help their fellow moms in need. How awesome is that?

That is what I call "peak villaging." And while the work that Hot Mess Express does is phenomenal, being a village mom doesn't have to involve founding an organization and conscripting hundreds of volunteers. There are a thousand different smaller ways to become a village mom, as exemplified by the support Jessica organized for Lindsay while she was recovering from her accident.

BE "A MOM WHO..."

I've been suggesting ways to make small, powerful mindset shifts throughout this book. But if I had to choose just one tweak to your thinking that will lead to major transformation, it would be this: learn to think of yourself as "a mom who helps other moms." The very act of thinking of yourself this way will color your choices, and it will make you more inclined to spot and act on opportunities to reach out and help other moms.

I recently saw this in action with my friend Danielle. I told her about the idea for this book, and when she came back from spring break with her family, she called to tell me that simply thinking of herself as a village mom had changed her behavior. She'd gone to New York City with her husband, Ben, and twelve-year-old son,

Felix. At school drop-off a few days before the trip, another mom, Malena, told her she was taking her two sons to the city as well. Danielle could tell during their conversation that Malena was hoping they could meet up, but Danielle had been looking forward to the time with her family and chose not to take the hint.

On the second day of their trip, however, Danielle thought of Malena and, feeling mildly guilty about their conversation, texted her to ask how they were enjoying themselves. Malena immediately replied that things had been a bit rough. Her younger son had come down with a fever, and they were all camped out in a Times Square Hilton. Danielle's first thought was, *Ugh—good luck with that!* But the idea of being a village mom had wormed its way into her consciousness. She was in a position to help out, and once the thought entered her mind, there was nothing she could do to quiet it except make an offer. She texted back to ask if the older son, Emerson, wanted to spend the day with them, secretly hoping that Malena would demur. Instead, she got an all-caps "OMG YES, HE'D LOVE THAT."

Danielle told Ben she was worried that she'd regret her moment of generosity—after all, they were going to have to look after another kid. What if he didn't enjoy her carefully planned outing to the Met? It had been hard enough to talk Felix into spending part of his trip to the big city at a museum. But as soon as Emerson met them on the steps, she knew she'd made the right move. He looked so happy to not be sitting in a hotel room, and Felix was glad to have another kid to giggle with when they got to the nude Greek statues. Danielle felt warm inside.

Felix had a blast with Emerson. Danielle and Ben marveled when the boys joined a pickup soccer game in Central Park, something Felix, a shy kid, would never have been brave enough to do on his own. The day they spent with Emerson was one of the highlights of the trip. Malena was beyond grateful to Danielle for taking Emerson out to see some sights while she tended to her sick kid. Danielle's moment of villaging had not only increased her own family's joy, it had also spread joy to another family. She told me that if she hadn't heard the term *village mom*, she probably would have stuck with her original plan. But the idea gave her the nudge she needed to take the extra step and make the offer. She was so glad she did.

WHAT VILLAGING LOOKS LIKE

Don't get me wrong. There is more to being a village mom than just shifting your mindset. It takes action, just as getting into shape takes more than *thinking* about going to the gym. This means that once you're thinking like a village mom, you need to behave like one. It doesn't mean you have to be the Mother Teresa of villagers, dedicating your life to the service of others. Instead, you need to develop an awareness of the many ways you can participate in your village and occasionally be willing to take action.

There is no formula for how to village. The only way to do it wrong is to not do it at all. Each of us will do it differently. While Donna might sign up to head the PTO, Alison may only have time to buy the paper cups and soda for the school dance. Both are villaging. This is a no-judgment zone, friends. Can't find it in yourself to chaperone a trip to the zoo? No problem. Another parent has your back today. Have a little extra room in your schedule? Great. Become the manager of your kid's baseball team. If the duties are overwhelming, delegate some to another parent. Giving to your village should feel *good*. It shouldn't drain your energy tank down to Empty.

When you have the resources to do so, helping other moms should be rewarding. According to psychologist Donna Pinker, "Reaching out to other women releases oxytocin...[which] not only offers pain relief and an immediate jolt of pleasure, it also reinforces your commitment to people in your inner circle. Oxytocin creates a feedback loop that rewards both the women who reach out to others at times of crisis and those who receive their help."[1]

Villaging *feels* good—and creates a stronger village in the process.

WAYS TO CONTRIBUTE

I don't need to tell you (again) how much day-to-day labor is involved in being a mom. But it lightens the load when we do it together. Following are some examples of ways you might pitch in and become an active participant in your local village.

> *Carpool.* You don't need to drive your kids to every prac-
> tice or rehearsal or to school every day. If you share
> the load with even one other family, that will cut
> your driving time in half. With the time you save,
> you can relax, get chores done, connect with a friend,
> or spend time with your other children. Plus, you're
> granting the same opportunity to another mom.
>
> *Take the snow day.* Snow days are magical...when you're
> a kid. When you're an adult, they turn your schedule
> into chaos. Offer to take another family's kids during
> a snow day. Not only will you be helping out another
> family, you will also be making your own day easier,

since your kids will be occupied and therefore less likely to pester you for endless screen time.

Lend a hand. Maneuvering a stroller or even holding a kid's hand makes the simple act of walking so much harder. Do a solid for a fellow mom and hold a door for her when she's got her hands full. Return her cart at the grocery store or offer to watch her bags at the airport while she changes her baby in the restroom.

Be the extra eyes at the playground. The playground is a proving ground for villaging. We all know how tricky it is to keep track of our own active children, especially if we have more than one of them. If you see a kid who is about to put a handful of sand in his mouth or a little one who is teetering dangerously close to a swing, mom up and steer him in a different direction.

Host the group playdate. There is strength in numbers. If you are having one kid over, it is only a teensy bit more work to have two or three over, and you'll be giving a couple of other moms a break.

Feed your village. Between meal planning, shopping, prep, cooking, and cleanup, feeding a family is a massive and unrelenting undertaking. Even when life throws you a curveball, appetites keep coming. So if a friend is in need, starting a Meal Train or even just dropping off an extra lasagna can feel like the biggest blessing.

Be the class parent. Being class parent is a baller village-mom move. You will be a hub of information, and people will rely on you to make sure the holiday gift gets purchased, the class breakfast is organized, and the email list is up to date. In exchange, you will get to know all the parents in your child's class, creating a sense of community that can last for years.

Share information and wisdom. Before there was the internet, there was word of mouth. We learn so much through trial and error that we could share with other moms. If you've had a good experience with getting your kid to sleep through the night or have found the perfect squeezy pack that doesn't explode in your diaper bag, spread the word.

Pass it on. Got a Toys"R"Us worth of old toys in your attic? Offer to let moms with younger kids come over and pick what they'd like to take home with them. Sort through your books and put the ones your kids have outgrown in the nearest Little Free Library. Ask local sports teams if they have an equipment donation program. Box up the best of your nursing clothes and hand them down to a pregnant friend if she's planning to breastfeed.

Be a good neighbor. Shovel a little extra sidewalk. Remind neighbors when street cleaning is happening. Offer to hold packages until a vacation is over. Share recommendations for good and bad contractors. Toss a newspaper all the way up onto the porch if it's on the sidewalk. Drag a fallen garbage can back into position—not because your neighbor will notice you but because the feeling that neighbors are looking out for one another strengthens our social bonds.

Teach your kids about community. Each one teach one. One way to ensure that we shift away from an isolation mindset to a communal mindset is to demonstrate village behaviors for our kids. Make a point of talking with your kids about what it means to deliberately connect with your community.

A WORD OF CAUTION

Before we move on, I want to offer a word of caution about when and how to help. While we should take our feet off the brakes when it comes to generous impulses, we should first make sure our wheels are heading in the right direction. Before rounding up a crew to do yard work for a mom with a broken leg, for example, or organizing a bake sale to raise money for a sick child, make sure the help you are offering is desired.

I know a mom named Natalie who was going through a rough patch financially after her husband passed away suddenly from an aneurysm. When the cold weather came around, moms in her neighborhood generously donated winter jackets to her three kids. While Natalie was overwhelmed by their kindness, she also wished that people had taken a minute to check in with her before contributing. She ended up with a total of eight winter coats. So lovely. So kind. But also a bit wasteful. Finding a place to donate the unused coats actually created extra work for her.

You don't need to ask a friend or village member to fill out a questionnaire detailing exactly how she would like you to pitch in, but when you are ready to village, a quick email or text describing what you're thinking of doing can ensure that your contribution is welcome. Include a line letting the person off the hook if what you are proposing isn't what she had in mind, so she doesn't have to do the emotional work of taking care of your feelings. Something like, "I was planning on starting a Meal Train for you next week. Would that be helpful? No hard feelings if that's too much for you to think about right now. I can circle back in a week or two." But do make the offer. It's like offering condolences to someone who has had a loss. It's better to do something than to do nothing. Don't let perfection interfere with your good intentions.

One other word of caution: don't forget the strong people. There are some lessons you have to learn over and over. For me, one of them is that the way people present themselves isn't necessarily indicative of what's going on under the surface. Even if you think a friend is handling her business like a pro, you can still check in to see whether a helping hand might be welcome. She may actually be as together as she seems, but if she's not, what a blessing to offer.

LIFT HER UP

As wonderful as it is for us to help one another out with the logistics of parenting, it is equally important for moms to take care of one another emotionally. We can buoy other moms up simply by noticing when they are struggling and acknowledging how hard it is.

You'd think that because Eric and I homeschool the kids, our family might escape the bugs that kids typically bring home from school. Alas, we do not. My kids get sick plenty, and when one of them does, it tears through our house like wildfire. The kids and I recently caught the bug from hell—the kind that doesn't just give you a drippy nose and sore throat but also eats your energy, leaving you achy, leaden, and unable to think clearly. For four days straight, while Eric was mom, dad, head cook, and chauffeur, I only got out of bed to make tea and instant ramen—and of course to use the bathroom.

When I was finally well enough not to run my business into the ground because of my addled thinking, my parents came over to watch the kids so that I could go to the office and catch up and so Eric could get back to work as well. I sat at my desk at Latched Mama HQ assessing what I had missed during the previous four days. My team had done a killer job of keeping the company running smoothly in my absence, but there were still dozens of tasks to handle. As I was assembling my urgent action list, my friend Hillary texted me. She had just finished lunch and was in the area. She wanted to know if I was up for a visitor. *Hell to the no,* I thought. I had to finish my list and get home. But I also knew that somewhere inside my "I must do all these things" brain, there was a need for connection and a need to process my feelings about leaving my still kinda-sick kids so I could get back to work. (Was I being selfish? Would they be okay? Would they break their grandparents?) I knew Hillary could offer me wisdom—or at least a sympathetic ear. So I took a deep breath and told her I'd love to see her.

Half an hour later, Hillary bounced into my office. She sat down on the chair across from my desk and passed me a plastic container. "You look tired," she said. "And hungry. Eat." I looked at what she had handed me—it was her leftovers from lunch. "I assumed you hadn't eaten, and I know you'll love this. Eat, and then we'll talk." I was dumbfounded. She could have brought me a five-course meal, but there was something in the simplicity of her leftovers that made my heart swell.

Building relationships in your village doesn't have to be a gigantic effort that involves spreadsheets and girls' trips. More than anything else, it has been the small moments that have rescued me in motherhood. I try to offer as many of them to my friends as I can.

You, too, can take small actions to boost the morale of your whole motherhood community, even those who are not in your inner circle. Below are a few ways.

Be generous with compliments. So much of the labor we do as moms is invisible that it can feel like no one notices. But that's not true. Other moms notice. We notice when you've taken the time to cut the crusts off of your kid's bread and when you wait in your car during baseball practice to save your teenager the embarrassment of being driven home by his mom and when you use a vacation day to attend a parent-teacher conference.

As reassuring as it is to know in our hearts that other moms pick up on these gestures of love, it's even better when we get to hear another mom actually say something about it. If you are ever wondering whether to pay someone a compliment, the answer is *yes*. Paying a compliment is so easy. It costs you nothing. Foster a mindset of championing other women instead of envying them. It also sets a great example for your children.

There's a real pay-it-forward effect with compliments, too. Getting them can inspire you to give them, creating a chain reaction of connection.

Treat someone. My friend Bella has a mom friend who routinely buys two of whatever item of clothing she's buying for herself when she shops so she can give the extra one to Bella. Bella hates to shop, so she appreciates the wardrobe refresh. Granted, Bella's friend is general counsel at a bank, so an extra sweatshirt doesn't stretch her budget. My acts of love, on the other hand, are a bit more modest. I like to buy double snacks so I can share them with my friend Lindi. I'll surprise her with a bag of trail mix or some Luna bars anytime I've bought some for myself.

Celebrate the win. We've talked so much about the challenges of motherhood in this book, but there are a lot of moments to celebrate as well. The ultimate compliment to a mom is to celebrate a win with her. My friend Heather showed up with champagne and chocolate-covered strawberries when I hit a major sales goal for Latched Mama shortly after baby number six, which I'll remember long after the money is gone. A card, a text, or a tiny houseplant can serve as a hurrah that says you see your people.

Cheer your heart out. Noticing the accomplishments of your fellow village members' children creates communal joy. Give your friends' kids high fives during their cross-country meet; yell "Brava" after the school musical; tell a young student "Good job" after she's done her Bible reading that week.

Send a check-in text. A check-in text is my favorite village-mom move. It sounds so obvious, but sometimes we forget to do it. You don't have to write a novel. Your text can be just one sentence letting someone know you are thinking of her—a quick "How ya doin'?" Or "Hey, I've been thinking of you this week—hope you're hanging in there." Or a follow-up to something you knew was going on in her life—"How did dinner with the grandparents go?" This lets your mom pals know they are not rolling solo through motherhood. Sometimes I even set a reminder for myself on my phone to check in with someone who has just told me she's had a bad day.

Speak mom. The routine of motherhood can be so mundane that we often decide it's not worth talking about—*Is someone really going to be interested in hearing about my kid's picky eating?*—but when we avoid talking about the texture of our days, we diminish their importance. So go ahead and tell that story about the time you were so tired you accidentally put diaper cream on your toothbrush.

If you are a woman in the workplace, making room for talking about motherhood can be especially tricky, but there are small ways to be there for other moms. You could ask a fellow mom how her kids are doing while you're waiting for a meeting to start. Or, if you are in a supervisory position, be up front about leaving early for a kid's clarinet recital instead of pretending you have a doctor's appointment. Bringing motherhood into the light helps all moms get the notice we deserve.

As your kids get older and you progress through various stages of motherhood, your contributions to your village will change. What you are able to give will also depend on how deep your personal well is. The important thing is to make participating in the community of motherhood a regular practice.

MAKE HELPING A HABIT

Supporting other moms is infectious. In any group, cultural norms influence people's behavior. When we make supporting one another the norm, it becomes an easy choice to put forth the effort. Sometimes peer pressure is a good thing!

My friend Laura's mom, Nancy, is seventy-four. She's been gathering with the same group of women for tea on Tuesday mornings for more than forty years. Nancy and her friends Judy, Pam, and Barbara met when their children were attending pre-school in Providence, Rhode Island. All four women were stay-at-home moms—more common in their generation than it is today. They spent so much time together during their kids' early years that the children took to calling each of them Auntie.

When their children were young, they had huge group play-dates, taking turns cutting cheese cubes and pouring Kool-Aid. They watched over one another's kids at the local pool, and they weren't shy about stepping in with a gentle correction when a kid acted out, even when it wasn't their own kid. As their kids grew, they kept up their Tuesday morning tea tradition, sharing details of the week and discussing ways they could pitch in to help one another out. They made a hand-me-down train for clothes and compared notes on teachers, and when one of them saw a good sale at the grocery store, she bought enough for the other families, too. They took turns hosting backyard barbecues in the summer and potlucks in the winter. The dinners weren't anything fancy—paper plates, Capri Suns, and sides of chips—but they were an important collective experience.

They were also there for one another in a crisis. When one of Barbara's seven kids broke his arm while her husband was away, Nancy grabbed her two girls and brought them for a sleepover at Barbara's so Barbara could take David to the ER. When Judy's daughter got pregnant unexpectedly in high school, the others made space for Judy's complicated feelings at the baby's birth. A few years later, when Nancy's older daughter got married, they threw an engagement party where they each gave her daughter a teacup. Today, all four women are grandmothers, and they continue to support one another in their empty-nest years. When Pam's mother needed to move to a retirement home the same week Pam's husband, Tom, had heart surgery, Judy took over making meals for Tom so Pam could help her mom transition. Helping one another out became a lifelong habit.

Some people might have #couplegoals. I have #villagegoals. When I hear about stories like Nancy's, I know that the effort I put into my village today has the potential to sustain me for the rest of my life—but only if I take care of it now. If you don't water your plants, they will wither and die. I have a nursery full of empty pots to prove it.

Few of us who are parenting these days can gather weekly, as Nancy and her tea group did, but that doesn't mean our bonds can't or shouldn't be maintained. There will be times when you are stretched so thin that even keeping up with friendly texts will feel like too much. But when you have the energy, consistent and regular acts of village momhood will create bonds that sustain you. The important thing is to keep it going. If you can find the time and energy to village, it will always pay off.

Build Your Village

Following are a few great ways to practice your skills as a village mom.

- *Turn your admiration into action.* Look for ways moms are handling their business, and when you spot one, try to drum up the courage to tell the mom you noticed. For example, if a mom keeps her cool as her kid is having a tantrum, you could just say, "You're so calm." Chances are she is feeling anything but calm inside, and your kind words will give her a boost.

  No need to limit your acknowledgment to parenting skills. If you walk past a mom who just squeezed into a tight parking spot, give her a thumbs-up. Or if you have a friend who always makes you feel at home at her house when you stop by, next time you see her make a point of telling her how welcome she makes you feel.

- *Find a way to help.* You know that guilty feeling you have when you could have done a nice thing and you didn't because you were too busy or because it might be awkward? There's a surefire way to eradicate that feeling: think of yourself as a mom who helps other moms, then *do the simple thing.* Could you offer to take another mom's kid for an hour while she handles a chore or just reads a book on the couch? Could you drop off a bouquet of flowers for a mom who just finished a difficult medical treatment? Could you dog-sit a friend's Lab while she's on vacation? Keep track of your generous impulses, then set the goal of pulling the trigger on one of them sometime in the next month.

- *Be a checker-inner.* Simply remembering details about what's happening in a friend's life is a wonderful first step to fostering a communal feeling. I sometimes send myself a voice memo or set a reminder on my calendar to check in on a fellow mom and follow up on how something went. You may not be able to accompany your friend to the dentist when her kid gets his first filling, but as a village mom, you can remember to reach out with a quick "thinking of you" text or a silly meme. Just knowing someone is thinking of you can create connection. You can send a two-line text to a divorced friend on Valentine's Day or a note to a friend who lost her dad on Father's Day. Don't worry if it's poorly phrased. Done is better than perfect.

Chapter 10

Be a Taker

ISOLATION MINDSET: Even though I am over-whelmed, I don't want to be a bother to anyone. I'll just soldier on.

↓

VILLAGE MINDSET: Being part of a village means asking for and accepting the help we need.

How does anyone do this? Megan asked herself. She sat in the doctor's waiting room with her twelve-year-old daughter, Mira, who had recently gotten her first period. Mira's little brother, Luke, age seven, was there, too. It was early August. No camps were in session, and the family had already maxed out their child-care budget in the first eight weeks of summer. Now Megan and her partner, Zach, were each using some of their vacation time to cover the weeks until school started. Megan knew that the last thing Mira wanted was her little brother coming into the exam room with them. The trouble was, Luke was an anxious child—so anxious that he resisted staying in the waiting room alone. He hated being left without an adult, so even though Megan had broken their no-devices-outside-the-house rule to keep him occupied, he was still a nervous wreck in the waiting room. He clutched at Megan's leg when they called Mira's name, looking at her with panicked eyes that said, "Don't go."

But she had to go. She didn't want Mira to have to speak to the doctor alone, so she promised Luke she would check in on him every few minutes. For the next twenty minutes, as they waited for the doctor to come to the exam room, she darted back and forth, checking in on Luke and then extracting herself from his grip and dashing back to Mira. She felt like a chicken with her head cut off. She cursed herself for not being brave enough to ask the lovely older couple next door to look after Luke during the appointment. Jack and Phyllis had always been friendly to their family and had grandchildren who lived out of state. They'd offered several times to keep an eye on the kids, but Megan had always demurred with a polite "Thank you—I'll keep that in mind." Why, oh, why hadn't she just said yes?

We moms are so accustomed to doing every darn thing our-selves that we frequently resist help even when it's there for the taking. How often do you say "I'm good, thanks" when you are anything but good? Or "I've got it" when you really don't got it? I can't count the number of times I've said no to help. One day I rolled a cartful of groceries to my car with two tiny people in tow. The nice kid who bags the groceries had asked me if I wanted help loading the items into my car, but I waved him off. There is a stubborn part of me that insists on doing everything myself, even when I know I'm risking a back injury (me) or a temper tantrum (also me).

IT'S EASIER TO GIVE THAN TO RECEIVE

As women, we are conditioned to be caretakers and nurturers—it's easy to forget that we, too, need nurturing and care. As much as I hate to admit it, sometimes I convince myself it is simpler just to do things myself instead of having to adjust to someone else's way of doing things. It can be less stressful to make a box of mac and cheese I know my kids will eat than to accept my friend's offer to let them stay at her house for roast chicken so I can have an hour to myself, because I know I will just spend that hour wor-rying that they are not eating because her meal "looks funny" or "isn't like you make it."

The reality is, it wouldn't be the end of the world if the kids acted like kids when they are served a meal that isn't exactly what they expect. It would be a great chance for them to practice the manners I've tried to drill into them. Most of the time, my concern about making sure everything is just right for them is misplaced.

They'll actually learn from experiencing something new if I can just be a touch less controlling.

There is also social pressure to receive help in a particular way. We are supposed to be visibly grateful and gracious—like Donna Reed accepting a dessert to serve at a dinner party—when the reason we need help in the first place is because our resources are stretched so thin we feel more like Medusa after a long day of turning people to stone. When I had my sixth child, my midwife asked me if I wanted her to set up a Meal Train. I knew very well what's involved in taking care of a newborn. The continual nursing, late night diaper changes, and endless swaddling would leave me mind-numbingly tired and not eager to cook for the rest of my crew. And yet I still said "Heck, no!" even though it would have made my life so much easier in those early, hazy weeks.

Why did I say no? When I imagined having to smile and socialize, even for five minutes, with someone bringing over a casserole, I just couldn't do it. I figured it would be easier to order pizza for twenty nights in a row. When we feel stressed and depleted, it can be hard to muster the energy to respond to someone else's kindness. Let's just admit that. So how do we accept that casserole and respond graciously without feeling obligated to invite the giver in for coffee?

When friends come to your aid, they aren't doing it for the thanks. They're doing it because they *want* to help, and they probably don't care whether you are the model of a gracious recipient. They don't want you to feel like you have to put on lipstick and pour them a glass of wine when they do you a favor.

It's strange: when we offer to help someone, we generally recognize that our motivation is to help that other person—not to receive thanks for the favor. However, we don't always extend other people the same courtesy when we think about their motivations for helping us.

For all the years I've spent building and participating in my village, I still suck at letting other people help me. Lucky for me, I have a friend who doesn't give up. On one particularly terrible mom day, Eric took Alex, our second child, to basketball practice, leaving me to make dinner for the other five children. Because I am a masochist, I decided to make meatballs—the messiest, most labor-intensive meal on earth. I was in a rotten mood because our dog had run off, and we hadn't seen him for hours. I was up to my wrists in raw meat and garlic, imagining how I was going to tell the kids that Lucky was lost, when I heard a glass shatter. Matthew, our sixth, had dropped it on the floor, leaving shards of glass everywhere. At that exact moment, Lindi called to ask me to write a Latched Mama email that would go out to approximately 150,000 people. I burst into tears.

I got off the phone as quickly as I could, wiped the meat off my fingers, and swept up, my tears mixing with the splinters of glass in the dustpan. Because she is a great friend, Lindi texted me to say she could tell I was in a rough spot and asked if she could bring dinner. Ugh. No. I wasn't going to waste all my efforts. Thanks, but no thanks. What could she do? she asked. *Nothing*, I shot back. There was nothing anyone could do to help me out of my funk. I didn't feel worthy of anyone's caretaking in that moment. I felt worthless and overwhelmed—but those are precisely the moments when we need to open ourselves up and accept care from others. We got through dinner, and as I was washing up, Lindi called to ask me to come outside for a minute if I could. I stepped out onto my porch and saw her there. She'd bought me a pint of my favorite ice cream, a pint for herself, and ice cream sandwiches for the kids. Eric (and Lucky!) had gotten home by then, so I tossed the sandwiches inside and sat on the porch with my dear friend and unloaded. She had wanted to help. She *had* helped. I shouldn't have made her read my mind. I should have just said yes.

Whenever I stumble under the weight of someone else's generosity, I try to remind myself that being part of a village is not a strict tit-for-tat relationship. I don't need to earn my place in the village through generous actions or by being the world's most together mom. There are going to be times when my role is to take and other times when my role is to give. The approach is holistic and communal, not transactional. I don't accept help from one friend knowing that I'll owe her one later. I accept help from a friend knowing that when I am in a place of strength, I will be able to contribute to the village at large. I think of it as a gift economy. We give to one another so there will be a well to draw from, a collective resource. We show up for the whole village, not just the people who have shown up for us.

YOU'RE DOING A FAVOR BY TAKING

Until you get used to the idea that you don't have to do every single thing yourself to be a great mom, saying yes to offers can be very uncomfortable. To help you get over your reluctance and accept support, how about this Jedi mind trick? Think of yourself as doing a favor for the person who is offering. She will enjoy the benefit of feeling good about herself for helping you.

I'm sure you've been in the position of wishing you could help someone only to have that person shut you down. You know how bad this feels—like your gift is being rejected.

Research shows that helping makes the helper feel less lonely and more connected, and we know what a blessing that is. Dr. Stephanie Cacioppo, assistant professor of psychiatry and behavioral neuroscience at the University of Chicago, told the *New York Times*: "For years people thought the best thing you could do for a lonely person is to give them support...Actually, we found that it's about receiving and also giving back. So the best thing you can do for someone who is lonely is not to give them help but ask them for help. So you give them a sense of worth and a chance to be altruistic. Even if we're getting the best care, we still feel lonely if we can't give something back. The care is extremely valuable but it's not enough."[1]

When someone does something kind for you, give yourself permission to accept it without having to put on a happy face in the moment. You'll be helping the giver as much as you'll be helping yourself.

ACCEPTING HELP

Just because accepting help doesn't come naturally to some of us doesn't mean you can't learn how to do it. And when we do learn, the results can be amazing.

A week after her harried doctor's appointment with her daughter, Megan took a COVID test. By the time the second line showed up, she already knew it would be positive. She'd taken a nap that afternoon. She never took naps. Plus, there were the aches and a sore throat and a stuffy nose—and the fact that Zach also had COVID. Great: right before she was supposed to host her in-laws for the holidays and finish up two huge projects for work. She was instantly down in the dumps. She did the responsible thing and notified everyone she'd come into contact with, including the parents of the kids her children might have exposed and members of her book club. Exhausted, she prepared for a repeat of lockdown. *This is the worst*, she thought. *The absolute worst.*

That's when the text messages started coming in.

I'm so sorry. Can I pick up Mira's homework at school and drop it at your house?

I'm heading to the supermarket. Do you need milk?

I'm making ginger chicken soup for another friend. What if I doubled the batch?

Megan's initial instinct was to shake off all the offers, but when she thought back to turning down her neighbors' help, which would have made things easier at the doctor's office, she decided it was time for a change. She thought through what it would be like to have help—really imagining that she didn't have to cook while sick—and she was overwhelmed with gratitude at the prospect. These people had offered without being prompted, and they wouldn't have done so if they hadn't meant it, right? Before she could change her mind, she texted back, accepting all the help she could get. She granted herself permission to say yes. Her skin hurt like someone had dipped her in boiling oil, but her spirits were sky-high. Over the course of the following few days, her sister sent flowers and a Whole Foods delivery. Mira got her homework assignments, and the family had homemade soup to keep them going until her symptoms were under control. This is the way it should always be.

The story of Michelle, mom to Noah, is a shining example of how powerful a community can be if you let yourself accept help. Michelle, who lives in Poughkeepsie, had recently gotten divorced when the unthinkable happened to her beloved sister, Nikki. In a nightmarish turn of events, Nikki was arrested and imprisoned for defending herself against her abusive partner. Michelle's world turned upside down in an instant. Nikki's children needed a home, and Michelle opened her door without hesitation. How could she do anything else? Nikki had been like a second mother to Noah, so she brought Ben, four, and Faye, two, to live with her. Michelle knew she was doing the right thing, the only possible thing, but she felt overwhelmed to the point of panic. How would she manage? She worked at a wellness center to support herself and eleven-year-old Noah, and she didn't have a lot of extra money saved up for the additional expense of two more kids. She didn't know how she was going to pull it off.

Straightaway, the sisters' community, mostly moms, stepped up to organize a GoFundMe campaign to raise money for the kids. People donated clothes, food, and gift cards to help the family stay afloat. During the holidays, so many people wanted to "adopt" Michelle's family that on Christmas morning the presents spilled out from under the tree, nearly covering the living-room floor.

You can imagine the emotional turmoil that came with the new family arrangement, but Michelle mothered her niece and nephew, not to mention Noah, with exquisite grace and care. While Ben and Faye struggled to adjust to their new situation, they eventually found a delicate equilibrium with the help of the mental health experts Michelle tracked down.

Michelle could tell that it was easy for people to give to the children. They wanted to do anything they could to ease their pain, even if it was to make only a small donation. Michelle understood that and appreciated the outpouring for the most innocent and vulnerable people affected by the tragedy. And so it was as easy for her to accept generosity on their behalf as it was for other people to give it. She got the feeling that people *needed* to give. It felt like a gift to them—as well as to her family—to be able to receive their generosity.

What was harder for her to accept was the support that came in for *her*, even though, in many ways, that was the support she needed most. While the majority of donors focused on the children's needs, there was a core group of women who took care of Michelle. She'd had her life ripped out from under her. She had taken a leave of absence from her job. Her sister was in prison, and on top of that, their mother was very ill. She couldn't be the mom she wanted to be to her son, and she spent any free time she had working to help her sister's lawyers exonerate her. She was completely depleted.

She appreciated the gifts that came for her—a certificate for a massage, chocolates, new clothes—yet it was the emotional support she got from the women who formed a committee to work on Nikki's case that transformed Michelle's life. These women became a lifeline for Michelle by putting in countless hours of legal work. What helped lift Michelle out of despair most of all was simply having them there to witness her new reality. She felt safe around them, able to vent about the strains of motherhood in a way she couldn't publicly. They filled the space that Nikki had left with a nonjudgmental compassion. She isn't sure how she would have gotten through her darkest times without them. Their dynamic went beyond friendship; it was a sisterhood. The message she got from this group of women was, *We see you. We see the burden you're carrying. We are here.* Having a group of women affirm how heavy her load was helped Michelle feel like she wasn't crazy. The situation really *was* as difficult as it seemed to her.

Experiencing that level of care from other people transformed Michelle. It forced her to ask herself what she would have done if she had been a bystander, not the person at the center of her tragic story. She suspected she would have read about her family's situation and thought, *That is really sad; maybe I should chip in*, and left it at that. No longer. Now that she understood the power of community, she would never sit on a generous impulse again. When a campaign comes into her inbox these days, she might not be able to give $1,000, but she can give $10, and she knows from experience how those small donations add up, not just in dollars but also in the feeling that people care.

ASKING FOR IT

Michelle was fortunate to have a community around her that took action without her having to ask. Moms aren't supposed to ask for help. We're the helpers—the organizers of schedules, the slicers of apples, the managers of academic careers. We're the ones other people rely on to get things done—organize the school fair, have uniforms ready for game day, schedule doctor's appointments. We're supposed to be able to do it all without complaint because being a mom is the most rewarding job in the world. And it *is* rewarding, but it is also difficult and draining and performed under the weight of impossible expectations.

As vulnerable as it can feel to put yourself out there when you are seeking connection, it can be even harder to ask for help—even from someone you have known for decades. Especially with those unrealistic expectations egging you on: "Just handle it yourself, girl. You've got this."

I think of our reluctance to ask for help as a cousin to what Sheryl Sandberg describes in her book *Lean In* as tiara syndrome. Tiara syndrome is the tendency of women in the workforce to grind themselves to the bone hoping that when someone notices how much they are giving they will be rewarded in some way—with praise, a promotion, a bonus. But as Sandberg points out, when we keep our heads down, we are in fact less likely to have the metaphorical tiara bestowed upon us than if we make a clear case for why we deserve some form of compensation. I catch myself in this trap frequently when it comes to motherhood. I want approval for doing it all—for all my feats of organization and nutritious meals and on-time arrivals—but no one is handing out an award for "most self-sufficient mom." In reality, my only reward for wringing myself dry is more work. So many of us moms talk ourselves out of reaching out for support. We exhaust ourselves and then we go to bed thinking, *Why isn't anyone helping me?*

PRACTICE, PRACTICE, PRACTICE

Even if you know intellectually that asking for help is nothing to be ashamed of and is even beneficial for the person you're asking, it can still be hard to take the leap. I am trying to get better at this myself. (Hence the reason so many of the stories in this chapter are about people other than me.) Below are a few things that can make it easier to start asking for what you need.

> *Ask for advice.* Asking for advice is a great warm-up activity. You're inviting a form of help that requires very little from the person you've asked and nearly nothing from you. You can act on the advice or completely ignore it. But reaching out to another mom—whether for her opinion on the best stroller cover or guidance on how to talk to your child's teacher about a delicate issue—is good practice in asking for something you need.
>
> *Find a proxy.* Sometimes it's easier to make a request on someone else's behalf because you have no skin in the game. If you find yourself in need of a helping hand but are unable to ask for it, recruit a friend who can make the request on your behalf. Maybe you can't

make your child's school play because of a work event—ask a friend if she can ping the class group text to request the recording.

Spread the ask. You might hesitate to send a request to just one person because you feel like you're putting her on the spot. If you can ask a small group of people, the request is less pointed. You'll have a good shot at finding someone willing to step up—and as a bonus that person will look like a hero in front of her friends. Keep the number of people small so people don't ignore the request because they assume someone else will do it.

Be direct and specific. That dreaded phrase "If there's anything I can do..." can feel like an empty promise, but try to regard it as a sincere invitation to make a concrete request. People like to be told how they can help. Once you identify areas where you could use a hand, identify specific tasks you could ask people to do. When you ask for help, couch it in gentle terms: "What I could really use right now is an hour alone. Could you take my kids for a bit?"

Volunteer to ask for help on someone else's behalf. If a fellow village mom is up a creek, step in to be the one to ask other villagers for a paddle. It's a great way to request help without feeling selfish.

Offer to reciprocate. You might be the one in need right now, but chances are, someone else will be in that position soon. If you're asking for someone to drive your kid to practice on Monday, offer to take the Wednesday shift in return.

Learning to receive is one of the hardest things we do as we build village connections. We must overwrite the belief that accepting help is equivalent to admitting that we have failed. But we shouldn't have to do everything alone. Each time we break with expectations by accepting help, we normalize momming together instead of in isolation. The next time someone offers to make your life easier, don't say yes just for yourself; say yes for the next mom who needs a village.

Build Your Village

Learning how to accept help might not come naturally, but following are a few things that might ease your way.

- *Admit you need help.* The first step in getting help is admitting you need it. For a week, note every time you yearn for an "easy button" you could push to streamline logistics. Keep track of when you wished there were someone who could help you. It can be anything from having to bring your toddler with you to run errands to the hour you spent arranging your schedule so you could get all your kids where they needed to be or fantasizing about washing the dishes without your baby strapped to your chest. Then imagine how much lighter you would feel if you had someone to lift your load. Would it be worth it to ask someone?
- *Actually ask.* It's so hard. I know. But it won't get easier until you try. Tell yourself you are worth supporting. Start small, with minor requests that are easily reciprocated. Direct your first requests to your inner circle, the people who love you the most. When you get a positive response, it will train your brain not to be so afraid next time you need something.

- *Practice saying yes.* You can take baby steps on the path to becoming a person who graciously receives help by accepting the tiny offers that pop up during your daily life. If someone offers a ride for one of your kids or a hand-me-down sled her kids have outgrown, try to say yes. See how it feels. If you can flex the yes muscle by accepting small gestures, it will be easier when you have a bigger need. I'm trying to practice saying, "That'd be great. Thanks so much!" The more I do it, the easier it gets.

- *Take a beat.* If you are lucky enough to receive an offer of kindness from a member of your village, before you reject it, put yourself in her shoes. What would you be hoping for in that moment? Would you be hoping for a rejection or an acceptance of your generous impulse?

- *Hold the thanks.* If you are stretched so thin you fear you will break at any moment, don't overextend yourself by pushing yourself to act like the most thankful person on the planet. Say thank you politely, then accept the help. Once you've gotten your strength back or your crisis has passed, you can thank the people who have supported you.

Chapter 11

The Emotional Neat Freak

ISOLATION MINDSET: My feelings are too messy and embarrassing to share with anyone else. If other people knew what was inside my head, they'd run away screaming.

VILLAGE MINDSET: Vulnerability is the portal to connection. Opening it can be terrifying, but the payoff is worth the risk.

When I first realized how badly I needed a village of people to support me in motherhood, I panicked. During those beautiful crisp mornings when I was walking around my new farm during lockdown, I tried to calm my nerves by taking stock. I knew I had made friends during my years of parenting, but where were they? What had happened to them?

To figure out what had gone wrong, I broke out my phone and scrolled through my old text messages. Public service announcement: unless you have self-regard to rival Kanye West's, do not do this. I was shocked by what I read. It was brutal to see how large the gap was between how I like to think of myself as a friend and how I came across in those messages. As I read, I winced at the many ways I had consistently let down the people I claimed to care about. When friends shared intimate details from their lives, I brushed them off with a "So cool!" or "That sucks!" I turned down offers to get together with "Can't, sorry!" and no further explanation. Worst of all, I ghosted—just evaporated into the digital ether without so much as a goodbye. So many of those exchanges made me want to crawl into bed in a roadside motel where no one would think to search for me. But it was the thread with Kim—she of the perfect parties—that really opened the floodgates of shame. Revisiting how I starved our friendship until it withered was truly painful.

EMOTIONAL NEAT FREAKISM

Months after Kim's Halloween extravaganza, I started to find my footing as a mom. I was far from thinking I had it all figured out, but by the time Nathan was ten months old, he took longer breaks between crying jags, and I got more sleep as a result. With more rest and more quiet, I was able to handle brief forays into the big bad world. I learned how to go out in public without shaking like a Chihuahua. Eventually, I felt strong enough to hang out with Kim again, but as I would soon find out, I wasn't ready for actual connection.

I wanted to sit together in a café and swap stories about cradle cap and exchange tips for getting a good deal on diapers. Kim had a different idea of what real friendship looks like—a better idea. The more we hung out, the more she let me see behind the scenes of her perfectly photographed life. She dropped hints that she was having a hard time.

Okay. They were more than hints. She flat-out texted me that she was struggling with her relationship with her husband. Things were so hard, she said, that she was about to lose it. I remember getting that text and wondering where this confession was coming from. Kim had always seemed so emotionally guarded. So tough. To be honest, that was part of what I liked about her. I appreciated the fact that hanging out with her hadn't put me at risk of detonating any emotional land mines. Now that she was trying to bring her home life up in conversation, it made me feel uncomfortable, and so I steered the conversation back to safer shores—the latest celebrity gossip or the most recent milestone our kids had hit.

Things went on like that for a while—she trying to have a real conversation and I willfully redirecting our exchange to lighter talk. But then one night, nearly three years into our relationship, we went out to dinner at our favorite spot. We had both had our second children by then, and I was feeling more confident as a mom. After the waiter took our drink orders, I looked up from my menu and saw Kim crying. I was one hundred percent not prepared for that. Where was my strong friend? Who was this person crumbling in front of me? She sniffled and said, "Melissa, I feel numb." I felt my shoulders tighten. I had enough presence of mind to ask, "What do you mean you feel numb?"

"I feel like my emotions are in a box in another room somewhere and I can't get at them. I know what I should be feeling, but I just don't. I don't know what to do." When I heard that, I actually leaned back in my chair. Then: I froze. Looking back, I hate what I see—I sat there as if repulsed, not wanting to get her feelings all over me for fear of contamination. She broke down in sobs as I stared helplessly.

I shouldn't have been so shocked. Even if I hadn't wanted to talk about it, I knew what a hard time she was going through. Her marriage had hit a bumpy patch. Her dad was dying. In addition, she was trying to raise two very young kids. She was carrying all that sadness, and it was too much for her to hold alone. No wonder she was having trouble accessing her emotions.

This woman, this incredible woman, was showing up with such depth, showing me real, precious vulnerability, offering actual connection, and I was having none of it. I looked at her awesome display of deep emotion and decided: *I'll pass.* I still cringe when I think about it.

I have no idea what I said to her in the moment. I think I told her that she needed to go talk to somebody and made a half-hearted offer to help her if she needed it, but I was miles away emotionally.

What was wrong with me? This woman I cared about had cut herself open and laid her heart out on the table. But I couldn't even acknowledge that, let alone match her offering. My own sense of balance felt too precarious to risk holding someone else's troubles in addition to my own. No one was going to weigh me down, damn it.

It is one of the great tragedies of my life that Kim hit the moment when she could be open with me before I could be a real friend to her. I just couldn't meet her where she was emotionally. Eventually, the friendship fell apart.

CONNECTION CONCENTRATE

Surgeon General Dr. Vivek Murthy wrote in his book, *Together*, that there are three categories of connections we need in our lives: "We all need close friends and intimate confidantes with whom we share deep bonds of mutual affection and trust. We need casual friends and social relationships that offer shared support and connection. And we need to belong to communities of people—neighbors, colleagues, classmates, and acquaintances—with whom we experience a sense of collective purpose and identity."[1]

I like to think of these three groups as the concentric circles of people in my village. The largest circle, encompassing both of the smaller ones, is the village at large, made up of folks with a shared sense that we're all in this motherhood thing together and will look out for one another, even if we don't necessarily know everyone's last name. These are the weak connections I wrote about in chapter 5. Then there is the slightly smaller but still substantial circle of people I am always happy to see. I think of them as my neighbors in the village. They are part of a metaphorical potluck dinner crowd. We gather together to enjoy one another's company and help out when needed. In other words, mom friends. Finally, there is my inner circle, made up of my family and my chosen family, the folks I keep closest to the home fires. We rely on one another to manage from day to day and to keep an eye on how we can help one another thrive over the long haul.

While you absolutely need the two wider circles, it is the inner circle that provides the most essential support in motherhood. The members of my village who fall into the inner-circle category could fit into a minivan. It is a small but mighty group, and now that I have an inner circle in my village, I don't know how I did motherhood without it. (Actually, I do—and it was much harder.)

When you're ready for an inner circle, you will level up your village. But when you are just easing your way out of isolation, how do you turn those weak connections into strong ones? One study showed that it can take more than 220 hours together before you consider someone a close friend,[2] so clearly you need to use the strategies in this book to make sure you spend time together. But it takes more than just time to turn a friend into an intimate connection. It also takes a willingness to be vulnerable with each other.

CLIMB VULNERABILITY MOUNTAIN

Being vulnerable is the hardest easy thing. Once you learn how to do it, it's so much less work to speak freely about your feelings than it is to contort yourself into a phony, fun-all-the-time version of yourself, spinning things to pretend you are fine. And yet relaxing the protective barrier between you and another person somehow takes more strength than holding it in place. What gives?

I think we're holding on to our emotional armor because the cultural pressure to do so is intense. A study conducted by the Pew Research Center found that the top three traits society values in women are

1. physical attractiveness;
2. empathy, nurturing, and kindness; and
3. intelligence.

For men it is

1. honesty and morality;
2. professional and financial success; and
3. ambition and leadership.[3]

Setting aside that first one for women—because OMG, are you kidding me; we're still talking about women being valued for their looks?—it's noteworthy, not to mention infuriating, that the second trait consists of being pleasant to other people. Contrast that with the top traits for men—honesty and morality—which entail being true to yourself. Can you imagine what it would be like if women, especially moms, were allowed to be honest all the time? Imagine the startled faces. The pearl clutching. The *freedom*.

Instead, the message we receive—from men on the street telling us to "Cheer up, baby" to being labeled angry or bitter or bitchy for expressing anything other than the lightest, happiest, most grateful emotions—is that we should be relentlessly positive. Anything less would be downright unmotherly. To be grouchy, resentful, or frustrated risks being considered the opposite of valuable and could be a reason for casting us aside in social isolation, so we bury our sadness. We bury our feelings of unworthiness. We bury our pain.

There is a vein of ironic commentary on motherhood, mostly found online, that masquerades as a type of honesty, or "realness." What passes for real, though, are wry comments about how much pinot we drink or how little sex we have with our partners. I don't want to sound like an internet grinch—there is a place for "I need more wine" memes—but we can't let them replace actual vulnerability between human hearts.

Our reluctance to be vulnerable with one another is a side effect of perfectionism and our desire for control. We wear emotional hazmat suits to keep the impeccably maintained selves we present to the world unsullied. Those hazmat suits are great at keeping other people's feelings out, but they also keep yours in, which, as I've tried to demonstrate, is bad for you.

Hiding your feelings is unhealthy. Research has shown that holding in your emotions suppresses your immune system, making it less capable of fighting off illnesses ranging from colds to cancer.[4] When you spill your guts to someone else, you are putting a name to those feelings, which has been proved to lessen the stress response to those feelings.[5]

TAKING A RISK

Fair warning: there is no guarantee that being vulnerable will result in increased intimacy and connection. What if you let your guard down, and instead of respecting your bravery, a friend takes advantage of you or laughs at you? On the other hand, what if you end up feeling less alone? More worthy of love and connection? That's what happened to my friend Samantha.

Samantha had never been especially maternal. Even as a kid, she preferred tearing around the playground pretending to be Wonder Woman to playing house. She wasn't one to dream about marriage and the long white dress, but when she met Adam during college, she was immediately drawn to his warm smile and calm demeanor. When they graduated, they scandalized their conservative parents by living in sin just outside New York City, where she'd found a job in tech. Eventually, Adam and Samantha made it legal.

In the early years of their marriage, Samantha was adamant that she did not want children. Although her own childhood had been idyllic, she'd just never felt the desire to have kids—just as some people have never felt the desire to bungee jump. It simply wasn't for her. Adam was happy to follow her lead, so they lived childfree. But as they entered their early thirties, their friends started having babies, and Samantha second-guessed herself. Did she really want to miss out on what everyone described as a peak human experience? Was she making a mistake? Slowly she changed her mind, and the couple started trying. A few months later, she was pregnant with their daughter, Erin.

To her delight, Samantha fell in love with Erin right away. But from the start, things were tough. Erin was a fussy baby and a highly sensitive toddler with big emotions. Little stumbles led to massive meltdowns that took forever to recover from. A dropped apple could mean forty-five minutes of soul-crushing tears. She would fall to the floor bereft every time Samantha left the house, even when Adam was home to take care of her. Samantha kept thinking that Erin would grow out of it, but as Erin got older, things only got more difficult.

By the time Erin was a tween, each day was a minefield. When life didn't go her way—when she didn't have enough time between activities, or when she wasn't able to watch her favorite show—she screamed and cried as if she were possessed by a demon. Samantha had no idea a child Erin's age could act like this. Shouldn't she have grown out of this behavior by now? She was also burned out by how much pain she experienced vicariously for her daughter. Samantha felt completely unprepared for how hard it was to try to help another person handle emotions that seemed too big for her. No matter what Samantha did, no matter what techniques she tried, no matter how much therapy she got for herself and Erin, nothing changed. Erin remained dysregulated. It was like she sucked all the energy out of the household. Every move Samantha and Adam made was calculated with Erin's response in mind. Samantha felt like she was living with an abusive spouse. She never knew when a misstep on her part might result in threats and yelling from her daughter, making her regret she had ever opened her mouth. She hated to admit it, but being a mother was making her miserable. She felt like she *couldn't* admit it. She didn't know anyone else who felt as conflicted about being a mom as she did. Samantha felt like a freak.

Samantha wished more than anything that there was a higher authority she could appeal to, a kind of school principal of parenthood who would help her figure out how to handle Erin's emotional volatility. She dreamed of spilling her guts to this person, admitting that her days were swallowed by her efforts to keep Erin from succumbing to panic attacks and screaming fits. Surely if she could only explain herself clearly, someone would see how impossible her situation was and help her.

When Erin was eleven, Samantha enrolled her in the local chapter of Girls on the Run, hoping that some regular exercise would help regulate her emotions. Samantha's friend Sandy, an ob-gyn whom she had known since she first moved to the New York suburbs, had a daughter, Bella, who was also in the program, so while the girls practiced their running form, the moms walked circles around the track—always where Erin could see them, of course; otherwise, meltdown city.

The two women had long been friendly. They lived in adjoining neighborhoods and knew most of the same people, but their

walks together were the first time they'd had one-on-one conversations. Over the initial weeks of practice, they stuck to
lighthearted discussions of their favorite restaurants and which
podcasters' voices made them crazy. Occasionally they'd share an
eye roll when one of their daughters came over and demanded—
without a please or thank-you—that her water bottle be filled.
They would laugh ruefully together about raising little princesses.

One beautiful October evening, Samantha looked at the girls
with their bouncing ponytails and wondered, with a heavy heart,
if hers was the only child who had thrashed on the floor for an
hour earlier that afternoon because she'd decided it was too hot to
practice. How had so many years of her life been held hostage to
her daughter's emotions? She was so caught up in her misery that
she almost missed it when Sandy said that Bella had nearly snapped
her head off when she suggested she eat an orange instead of the
bag of Doritos she'd chosen as a snack. Samantha laughed sympa-
thetically and commented wryly that sometimes she thought Erin
had fangs instead of front teeth. Sandy nodded and said she would
never have dared to talk to her mother the way Bella spoke to her.
Samantha said she could certainly relate.

Before long, they were deep into a real conversation about
their daughters' difficult emotions. Samantha was surprised by
the way Sandy described Bella's behavior at home, because Bella
had always seemed like a good egg, the type of kid who compli-
mented other girls on a fast run. Samantha had never pictured her
as a challenging child. Once the subject was on the table, though,
the moms' exchange accelerated almost like flirtation, as if they
were daring each other to share more. With each confession about
their household dynamics, the stakes felt higher, and Samantha
felt a dizzying sense of lightness. Finally Samantha blurted out
something she had thought ever since she brought Erin home

from the hospital but had never dared utter aloud: "Sometimes I wonder if I am cut out for this motherhood business at all."

She looked over at Sandy, expecting her to respond with "Oh, don't be silly—of course you are." Instead, Sandy said, "I question my decision to have kids at least three times a week."

Samantha couldn't believe what she was hearing. This woman was an *obstetrician*. She had dedicated her life to babies, and here she was confessing that she, too, had had doubts about being a mom?

Samantha described the experience of hearing Sandy's confession as similar to going to a party in a cocktail dress only to find a roomful of people wearing cutoffs. You feel horrifically out of place until you catch a glimpse of another woman across the room who had also donned a flouncy dress, and you feel a flash of recognition. *We're the same! This is fine. I am fine.*

Once Samantha had voiced her greatest fear, its intensity lessened slightly. For the first time, she felt an easing of the shame she felt in her heart. She didn't have a solution to her problem, but at least she no longer felt like a mutant for questioning her decision to have children.

Samantha and Sandy had climbed vulnerability mountain together.

THE THREE STAGES OF VULNERABILITY

When you climb vulnerability mountain with a friend, you walk side by side with each other toward greater heights of intimacy. As you climb, you feel increasingly open and exposed. You reveal everything from your feeling of inadequacy in motherhood to money fears until, after a long haul, you are rewarded. I like to think of the hike up the mountain as having three stages.

Stage 1: Sharing minor imperfections. Stage 1 is the equivalent of mucking around in the foothills. There's not much of a grade, just some pleasant, well-worn paths that are comfortable to stroll along. In a relationship, stage 1 is made up of finding shared ground and copping to the little ways you might be judging yourself— things such as running late for work, eating fast food six meals in a row, getting your car towed for parking illegally, or putting your kid in front of a screen so you could have a much-needed moment to yourself on the porch.

Stage 2: Sharing mistakes and misjudgments. Stage 2 gets your heart going a little faster as you put in some work. There's elevation to deal with, making the hike more challenging, but it's still manageable. In your relationships, stage 2 is made up of mistakes you feel guilty about, the kinds of actions that have real ramifications but aren't life-altering. You didn't sign your kid up for her favorite camp, and now she has to attend six weeks of a boring craft camp she hates. You fired off a spiteful email to the principal about a new teacher after just one week of school. You blamed another child at the playground for pushing, then didn't apologize when you found out later your kid was the instigator. You spoke badly of a colleague, and now others are avoiding working on a project with her.

Stage 3: Sharing feelings of deep unworthiness. Stage 3 is where the path narrows. It's not for the faint of heart. You need to choose your footing carefully and only proceed if you can trust your hiking partner to have your back. When you hit stage 3 in a friendship, you are taking a real risk in sharing. Stage 3 vulnerability issues are intractable; you can't see your way out of them, and they seem to reflect an unfixable flaw in your character. You can't afford to live in a neighborhood with good schools because your finances are a wreck. Your mental health status has reached a crisis point. You failed to notice that your child has ADHD despite the fact that he's been struggling in school and daydreaming at home.

Climbing the mountain can be terrifying, but the rewards of having a new perspective once you reach the top—a clearheaded assurance that lets you see that you are still worthy of connection no matter what secrets you hold—are worth it.

By daring to let ourselves be seen, we transform our insecurity into a bond with other moms over our shared, stumbling journey. The confessing is where the connecting happens. I promise you there is no thought you have had about yourself that another mom has not had about herself.

MY FIRST STEPS

My own climb up vulnerability mountain began with finding a therapist. I sat down to write an email to the first person a friend had recommended, and I stared at the computer for what seemed like half an hour trying to figure out a subject line. "Appointment?" "Accepting new clients?" "Is something wrong with me?" I finally settled on "Consultation?"

In the body of the email, I wrote, "I have never really done the whole therapy thing, but I feel like I'm finally at a place where I feel confident, settled, and overall healthy enough to explore some places where I know there is an opportunity for some growth."

Total BS, but come on—baby steps. Within hours, I had my first appointment scheduled.

I showed up for weekly Zooms with Donna. I paid the money. I talked about the people and the things—how busy I was, what was going on with the kids, with Eric. I patted myself on the back for being an A-plus patient.

I thought I was crushing therapy, but one day around six months in, as the session was ending, Donna said, "You know, Melissa, I don't think you're hearing me." What was she talking about? Hearing *her*? Wasn't *she* supposed to hear *me*? I left that session grumbling to myself about the fact that I had clearly chosen the wrong therapist. But as the days passed, I wondered if Donna might be right.

When I mentally reviewed our talks over the previous months, I could see I was in the habit of deflecting her whenever things got vulnerable. When she brought up my relationship with my mother, I pivoted to talking about something safer, like Eric's driving me up the wall. When she tried to get me to open up about my loneliness, I made jokes about being too busy to let myself feel lonely. The more I thought about it, though, the more I had to face facts: I was stonewalling her so hard I might as well have been talking into a tape recorder. It was Kim all over again—the flow of connection was only going one way. Donna was telling me to knock it off. She wanted me to let her in.

The idea of leaning in to my relationship with Donna, of letting her see beneath my "I've got this" exterior, scared me to death, but I did it. I faced my insecurities. I began confessing all the ways in which I believed I was unworthy of connection. I knew she had to listen—after all, it was her job—but still, part of me worried she would get up and leave when I showed her who I was inside. It was a mess, but like most meaningful relationships, a beautiful mess. She held the line and showed up each week with compassion and care and continued to do so throughout our relationship.

I started to open up to her more, letting her sit with me and hold what I felt was heavy, and after a while, the heaviness lifted. It took a while, but after around a year of this new dance, I felt strangely... good. And slowly, my life started to change. I didn't feel so mind-bogglingly overwhelmed and pressured every waking moment. I let myself unclench. There was something about taking that hour to share the load each week that settled my entire nervous system down. It helped to have a caring, compassionate individual to help me hold all my motherhood struggles. Yes, I was doing it all in the safe space of a therapist's room, but I was climbing the mountain.

I've brought what I've learned with Donna into my other relationships. I'm trying to create safe places where members of my inner circle and I can show up as a total shit show, because that is motherhood on most days. But it's a delicate dance. I'm trying to go slowly enough to move at the same pace as the person I'm connecting with so that we can arrive at vulnerability together.

Finding the courage to connect with another person, whether it's your therapist, your partner, another mom, or your sister, is ridiculously hard. Putting aside decades of messages and cultural assumptions about how we should present ourselves and having the courage to show someone what's hiding under your armored self is a heavy lift. You have to break through a lot of crap to be able to build something. The very fact that anyone has close connections at all is incredible. You need to find the time, muster the energy, match with the right person, and allow vulnerability to flow between you. But when you take the risk, you will build a powerful part of your village.

These days, I live life publicly for my business. I blog and I podcast and let people see a lot of my personal life. I know I am opening myself up to criticism and judgment. I bring that same openness (and more) to my most prized relationships because the same channel that leaves me vulnerable to criticism lets in love, connection, and support. I'm not going to close it up. I'm going to get out there and talk about my self-doubt and the insecurity that continues to run through my veins no matter how often I prove to myself I'm good enough. My new attitude is, I'm going to embrace my mess, and I'm going to accept yours. Let's all peel off our hazmat suits and get a little messy together.

Build Your Village

As you prepare to open yourself up to vulnerability in relationships, below are a few suggestions to guide you.

- *Go slowly.* As you climb vulnerability mountain, take baby steps, not giant leaps. Start by sharing your laughable imperfections and foibles before you delve into your deepest, darkest secrets. Go stage by stage. It can be so heady to experience real stage 3 vulnerability in a culture that discourages it that once you try it, there is a temptation to be all disclosure all the time or to expect the same from others. Being vulnerable is exhilarating, but don't let it crowd out the more common, still fulfilling forms of communication such as laughter and debate and storytelling.

- *Initiate a do-over.* We all can think of times when we wish we had said something different in the moment and only come up with the perfect thing to say much later. Usually, we experience this when we want to deploy a clever zinger or an effective retort. What if instead you think of a time where you had the option of saying something candid or vulnerable and chose not to? If it was with someone who makes you feel comfortable being open, next time you see that person, bring it up. Say something like, "Hey, the other day when we were talking about *x*? I made that joke about *y*? I think I did that because I wasn't comfortable talking about *z*. But I really wish I'd said..."

- *Give-and-take.* Your friends are not dumping grounds for your problems. You will build a truer, stronger connection if you are willing to listen without judgment to your friend's confessions as well as sharing your own. If what you hear from the person across from you sounds familiar, say so! Nothing builds connection faster than a "Same, girl; same."

Chapter 12

The Path to a Village Is a Squiggle, Not a Straight Line

ISOLATION MINDSET: I've tried making friends, but I feel as lonely as ever. I give up.

VILLAGE MINDSET: There are going to be setbacks, heartbreaks, and WTF moments when building a village. When they happen, we've got to pick ourselves up and try again.

*K*atie couldn't remember the last time she'd been this nervous. She slipped the piece of paper into the mail slot and dashed down the sidewalk so quickly that she worried people would think she had stolen something. Minutes later, even though there was no possible way Jean could have read her note, Katie pulled her phone from her pocket, checking her texts for Jean's response.

Katie had met Jean in a Mommy and Me yoga class. It was right after COVID, so folks would bring their yoga mats to the park, where an instructor led parents and kids through a series of child-friendly poses. Katie had hoped the class would be a good place to meet some fellow moms. She'd been in a bubble with her immunocompromised mom during lockdown, so she had cut herself off from the world for nearly a year, and she knew she needed to jump back into socializing. Katie's three-year-old daughter, Mandy, generally seemed to enjoy the class, doing her best to mimic the postures. However, on the day Katie met Jean, Mandy was not having it.

After doing one or two half-hearted tree poses, Mandy wandered off into the field to pick dandelions in the shade of actual trees. Katie decided she should model stick-to-itiveness for her daughter, so she stayed on her mat while watching Mandy out of the corner of her eye. Around halfway through the class, she noticed that a little boy had left his mom and sister to join Mandy in the spot where she was kneeling next to a big patch of dirt. Katie knew Mandy would much rather play with another kid than do more downward dogs, so she took that as her cue to slide away from the group. She dug through her bag, found the little pail and shovel she'd brought with her for after class, and offered it to Mandy, saying, "Why don't you see if your friend would like to dig with you?" Then Katie relaxed on the grass while the kids played. At the end of the class, the boy's mom brought his baby sister over and thanked Katie for being so nice to him. She introduced herself as Jean, mom to Jayden and baby Mina.

A few weeks later, Katie and her husband, Carlos, took Mandy to a restaurant where they ate outside. At the table across from them were Jean and Jayden, out for a special mommy-son dinner. The two families started talking as they waited for their food to arrive. It turned out that Jean ran a kosher catering business. Katie recognized the name of it from a small commercial strip in their neighborhood. She wasn't especially religious, but she was always up for meeting people who shared her Jewish background, and Jean was *so* interesting.

Jean was one of those rare people who skipped the small talk and got into substantial topics right off the bat. Having grown up in Hungary, Jean had traveled to countries Katie had only the most glancing familiarity with, and she seemed to have read everything ever written, though she wasn't show-offy about it. Katie talked so much about how much she liked Jean on the drive home that Carlos started teasing her about it.

Over the next month or so, Katie ran into Jean on the street a few times and exchanged "How are you?" greetings with her. Each time left her a little giddy. After their third encounter, Katie made a decision. She was going to make a new friend. When she got home, she went straight to her desk and wrote a note saying, "Hey, I'm always so happy to see you out and about. If you ever want to have a playdate or just hang out, here's my number." She folded it up and set out to Jean's catering business to put the note through the mail slot.

Katie must have checked her phone fifty more times that day. When she didn't hear back right away, she told herself that Jean must be busy. The restaurant business is notoriously demanding, plus she had those two kids to take care of. Maybe she hadn't had time to check the mail. But as the days went by, the narrative in Katie's head morphed from *Jean must be busy* to *Katie must be a fool*. What had she been thinking? Why had she been so brazen? What made her think someone like Jean would want to hang out with someone like her? She burned with embarrassment.

I feel Katie's pain. One of the hardest things about taking emotional risks as you attempt to build a village is that they don't always pay off. That's the risky part. You simply can't predict when a relationship will blossom and when it won't. Everything about a potential new friend can look perfect on paper. Your kids go to the same school; you have the same favorite seltzer; you read the same books. You hang out a few times; you get butterflies and feel a rush of energy. Before you know it, you're spending hours after the kids go to bed scouring VRBO for a beach house that will fit both families for a fantasy vacation. But then the texts stop. You don't see her at school pickup. The coffee you left on her front porch is received with a flat "Thanks. Sorry. Life has been crazy" text. You see on her social feeds that she's still finding time to go out with other friends and that she seems really happy. Ugh. The shame. It's enough to make you want to swear off trying to establish new connections forever.

Most people don't marry the first person they date (and I, for one, am very happy about that—sorry, Matt Stewart; I wish you and your lovely wife nothing but the best). Similarly, not every attempt you make at friendship is going to lead to a connection. Not every person you ask is going to jump at the chance to come over and watch *The Bachelor* with you after the kids are asleep. Not every first coffee date is going to be followed by a second date. Not every mom is going to be a member of your village no matter how ideal she seems for the role.

Much as I wish it were otherwise, the journey to a village is not a linear path. It's more like a squiggle—surging forward, looping back, and leaving you occasionally twisted and confused. Friendships are going to fall apart. You're going to get ghosted. You're going to wish that you hadn't told that one bigmouth your secrets.

It sucks when we moms get hurt. Unfortunately, the demands of motherhood don't go away when someone hurts our feelings. We still have to show up to wipe the noses, kiss the knees, and cut the carrots. We can't hide under the covers watching rom-coms and eating cheese puffs all day. But if I have learned one thing about pursuing a village, it's that in the long run, it is worth it to keep trying. The risk does pay off.

TRY, TRY, TRY AGAIN

As the seasons changed, Katie occasionally saw Jean on the street, where they exchanged polite hellos, but she never did get a response to the note she'd left. She had to work hard to get over the sting of rejection. When she put herself out there, she knew there was a chance that Jean would leave her hanging—she just hadn't realized how much it would hurt. The thing is, Katie's first impulse—assuming that Jean's silence wasn't necessarily a reflection on her own worthiness—was the right one. Just because Jean didn't get back to her didn't mean she was worthless. It just meant that one person, one time, hadn't taken her up on her offer for reasons she could only speculate about.

Society tells us we're supposed to keep dating until we find a partner, so despite being emotionally hurt, we keep swiping left (or is it right?). But what society doesn't tell us is that it is imperative to our emotional and physical health to do the same when building our village and finding friends. Finding the energy to persevere through all the false starts can be one of the hardest parts of this process.

It took a while for Katie to acknowledge that there would be other chances for connection—and to pull back far enough to see that despite this blow to her ego, she did have a number of friends who cared about her, which seemed like proof that she wasn't a total troll. The next time she had the urge to "ask out" another mom, she did it in a much safer, more low-key way. There was a mom of a four-year-old girl she'd talked to at the playground dozens of times, and with whom she already had a very established connection, and she asked that mom if they could exchange numbers. That mom said yes, and she and her daughter became playground buddies with Katie and Mandy. That success fueled her desire to keep trying.

Working on her village was like building a muscle. Each rep made Katie a little stronger, a little more confident in her abilities. Not every mom she talked to became a friend, but enough connections flourished for her to feel emboldened. The more success she had, the less the failures hurt. She and Carlos talked frequently about how good it felt to have a community of parents in the neighborhood and what a joy it was for Mandy to have a community of friends. Katie felt proud that she had provided that for her family.

We could all take a lesson from Katie. She figured out that while it hurt like heck to be rejected, she lived to mom another day. When she found the strength to try again, her setback with Jean became a way station on her journey to creating a village, not the end of the line.

THINGS (SEEM TO) FALL APART

Even more scarring than friendships that fail to launch are those that get off to a promising start only to crash and burn. These experiences can leave us feeling bruised, battered, and humiliated.

Almost immediately after I started Latched Mama, Tess and Lily joined the company. In those days, we were still a scrappy little start-up with just a handful of employees tossing ideas around my dining-room table. Tess and Lily, both in their early twenties, were new moms, and they threw themselves headlong into parenting in a way that left my late-thirties self breathless. I loved their openness and youthful enthusiasm and what that brought to the company.

After long days in the office together, I began inviting Lily and Tess's families over for weekly family dinners. Every Friday, we had a big, happy, brilliantly chaotic meal. It wasn't organized or quiet, but it was fun and fulfilling. People talked over one another. No one stayed at the table for more than a few minutes at a time, and more food ended up on the floor than in our mouths. And yet as I washed the dishes next to Eric each week after everyone had left and my own kids were tucked in, I was filled with a deep satisfaction. It was a time of fullness in my life. I'd had my fourth baby in six years. Latched Mama was moving and grooving. I was keeping it together—even if doing so required the coordination of one of those plate spinners. Everything needed to be spinning just so for the show to go on.

For a while, a perfect balance held. But then one of the plates came crashing down. A key babysitter quit right before the holiday season, the busiest time of year for our company's sales—and, as everyone knows, a frenzied time of year for almost any family. This had a terrible domino effect, and soon there was mess everywhere. Appointments were missed, meetings canceled, orders lost. For a control freak like me, it was hell. I was terrified that I wasn't going to be able to see my family or the company through the storm. I needed to triage, and one of the first things to go was the time I spent with friends, including Lily and Tess.

Though I cherished my relationship with them, I just couldn't find the time to be part of their lives. All my energy was suddenly needed for work and the kids. I stopped inviting the girls over to our house for those family dinners. I let their texts go unanswered. I couldn't find the time to stop by their desks during the workday. I kept telling myself I'd make it up to them. In the meantime, they stopped trying to reach out. Eventually, there were no more (unanswered) texts from them asking if I wanted to hang out. And by the time I was ready to show up for our friendship again, they had moved on.

I should have seen it coming, but losing their friendship was devastating. Seemingly overnight, my kids lost their beloved "aunts." I tried to explain their absence the best I could to my family, but the children's blank expressions told me they understood even less than I did.

Even though I didn't have the wisdom to recalibrate my priorities and move connection back to the top of my list, I kept tabs on Lily and Tess and loved them from a polite, professional distance with the hope that our paths would cross again.

In the years that followed, they both got divorced and remarried, and each had another child. Here's where I feel stunned by my good luck: Recently, the iciness between us thawed. Lily and Tess put out a few feelers, and this time I leaped at the chance to bring them back into my personal life. I committed to putting our connection first. My entire world lit up again. I wasn't certain what brought them back, but I wasn't about to question a blessing.

A few weeks into our revival, I sat across my dining table from them as we had in the "old" days, drinking margaritas and eating our weight in chips and salsa as they held their new babies. At one point, as Lily fed her child, she casually said, "You know, I'm sorry about all that happened. I just didn't get it. I didn't understand how much was on your plate." It meant the world to me to hear that she understood that my pulling back hadn't been a reflection of how much I loved and cared about her but rather of the way the demands of life can interfere with connection. I didn't need her to say any more. I was just so happy to have my friends back.

THINGS REALLY DO FALL APART

Having Lily and Tess by my side was instrumental in helping me survive what happened next.

Shortly after I started writing this book, the village I'd built within the walls of my company was decimated. Latched Mama had grown beyond a small family-run operation driven by heart and good intention. We had more than fifty employees and had officially reached what business analysts call the "teenage years." This stage of growth is just as miserable as it sounds. New employee concerns popped up every day. I let someone miss work because her kid was sick, but someone else in the same situation didn't know that was an option and got extremely upset when she found out I'd granted that favor to another employee. I DoorDashed dinner to an employee who was home with the flu, but I was unaware of another employee who was momming alone while her husband was in the hospital, and I got blowback for not helping her as well. I bought diapers for one of our single moms, but didn't I know that she wasn't the only one struggling? Suddenly I was drowning in paperwork, handbooks, and HR audits. The more I learned about the ways my good intentions were going sideways, the more afraid I became. I was doing my best to show up for other people, but I was apparently getting it really wrong.

The worst of it started after I had a difficult conversation with an employee that didn't sit right with her, and she subsequently quit. After she left, there was a mass exodus from the company. I could have put the resignations in the "It's just business" category, but some of the people who left were people I had considered friends. As they left, it was as if they'd thrown a grenade of hurt and destruction over their shoulders as a parting gift. It was one of the most emotionally challenging experiences of my adult life.

I had worked really hard on those relationships. These people had meant so much to me: we'd passed our newborn babies around the warehouse, shared home-cooked meals and late nights at the office, laughed and celebrated success together. And in the blink of an eye, it was gone. I had let them see me. All of me. And apparently, they hated what they saw.

I reviewed every interaction I'd had with the people who left, wondering exactly where I went wrong. I spent hours mentally rewriting conversations I could never have again, trying to will a different outcome into existence. Many nights, I crawled into bed and let the tears roll down my cheeks, pledging that if I was able to see my way through the implosion of my village, I was never going to rebuild anything. The hurt and failure affected every aspect of my life—my health, my sanity, my marriage, and my ability to parent. I was short with my kids. I couldn't hide my pain and fear from them. My relationship with my husband was a wreck. He wasn't saying the right things, and the kind words he *was* saying I couldn't hear through the hurt. I couldn't go to the office without being haunted by the ghosts of those relationships. I thought, *If this is what happens when you open your life and heart to people, maybe creating a village isn't such a good idea after all.* Screw the research. Screw the experts. It's solitary me versus the world forever and always.

The negative self-talk played on repeat: "What is wrong with me?"

I'm sure you've said the same thing to yourself when a relationship imploded. *Did I say the wrong thing? Maybe I came on too strong. Was it because my kid didn't say thank you?* We all do it.

So what do you do when you feel eviscerated after a relationship crumbles? I'll tell you what you *don't* do: give up.

GET UP, DON'T GIVE UP

No amount of self-confidence will ever totally silence the voice in my head saying that these people left me because I wasn't worth sticking around for. As deeply as I know that it was a two-way street, admitting to this failure, confessing to this loss, feels like confessing that I am a fraud. My village fell apart. Who am I to offer advice about how to build a strong one?

Putting myself back together again was one of the hardest things I've ever had to do. Thank goodness I believe strongly in the need to repair and start again.

My personal earthquake led to a controlled burn of my village. Now it's greener and richer on the other side. I am much more self-aware and confident. But it was rough. Really rough. I will probably never understand exactly how things went south with my Latched Mama village. If I could turn back the clock, there are many things I would do differently. I know, though, that I can only control my response to the way those events unfolded, so I look forward, not back.

I hope you never find yourself in a similar situation. But if you do suffer a painful setback, like mine or Katie's, following are a few things I recommend trying. Doing these things helped me find the strength to get back out there and begin rebuilding.

I acknowledged my loss. When the shit was hitting the fan, well-meaning friends said things like, "You don't need those people! You're better off without them!" While I appreciated their cheerleading, it made me feel worse. I *did* need those people. I *wasn't* better off. I was devastated. Rather than blast toxic positivity at my feelings, I made space for them. I acknowledged that losing those relationships was hurtful and I mourned what I had lost.

I talked about it. The last thing I wanted to do was let other people know how abandoned I felt. It was embarrassing to confess how many friends had walked away, but secrecy is fertilizer for shame. We moms are so addicted to being seen as strong that it runs against our instincts to admit vulnerability. However, each time I got brave enough to share what was going on with a trusted friend, I felt a little lighter.

I got real. It was tempting to go on a self-hate spree, telling myself I was destined to be alone forever because I was obviously unworthy of companionship. But I tried to take a step back and ask myself whether my interior monologue was true. When I did, I saw there was an awful lot of data to contradict that narrative. I reminded myself of my friendships that remained intact, like my relationship with Lindi, whose love for me is as unconditional as my love for her. Focusing on those bonds buoyed me.

I jumped back in. Losing a big part of my village meant I suddenly had a lot of space in my life. I could either fill it with self-pity or get back to work. I chose to get back to work. If I've made mistakes—and Lord knows I have—I know I'm not alone in that. It's just another thing I have to bond over with my fellow flawed humans. The best way to end up without a village is to not try to create one.

WHEN YOU ARE THE ONE TO LEAVE

At some point on your journey, you may find yourself in the position of pulling back from a relationship. We hold on to some friendships longer than we should—sometimes out of habit, sometimes out of guilt—but there is freedom in granting yourself permission to move on when the time comes.

There are all kinds of reasons to say goodbye to someone. Some relationships are perfect for a particular stage in your life, but they may no longer serve you after that stage of life is over. The mom you ran the middle school PTA with may fall out of your circle when your kids go on to separate high schools. Hanging with a mom who moves across town may no longer fit into your schedule. A friend whose kids' lives are suddenly ruled by travel hockey may have different priorities. Or a mom who seemed like a good match for you when your kids were infants might reveal herself to be so overprotective of her child that you have trouble agreeing on a way to spend time together that feels good to both of you. There's being polite and compassionate, and then there's bending yourself so much to try to fit a relationship that it becomes untenable. I like to think there are people who are just right for a season of our lives. You can honor the time you spent together best by not keeping a friendship on life support out of a sense of obligation.

You have permission to make healthy decisions for your family. Your role isn't to be the welcome-all-comers of villagers. Sometimes you need to make a difficult call.

I went on a really weird walk one day with a woman whom a friend had introduced me to because we both run our own businesses. The walk started out normally enough as we commiserated about the difficulties of running a tight ship while keeping our employees happy. As we talked, we learned that we had a lot in common. We both homeschool our kids, we both used to work in real estate, and we even went to the same hairdresser. I made a mental note to thank the friend who'd set us up. Then the conversation took a sharp turn. Out of nowhere, she told me that her dream in life was to have an open marriage. She and her partner had started watching videos of threesomes together, but that wasn't enough for her. She wanted the real deal.

Okaaay. We'd just been talking about learning modules for math, so I was taken aback by the abrupt change in topic.

I am not about to tell anyone what to do behind closed doors. I hope she found fulfillment. It was clear, though, she was going through something and needed someone with whom she could talk things over, but dude, this was our *first walk*. I had not had enough sleep or alcohol to absorb that level of overshare. She'd jumped into the deep end while I was still in the kiddie pool.

As women, we are conditioned to sidestep confrontation, to say yes, to avoid rocking the boat. Most of us hate letting people down. For my part, I don't like the idea of anyone regarding me as anything less than Disney Princess nice. But when I looked into my heart, I knew this woman wasn't going to be part of my village. I wasn't going to be able to show up as my full self in a friendship with her because I'd perpetually be on the lookout for another emotional oil spill. That wouldn't have been fair to either of us. I politely turned down her next offer to go for a walk, and I never invited her on one again.

There's a unique blend of chemistry and convenience that leads to a good match. While I've learned to turn down the volume on my judgment, I also haven't welcomed just anyone into my village. We have the right to be selective so we can find a village that lifts us up instead of weighing us down.

No village is perfect—nor is a village a fixed state. The best of them are continually in flux, changing to meet the needs of the people they contain. If a storm hits your village and you lose members, you grieve, learn what you can, then pick yourself up and keep looking for your people.

Build Your Village

When you hit a rough spot as you build your village—and you almost certainly will—following are a few tips that might help you get through it.

- *Check yourself.* When a connection fizzles out—or fails to catch in the first place—and you notice yourself spiraling into self-criticism, ask yourself if the negative tale you're telling is based on fact. Practice asking, "Do I know for certain this story is true?" If not, allow for the possibility that there is something going on in the other person's life that may have prevented connection.

- *Take inventory.* When you suffer a setback—when a relationship peters out or goes down in a blaze of glory—and you're worried you'll be doomed to a life of solitude, take stock of the relationships you do have, those that make you feel comfortable and confident. Then make a list of all you have to offer—maybe you're unusually empathetic and people feel seen by you; maybe you're quick to lighten the mood with a joke; maybe you are a refreshing straight talker. When you're feeling down, remind yourself that those qualities are not going to go to waste. The right relationship will blossom under their glow.
- *End a bad relationship to make room for a better one.* Is there someone in your life who drains your energy instead of boosting it? Consider that it might be a favor to both of you to find a way to ease out of the relationship. It's not fair to the other person if you bring a hesitant self to your interactions, and it's not fair to you to spend time with someone who doesn't enrich your life. Focus on the people you care about, those who light you up. Don't give your precious energy, heart, and mind to a person who isn't doing the same for you.
- *Make a date.* We've all had the experience of getting turned down when we extend ourselves. Next time you get burned, set a date with yourself—actually mark it on your calendar—to try again. It can be with the same person or someone else, but hold yourself accountable to the process of actively building a village.

Chapter 13

Family Matters:
Alloparenting 101

ISOLATION MINDSET: For better or for worse, the family I'm born into is the one I've got.

VILLAGE MINDSET: Our idea of family can expand to include new members—and new relationships within our family of origin.

*C*larissa's boss had run out of patience. When she'd first asked for time off to drive her son Diego to his weekly physical therapy appointments, he'd been very understanding. "Do whatever you need to do," he'd said. "Family comes first." Fifteen-year-old Diego had twisted his ankle badly in a volleyball match, and his doctors had put him on a rigorous PT schedule to heal the joint. She'd driven him to his first two appointments without any resistance from her boss. But now, after two weeks, he seemed to have changed his tune. She could have sworn she caught him rolling his eyes when she slipped out to pick Diego up that morning. Clarissa got the message: find someone else to drive Diego. Thank goodness for her nearby family.

Clarissa's grandmother, mom, and two aunts live together in a house a block away from Clarissa in their Houston neighborhood, so close that after her washing machine had broken the previous month, she was able to walk her basket of clothes over to their house. Clarissa's mom, Aileen, had joined her relatives there when she first came to the United States from El Salvador. At the time, Clarissa was four, and her sister, Gabriela, was just a baby. The family nest had been the setting for Clarissa and Gabriela's entire childhood. Every day after school, every summer vacation, every holiday was spent at that house in a big jumble of relatives. The sisters often joked that while other people had friends, they had cousins.

After her husband left her, Clarissa was raising their twin boys, Diego and Miguel, on her own; she was overwhelmed. She needed all the women in her family for support, but she relied on her mom most of all. Aileen drove her grandsons to practices, hosted them for dinners, and generally kept the boys in line. When the twins wanted to go to separate summer camps, Clarissa was able to take Miguel to Rice while Aileen took Diego to volleyball camp in Huntsville. Her mom did so much for her that Clarissa nicknamed her Wonder Woman. The logistical support was terrific, and Clarissa was grateful for it, but it was the sense that she wasn't alone in her parenting, that there were other people looking out for her and her family, that she couldn't live without.

Clarissa had been only twenty years old when her twins were born. As a young mom, she remembered feeling clueless about how to take care of herself, let alone two infants. Fortunately, Aileen had been there to hold her hand through all of it. Clarissa had moved back in with her mom for the first forty days after they were born so she could recover from her C-section. Her mom fed her the traditional Salvadoran diet of charred tortillas and chocolate to increase her milk production, and Aileen made sure Clarissa didn't go outside or shower too often, as she had been taught when she herself had been postpartum. Clarissa's mom patiently taught her how to hold a baby while breastfeeding, the best way to swaddle, and soothing songs to sing at bedtime. When Clarissa had questions about potty training a few years later, her mom was there to tell her what had worked for her and Gabriela. As the years passed, the wisdom Aileen passed down shifted from practical to emotional. She taught Clarissa to trust her instincts and to believe in her ability to raise the boys to be good people, prepared to face the world on their own. *You can do this*, Aileen told her often. That belief kept her going when things were hard. Her mom earned her nickname every day.

And now, thanks to her mom, Clarissa would be able to keep her job while keeping Diego on his PT schedule. For the rest of his appointments, Aileen took time away from her work as a seamstress to drive him. When Clarissa looks around and sees other single moms who don't have the kind of family support she has, she wonders how they do it. Her life isn't easy, but it's joyful because of her village.

These days you might think that Clarissa and Aileen's proximity is unusual, but it's not. It may surprise you to hear that today, Americans typically live an average of just eighteen miles from their mothers,[1] and grandparents are increasingly acting as caregivers for their grandchildren, especially in low-income families.[2] And yet many people, especially college-educated and high-income families, do not rely on grandparents for childcare and support.[3]

For years, I fell squarely into the group of people who had minimal help from the grandparents. If you had told me in 2019 that I would be cool with my in-laws just dropping by unannounced on a weeknight, even with pizza in hand, I would have called you crazy. But oh, how things have changed.

When Eric and I first started having kids, our parents lived in Florida, South Carolina, and the other side of Richmond—which at times felt several states away. Eric's parents got divorced when he was thirteen, so he brought two sets of incredible in-laws to our union. During the first few years of our marriage, Eric and I made a point to celebrate holidays with our extended families. We gathered with them for birthdays and life milestones. We'd spend a week in South Carolina each summer close to Eric's dad and stepmom's condo, and my parents would travel up from Florida for each of the kids' birthdays. Eric's mom and stepdad, the local set of grandparents, would share a meal with us every now and then. They were all very loving, just not terribly involved in our day-to-day lives. It worked. And honestly, it felt like we were doing it right.

A few years later, things began to shift, and we started seeing more of our parents—all six of them. Shortly after we moved to the farm, Eric's mom announced that she and her husband were searching for a home closer to us. Then his dad built a house in the same neighborhood as his mom. And then *my* dad announced that he had requested a transfer from Florida to Virginia and would be the friendly neighborhood optometrist. I'm not going to lie: there were a few moments when I wondered whether they had all jointly decided that I was failing the kids so badly that they needed to intervene.

I have since realized that of course this wasn't the case. They hadn't all secretly decided to move closer and get more involved because I wasn't up to the task of parenting my kids. What actually happened was that I had become more open about how overwhelmed I was, and I'd started asking them for the help. Instead of hiding behind the pretty moments of holiday dinners and themed birthday parties (which always came after rage cleaning for hours and screaming at my kids for being excited kids), I began inviting our families into the real version of our life. I went from not even considering asking my parents for help to asking my mom to come up to Virginia for "a few days." Eventually, those few days grew to be ten or more days. She returned to Florida only after I had gotten some rest, the laundry was caught up, Eric and I had a date night, and the kids had enough "Lala" time to feel connected and loved. Eric's mom now randomly brings dessert over on weeknights in exchange for hugs, and I no longer speed-clean or make sure the kids are properly clothed prior to her arrival.

As I've worked on my village, I've learned that help given is not a judgment. My parents and in-laws are not showing up at my doorstep because they think I have blown it with the kids and they need to rescue them from my incompetence. They aren't there because my kids have bad manners and they want to teach them how to look people in the eye and speak clearly. They are there because my kids are freaking awesome and they want to be part of their lives. I've softened, and it's made a difference. I feel much more intimacy, a much greater sense of being intertwined with the older generation, now that I have a close-up view of the beautiful flow of love between them and my children. Funny how when you're not actively pushing people away, they can get close enough to help.

The next level of villaging is bringing people into your life in an intimate way, integrating them not just into your day-to-day logistics and emotional life but also into your family. The official term for this, coined by sociobiologist Edward O. Wilson, is alloparenting, defined as care given to kids by people other than their parents.[4] An alloparent can be anyone who helps raise a child, from a grandparent to a trusted neighbor to a paid caregiver.

Alloparenting is the ultimate rejection of go-it-alone (aka isolation-mindset) parenting. There is nothing frictionless about it. When you invite other people into your family life, you allow complicated individuals with their own emotions and perspectives to influence your world. It can be messy. It can be awkward. But it is the best imaginable cure for the isolation and burnout of motherhood.

I'm still at the beginning of the process of welcoming other people into my village as full-fledged alloparents, but below are a few of the benefits I've experienced so far.

A chance to learn. Eric's stepfather never had biological kids of his own. He never spoon-fed anyone. Never changed a diaper. This is his first time putting a kid down for a nap. Now he spends hours a week with my children, and watching him is so inspiring. He doesn't feel the pressure I do to make every interaction with them awesome. He doesn't second-guess himself about whether he is doing it wrong. The little ones ask him for his phone, and he happily pulls up Disney+ and hands it to them. He actually said out loud to me, "I feel like all I have to do is show up and love them." Boy, could I ever learn from that.

A chance to heal. We come into motherhood carrying the weight of the way we were parented. No one is perfect, so no one was parented perfectly. We all have our scars. The wonderful thing about alloparenting alongside our own parents is that it offers us a chance to heal, a chance to rewrite the scripts of our own childhoods. Welcoming our parents into our village allows them to have another try. They are able to learn from us, watch our parenting, and build the kinds of relationships with our kids that maybe they didn't have with us.

My mom was very much of the "you'll figure it out on your own" school of parenting. We didn't talk a lot about feelings when I was growing up, and so when my mom started showing up regularly to help with the kids, she witnessed a version of me she had never met before. She watched me apologize to my kids for being short and grumpy. She watched me talk to them about how I was feeling and acknowledge their feelings in return. Something started to shift in our relationship.

Today, my mom is not in the same place in her life as she was when I was a kid, and as a grandparent, she is getting a chance at a do-over. She has learned to parent in a new way with her grandchildren, slowing down and talking to my kids about how they are feeling. This has been healing for both of us. I'll be honest: when I watch her gentleness, there are moments when the younger version of me grieves over what I didn't receive. But it warms my heart to know that she's giving my kids something I did not have and that she's also healing some of her own wounds through her relationship with them. And isn't embracing growth what being human is all about?

Proof that the world won't end if I show my flaws. Who among us reaches adulthood secure enough to be ourselves without worrying about the judgment of other people? For years, every time my mother-in-law was coming over, I burned through a pack of Magic Erasers cleaning the baseboards to impress her. I have since realized that this woman already knows every detail of our family's life. Who am I trying to fool? I can't stop her from judging me when the house is a mess. I can, however, stop myself from giving a hoot. I now look around at the mess and think, *Well, this is us— take it or leave it. If you want the hugs and the laughs, you gotta be okay with stepping on Legos and cracker crumbs.* And you know what? She still comes over, and she hasn't kidnapped Eric and the kids to remove them from my sloppy presence. She walks in, looks around, and then gets back to loving my children.

I've learned that the more I can remove the protective shell I've built around myself, the more joy and connection flood into my life and into my children's lives.

BEAUTIFUL THINGS HAPPEN WHEN
YOU SHOW YOUR TRUE COLORS

The end of Valentina's marriage came at her like a wrecking ball—starting high and far away, then beginning a downward swing that picked up momentum as it raced toward her and the kids. Her husband had gone from being a steadying influence in her life to a controlling and possessive jerk who made her doubt her self-worth. She knew she needed to get herself, nine-year-old Stephanie, and five-year-old Sebastian out of harm's way. The day she finally decided to leave, she and her husband had had a terrible fight about the way she spent her time—apparently she spent too much of it on herself. She needed to clear her head so she could calm down enough to find a way forward. She decided to go for a walk.

Now what? she asked herself as she rode the elevator down to the lobby, feeling unmoored. She needed an anchor to keep her from losing her way. She walked out the front door of her apartment building in Chicago, and there was her friend Nicole. The two women had been texting all afternoon, and Nicole had sensed that the end was coming, so she made her way across town to be there for her friend. Of course Nicole would be her anchor. Valentina nearly collapsed in gratitude as the two hugged. "What am I going to do?" Valentina said.

Nicole held her friend, then pulled back and said, "Here's what you're going to do. You're going to go back in there. You're going to get the kids, and I'm going to call an Uber, and we are all going back to my apartment. We'll figure it out from there." And that's exactly what they did.

The two women had first met nearly fifteen years earlier, when Nicole volunteered for the youth baseball organization in Chicago, where Valentina worked. They became fast friends, going out for Korean BBQ one night after practice and then meeting regularly for drinks and dinners, where they laughed and commiserated about the ups and downs of their early careers and the difficulties of dating in a big city. They were kindred spirits—both smart, funny, quick to smile, and just as quick to tell people when they'd crossed a line. It wasn't long until the two thought of themselves as something like sisters, sharing everything with each other—mistakes, regrets, screwups, and all. Their vulnerability allowed them to show up for each other in the right ways.

The two friends were so close that by the time Valentina got married and had kids, it was only natural that Nicole would be close with Valentina's kids, too (though with Valentina's husband, not so much). There's no religious component to their relationship, but Nicole describes herself as the kids' godmother to indicate that she has a role in their lives beyond "friend of the family." It's not precise, but it does the trick.

Nicole had decided in her early thirties that she did not want to have children of her own, but she adored Valentina's kids. Just because she had chosen not to have her own kids, that didn't mean she didn't want to be part of a family unit. Valentina's family offered her the opportunity to fill her need to belong to something larger than herself. As she saw it, she got to have all the love and joy with none of the sleepless nights and frustrations. Best of both worlds.

In the weeks following the end of Valentina's marriage, Nicole was a true partner to her. She sent emails to Valentina's work about her FMLA benefits. She made sure the kids were clean, fed, and dressed for school. She liaised with the broker when Valentina bought an apartment, which happened to be in her own building. Nicole also started picking up tasks that would usually be done by a parent. She got the kids off the bus, took them to practices and birthday parties, helped with their schoolwork, and attended their events. Valentina didn't even have to ask. If one of the kids had a big performance coming up, she would just let Nicole know so that she could pencil it in on her calendar. The two women know many people who think Nicole is the kids' second mom—and in a way, she is. She's just not Valentina's wife. They are a chosen family.

Not everyone is unconditionally supportive of the way Nicole and Valentina are modeling village life. Some of their friends have mixed feelings about their closeness and about the amount of time they spend together. A few people have suggested to Nicole that Valentina is taking advantage of her generosity, which just makes Nicole laugh. Being part of a family where we feel a sense of unconditional belonging is one of our deepest, most pressing desires. She finds the relationship fundamentally fulfilling. The two women feel so strongly about their bond that they refuse to alter it to make other people more comfortable. Besides, Valentina reasons, having kids is so demanding that she wouldn't have the bandwidth to show up for her other friends if it weren't for Nicole's help.

Nicole has had to bring up their relationship with the men she's dating, because she's found that men don't always understand the importance of female friendships, let alone the closeness she has with Valentina. She's learned to broach the subject early, to let men know that she and Valentina's family are a package deal. She recognizes that it's a bit unconventional, but it's so important that she communicates it up front.

Over the years, Valentina's idea of what friendship can be has expanded radically. Before she met Nicole, she had no idea that people who aren't related could be there for each other with the depth and consistency the two of them share. Sometimes, Valentina looks back on the week after her daughter was born. Nicole showed up at her apartment with a coffee just the way Valentina likes it, and Valentina immediately burst into tears. She hadn't asked for a coffee, and she had no way of reciprocating the gesture while she was still in her postpartum days. Nicole just brought it. Valentina realized that her old idea of friendship meant that if someone did something nice for you, you did something back. But there was Nicole with a nice drip coffee with cream because she thought Valentina would enjoy it. Back then, her bar for being taken care of or for having a supportive friend was so low that a gesture that small touched her deeply.

Neither woman had parents who reached beyond their immediate family for support. Nicole can't name a single other woman who was around consistently when she was a kid, but now the idea of life without Valentina and her family is unthinkable. Because she has chosen not to have kids, she has had to be very deliberate about forming a kind of chosen family for herself. Even though her blood relatives live hours away, she gets to have family dinners just by walking down a few flights of stairs. She gets to have the joy of going to the circus with the kids and watching their faces, taking Stephanie shopping for a special birthday outfit, and watching *A Christmas Story* on television with them each year.

Their relationship is brilliantly effortless from day to day, but that doesn't mean it didn't take a lot of work to build it. Creating the closeness they have took a leap of faith and a lot of commitment, including the commitment to being willing to bare it all to each other.

I think that sometimes, as moms, we minimize what we offer the world. There is so much value in bringing people into our village who aren't in the trenches of motherhood. You know those smiles and silly moments with your kids that make your heart stop? They can have that effect on your chosen family, too. Every time you invite people into your village, you are giving them a potentially meaningful experience just by being around you and your family.

Valentina and Nicole's story proves that we aren't beholden to our upbringings. Our village can be made up of our chosen family. We get to decide what that village looks like and who will be in it. Better yet, we can model new ways of forming mutually supportive relationships for other moms and our own children. We can normalize village life.

THE TOTAL PACKAGE

Nicole and Valentina have such a close connection that they are truly family to each other. This close familial bond is different from other types of village relationships. It's a mutual holding of one another with unconditional love and belonging. We don't get to pick and choose what parts of a person to accept. We accept the total package, and in exchange, we bask in that person's acceptance.

Welcoming an alloparent into the family comes with responsibilities. That word—*responsibilities*—always sends a chill down my spine. As if I need more responsibilities. I'm barely keeping up with the ones I already have. I admire people like Mary and Christopher, a couple with two kids who welcomed the additional responsibility that came when they built a close relationship with a friend named Janice.

Mary and Christopher had settled in Ann Arbor in the early 2010s. Mary taught at the University of Michigan while Christopher finished his PhD in philosophy and worked in a coffee shop. They were both obsessively into board games and loved hosting game nights for friends at their house. During his breaks at the coffee shop, Christopher liked to visit a game store a few store-fronts down to talk to the owner, a woman in her sixties named Janice. One day, after a visit with Janice, Christopher came home and told Mary, "You know, I'd really like to own a game store someday." Mary was all in on the idea—it seemed like as good a career as any for a philosophy PhD—and she immediately suggested that he talk to Janice about what it takes to run a successful store. When Christopher broached the subject, Janice thought it over and came back with an offer—why didn't Christopher come to work for her instead of at the coffee shop? That way, she could teach him everything she knew. Christopher leaped at the suggestion, and as he learned the ropes, Janice became not just a mentor to him but also a friend to the couple.

A year or so later, when a cancer diagnosis sent Janice to the hospital for a month, she asked Christopher to step in and manage the store. Christopher excelled at running the business, and that convinced Janice that he was the right person to take over the store when the time came. After Christopher and Mary gave birth to their daughter Kiara, in 2015, Janice decided it was time to sell them the store. Janice still stuck around a lot—after all, she'd owned the business for nearly forty years.

Mary's teaching schedule meant she could be home with the baby most of the time, and when she couldn't, Christopher brought Kiara into the store. That's when the couple noticed something odd about Janice's hours. They seemed to coincide with the times when Kiara would be there. Before Janice showed up, she would email to ask, "When is the youngest staff member going to be on the premises?"

Mary describes an unusual game night at their house as the first sign that Janice's role in their lives was about to change. She and Christopher had invited Janice over for board games with friends, and they'd assumed she would come at six thirty and play a few rounds of Ticket to Ride, per the invitation. Instead, she showed up two and a half hours early and spent most of that time walking Kiara around the backyard, pointing out the cardinals and the robins digging for worms. Mary remembers thinking, *Well, that was weird. She didn't even stay for the games.* And then it clicked: Janice was clearly smitten with the baby.

When it came time for Mary to pick up a full teaching load again, the couple realized that they had a gap in their childcare coverage, albeit just a couple of hours a day. They knew they could advertise for a graduate student or a part-time nanny to fill the gap, but they had a better idea: Janice. When they brought up the idea with her, she was over the moon. They started to talk about how much they would like to pay her, but she wouldn't hear a word of it. To her, the pleasure of spending time with Kiara was more than enough to compensate her for her time. She'd never married or had children of her own, though she adored them, so she treated Kiara as a beloved grandchild.

The first time she left Kiara with Janice, Mary had to quell a queasy feeling in the pit of her stomach. She had seen the two together so many times, and she had no doubt that Janice cared deeply for Kiara, but she'd always been there to keep an eye on things. What if Kiara got fussy and Janice couldn't calm her down? What if Janice couldn't remember how to turn on the bottle warmer? She spent her entire first day back at work with her mind still at home. She begged Christopher to call her the moment he got home to tell her how Kiara seemed. When her phone rang, she answered it before the first ring ended. "She's fine. She's happy. Everything's great," he told Mary. She could feel her body unclench. Mary didn't quit worrying completely, but the volume turned down to the point where she could enjoy doing her job.

Over the following three years, Janice took care of Kiara regularly. She taught her how to make pizza and how to eat a pomegranate. She downloaded toddler apps on her iPad and generally doted on her. Mary was impressed by—and frankly grateful for—Janice's efforts to ensure that Kiara grow up to be respectful and a good listener. At one point, Mary overheard Janice telling Kiara the story of David and Goliath, except with a twist—she said that some people thought David might have been a girl. Mary knew that wasn't biblical scholarship but rather Janice's belief that Kiara could be as mighty as any foe. It warmed her heart to have another person in Kiara's corner. When Christopher and Mary's second child, Cecilia, was born, the couple wasn't sure Janice would be up for looking after two kids, but she managed it beautifully.

Janice's cancer went in and out of remission as she aged, and Mary and Christopher started to worry that Janice wasn't catching everything the doctors had to say, so they began going to appointments with her. When Mary visited her in the hospital, she identified herself as Janice's daughter-in-law, since there's not really a word for what they are to each other. After Janice had a few health scares in quick succession, Mary and Christopher decided it would be better to have her closer. They searched for a house with an in-law suite so they could move Janice into it and keep her close. In a great stroke of luck, the house across the street from them went on the market, and Janice moved in, so she could come over in minutes, and they could do the same.

At one point, when Janice was recovering from a procedure that required her to stay on her back for hours at a time, Mary held her iPad above her and played videos of the kids when they were tiny, and she could watch Janice's heart rate and blood pressure normalize on the monitors. What better proof of how important they were to her?

Mary uses the word *enmeshed* to describe Janice's relationship with her family. They're inexorably joined. What affects Janice affects the family, and what affects the family affects Janice. Janice takes care of the girls. Mary and Christopher take care of Janice. It is a wonderful circle of mutual love and support.

In welcoming Janice into their family, Mary and Christopher welcomed *all* of her, not just the part that saved them thousands of dollars in childcare. Janice truly became like a grandparent to their daughters. Janice describes the seven years she's spent with the kids as the best of her life. She can't believe her luck: she gets to witness two incredible people experiencing the world for the first time. She gets to hear their laughter, introduce them to new games, and get stumped by their questions about why the sky is blue and who made the ocean so salty. The girls get another person who loves them completely, not for anything they achieved or made but just for being themselves. Who wouldn't want that?

OPENING UP TO A NEW IDEA OF FAMILY

I've been able to experience the beauty of alloparenting in my own family with my beloved friend Renée.

When my Latched Mama village fell apart, I wasn't the only one shaken. My employees suffered aftershocks, too. A lack of trust seeped into the interactions we had with one another around the office. I was used to an ease with my coworkers, and this new dynamic felt bad. I'd never had to navigate such turbulent waters as CEO, and I was at a loss for what to do.

One evening, I was laying out my troubles to a friend. I wasn't looking for advice, but when she told me that she knew a great employment lawyer, I sat up straighter in my chair. Was she suggesting that I needed an employment attorney at my company—a

company with a culture I'd intentionally built on grace and understanding? No way. That didn't sound like us. We were far too
evolved. We cared far too much about one another. I said thanks
but no thanks. And yet as I thought about it over the following
couple of weeks, I couldn't deny that things felt unstable. It was
time to admit I was out of my depth. So right before Christmas, I
texted my friend and asked her for the referral.

It was almost Christmas Eve when my friend sent me the
number just as I was about to pull out of the mall parking lot.
What attorney was going to answer the phone at this busy time
of year? I watched the last-minute holiday shoppers and families
laughing and bouncing to their cars with excitement. I knew if I
didn't reach out then, I'd put it off until after the new year, and it
would weigh on me while I should have been enjoying my family.
I dialed the number.

"Hi, Renée. My name is Melissa Wirt. I run a company
called Latched Mama, and I really need some help," I said. I held
my breath, half expecting her to snap at me for interrupting her
afternoon.

"Whatcha got?" she replied. "I'm on my way to my parents'
for the holidays. I have all the time in the world." All my doubts
and insecurities came pouring out. I tried to explain what had
happened to my company. I cried, I laughed, and I swore a lot.
When I was done, I gasped in sudden horror. "Oh, my gosh—are
your kids in the car?"

"Nope," she said with a laugh. "It's just me and my dog, Van,
and he's heard much worse."

After the start of the new year, she met me in my office, and
although I felt like my world was falling apart, I immediately
sensed that everything was going to be okay.

I looked forward to our meetings, even though they were ostensibly about a potential lawsuit. I just liked being around this woman. I suspected right away that we could be close friends. Her life couldn't have been any more different from mine. She lived in a one-bedroom apartment in the city with her (very low-energy) dog. She walked to work. She made her bed every morning, and she wore dry-cleaned suits and matching socks. She's on Tinder and takes a weekly hip-hop dance class. But despite our differences, I found that being vulnerable with Renée was easy. In the year that followed, she was by my side with legal advice, but mostly she was sheltering me from the storm that was decimating my village. Through it all, she reminded me that I was worthy of connection and support.

I started to think she could become part of my inner circle. At the same time, a little voice inside me said, "Renée doesn't have kids. Can she really be part of your village? What would she possibly get out of that?"

The first time I invited her out to the farm, the kids were confused. Who was this lady? Where were her children?

"But why don't you have kids?" they asked. "Do you not want to be a mom?"

It was awkward—like, my-kids-are-the-rudest-human-beings-alive awkward—and I worried for a second that Renée was going to turn right around and head back to her fabulous life, but instead her face lit up at their questions.

As the afternoon unfolded, I watched her become enamored of my kids in real time. It was as if their constant movement and activity animated her. She got down onto the floor, seeing things their way, and she was way, way more patient than I was with their long explanations of their complicated games. For their part, my kids quickly realized that the excellent thing about having a childfree adult in the house was that they didn't have to share her with other kids. Plus, she was younger and cooler than their "boomer" mom.

Renée came to the farm regularly, and our relationship gradually grew from professional to personal. I kept looking over my shoulder, waiting for her to run away when I wasn't paying attention. I fretted that, like the village members who abandoned me, she'd jump ship, but eventually I realized that she wasn't going anywhere. And I was so very, very glad. I appreciated the fresh energy, ideas, and skills she brought to our home. When Alex joined a basketball team for the first time at age ten—a sport that I have never played or particularly enjoyed—it was Renée who helped him learn how to use his size to his advantage. When Nathan's teacher assigned him to research a new state law, it was "Aunt Renée" he called to help him understand the nuances of the bill. At my last swim meet, Renée brought poster board and markers and sat in the stands with the kids and Eric making signs, cheering, and waving their homemade signs. She's just good people.

Renée can't always meet me where I am with the heaviness and exhaustion of motherhood, but I also can't meet her on what it feels like to be the only woman in the room trying to negotiate an agreement with the unions that bring all the imports into the state of Virginia. But isn't that true for every relationship in life? We must share ourselves and our realities so that we can try to understand one another. What makes my relationship with Renée work is that we communicate, and I (sometimes begrudgingly) let her see the motherhood mess.

On one occasion, Eric took our three oldest kids to the beach for the weekend. I remained at home with the three little kids, four dogs, and a very pregnant heifer (that's the term for a first-time mama cow). I knew the parenting would be better with another adult, so I shushed my inner critic, who told me I should be able to handle it all by myself, and asked Renée if she wanted to lend a hand for the weekend. A few days later, she arrived carrying dino chicken nuggets, s'mores supplies, cinnamon rolls for the kids in the morning, salmon and veggies for a grown-up dinner for us, and a full science kit in her bag. She showed me the mile-long list of things she wanted to do over the weekend. I laughed, knowing there was no way things were going to play out as she imagined, but I was touched by her thoughtfulness.

I spent the weekend walking the fine line between tempering her expectations with my tired mom perspective and allowing her to find as much joy as possible during her time at the farm. We half-assed our way through the science experiments, laughing a lot, barely reading the directions while trying to prevent my two-year-old from eating straight baking soda. We ate our salmon standing up while cleaning up a dino nugget–ketchup explosion, and at dessert, we roasted the marshmallows on the stovetop, too tired to make a fire. She didn't need to be a mom herself to know how to love and show care for us all. She cooked, cleaned, laughed, and village-personed hard the entire time she was with us. Having a second set of hands and another heart to love my babies for the weekend was a total game changer for all of us.

It took months of mutual vulnerability and trust to allow our relationship to evolve into what it is today. At the beginning, when her evening texts to me would go unanswered until the next day, she was hurt and confused. But allowing her to see what those hours looked like in my life was key to her appreciating my reality. Not only did witnessing the absolute chaos that is dinner and bedtime with six kids help her understand me better, it also allowed her the opportunity to learn how to be helpful and supportive. Some nights now, I'll finally get the kids down, check my phone, and there will be a text from her saying something like "I know the evenings are rough—you're doing great." Who doesn't want to hear that? I am so grateful that I gave our friendship a chance, and I am proud that, in the moments when I felt she'd never "get it," I didn't give up and instead found the confidence to invite her in further. In the end, Renée gets to be there for my children and they are better because of her presence. We are communing, we are momming, we are villaging.

I hope that if my own kids have children, there will be a neural pathway in their brains somewhere that says, "Oh, yeah, it's normal for another adult to get in here and help. We don't have to do this all alone." Caroline, my youngest girl, told me recently, "When I have kids, you are going to come over to my house, and we are going to eat chips and salsa and drink kombucha." Maybe it will be me, maybe it will be Eric, maybe it will be a friend they have yet to meet—but the model for having a village is there. We set a new pattern by breaking the old one.

Build Your Village

Ready for Alloparenting 101? Below are a few tips to get you started.

- *Parent for real.* One of the secrets of successful alloparenting is being your full parenting self—audible sighs, raised voice, and all—in front of another person. Letting yourself parent without pretense, without trying to impress anyone or live up to anyone else's expectations, is one of the things that distinguishes your relationship with a real alloparent from the relationship you might have with, say, a helpful fellow villager. Go ahead and do a half-assed rinse of an apple before feeding it to your kid. Let the kids have screen time to keep them quiet while you make a phone call. Hold fast to rules even if you know with one hundred percent certainty it will result in a record-setting meltdown.
- *Let alloparents do it their way.* It is so, so tempting to "encourage" helpers to do something your way (aka the right way), whether it's holding your baby or feeding your toddler. But our kids are not porcelain. They won't break if someone adds peas to their macaroni or puts their shoes in their closet instead of by the front door. Allowing a little wiggle room will not only create more space for people to feel comfortable helping you, it will also show your kids (and you!) a new thing or two.
- *Brag about it.* One of the best ways to change a paradigm is to change the way we talk about it. The more you can spread the word about the benefits of other adults helping to raise your kids, the more we will normalize a better way of villaging. Be loud and proud when you trust someone else to comfort your kiddo after a bad day or to be the one to teach him a new skill.

Chapter 14

Go Easy on Yourself

ISOLATION MINDSET: I've been working on this "village" thing for a while now, and it doesn't look or feel like a series of perfect concentric circles of relationships. I must be doing it wrong.

VILLAGE MINDSET: Every village is a work in progress. The only wrong way to build a village is to let an isolation mindset prevent us from trying.

*J*enna was running late—so very, very late. She had every intention of being at the mini-golf course on time. She'd even woken up an hour early to pack peanut-butter-and-jelly sandwiches and clementines for emergency snacking. But six-year-old Jackson didn't care about being on time. No matter how many times Jenna explained to Jackson that his friend Will, and Will's mom, Nadia, were going to meet them at Putt-Putt at 10:00 a.m., he kept asking for just five more minutes to work on his Minions' Music Party Bus Lego set. To avoid a meltdown, Jenna acquiesced a couple of times. But as the clock crept closer to their scheduled departure time, she knew she'd have to put her foot down.

Finally, as gently as possible, she told Jackson there would be no more building until they got home. And...meltdown. For the next fifteen minutes, Jackson stomped and yelled and cried as if she had just thrown the Minions into a fire. The tantrum sucked, but what sucked more was the anxious feeling she got knowing that they were already late for the playdate. Jenna snuck away from Jackson midtantrum to text "Running behind!" to Nadia, which technically bought her some time, but ugh, she hated, hated, hated being late. She'd already canceled on Nadia twice, once because Jackson had gotten sick and once because of a work deadline that had popped up. Her husband, Scott, was continually ribbing her about her "early is on time, on time is late, and late is unacceptable" approach to life. It was true that being on time was important to her, but that was because she saw it as a show of respect for the other people involved. She felt awful knowing that Nadia was probably watching the front gate and wondering where on earth they could be.

When Jenna and Jackson finally arrived at the mini-golf course, Jenna spotted Nadia over by the snack bar, scrolling on her phone while Will tried to balance his club on its end. Jenna practically vomited her apology on Nadia. She couldn't get her words of explanation out fast enough. When she'd finished, Nadia just looked up at her and laughed. "Don't even worry about it. We've been perfectly happy here. Will has been checking out the fish pond, and I've been watching TikTok." Jenna's whole body relaxed. Something shifted in her. If Nadia could be understanding about how her perfectly laid plans got hijacked by a clash of wills, why couldn't she grant herself the same understanding?

I have been in Jenna's position more times than I can count. As a mom, I have devoted a good part of my brain space to my kids. Where are they? Are they safe? Are they happy? Have they eaten? What is the next item on our agenda? This makes it incredibly difficult to be the kind of friend I hope to be. Since I became a mom, accepting this reality is one of the hardest mental adjustments I've had to make. I recognize that I can't be fully present in every interaction, and I try to cut myself some slack. I know I'm going to mess up more in friendship than I would at another stage of my life simply because I'm always distracted—and that's okay.

That's why my bestie, Lindi, and I have an understanding. Our default mode with each other is "I gotcha. No explanation necessary." We trust our bond to be stronger than the obstacles that put pressure on it. We know that it is impossible to answer every text when a three-year old is stepping on your chest, trying to get your attention. When we get together, we know that one of us might suddenly have to ditch if we get a call about a kid having a bloody nose or not being able to find a favorite stuffie at bedtime. We know that last-minute cancellation is always a possibility. We accept that we can't always be the friend we want to be—the friend we aspire to be. We're okay with that, and we grant ourselves and each other grace.

This is the message I want to end the book with: as we assemble our village, we need to traffic heavily in grace. There are already so many barriers to connection. Let's not erect additional barriers by judging ourselves for not living up to an idealized version of what our village should look like. We need to let go of the unrealistic expectations we hold for ourselves and others in order to embrace the beautiful reality we have in front of us.

BATTLING VILLAGE ENVY

It's been hard for me to let go of my expectations for what my village should look like. Once I experienced just how life-changing it could be to have supportive mom friends, I did a very "me" thing. I started comparing my village to those I saw around me and wondering why mine didn't measure up.

I compared my village to the book club I had belonged to briefly in my late twenties. I'd joined when I was first dating Eric, after some of the employees at his company invited me to be part of their group. Most of them were a couple of decades older than I was, and to this day I have no idea why they were so friendly to me. Their kids were in high school and college. Some even had children who had finished college and were close to my age. These women, like Laura's mom's tea group, had grown up together as mothers. They were woven into one another's lives. They worked together. They talked about books together. They went to Virginia Tech football games together. They even went on cruises together. After Eric and I got married and I got pregnant, they threw me an incredible baby shower. Each of these women wrote down something she had learned about motherhood on an index card, and they took turns reading their wisdom to me. I thought that was how my life would be once I became a mother—surrounded by a posse of amazing moms. Then motherhood hit me like a freight train, and I never went back to the group. My village today looks nothing like that book club.

I compared my village to my friend Holly's. She lives in the same city as her sister and her childhood best friend, who happened to marry her brother. The three friends share the closeness of a touring band. They do *everything* together. Their daily routines overlap completely. They take turns hosting dinner, and their kids act like they have three homes, not one. Nearly every aspect of child-rearing is a shared endeavor. They're like the world's smallest kibbutz. I don't have a village that looks like that, either.

I even compare my village to my sister-in-law's. Diane is married to Eric's brother, and she lives on the same cul-de-sac as her parents. Her sister and her four kids live right next door. And her brother and his family just four doors down. It's true that Eric and I have radically increased the amount of family support we have in our lives, but it is nothing compared to what my sister-in-law has with her family. It's like they were transplanted to the present from a much earlier time, when village life was the norm. Again, my village looks very different.

Sometimes it feels like those villages are taunting me. In my new connection-focused world, keeping up with the Joneses no longer means being jealous of someone's perfect yard or new Tesla; it now means being envious of other people's support systems. Sigh. Perfectionism. Sometimes it seems like we just can't win, doesn't it?

In those moments of *What is wrong with me? Why don't I have the friendships and support they have?* self-talk, I try to remember that every village is unique, shaped by the people in it. There's no rubber stamp for making a village. And thank goodness, because the range of what people need from a village is as wide and varied as the incredible women who need them.

Sheila's village might consist of four moms who live on her block who watch the same shows and all have a passion for pickleball. But Sita's village might be made up of her dance class, the PTA roster, and the staff at the restaurant she owns. Rhonda's village might be her sister and the people she runs into as she does errands—her dry cleaner, her grocer, and her favorite barista. The last thing I want to do is to give you an impossible fantasy to live up to. You know the one I mean—the one in which you meet people who are so good for you in every way that you never need to meet another person again. They make you feel amazing. They respect all your ideas. They're funny. They're smart. They are all your BFFs. But that is bullshit. No one has that. And buying into this fantasy version of a village undermines your ability to feel good about what you do have.

There's no point in replacing a broken system with the unrealistic expectation that you'll soon have a girl squad to rival Taylor Swift's. Even Taylor Swift's girl squad isn't perfect! What works for one mom might be a nightmare for another. The trick is to find the folks who fulfill you and invite them in.

I may not have a weekly wine night with a bunch of other moms or a long-running book club or family members who live on my block, but I do have friends who will make sure my kid gets home from her soccer game if I can't be there. I may not have the bandwidth to see my swim friends much outside of the pool, but I know they will be waiting for me every morning to connect and catch up between sets. I don't see my old neighborhood friends every night, but I know with a simple text, I could reach out and have a house full of people on a Saturday night. Most important, I have Lindi. We trade off making double dinners for our ridiculously large families, and I know she will always pick up the phone when I need her. It's not picture-perfect, but it's perfect for me.

I STILL FEEL LONELY SOMETIMES

Occasionally, even when we love the village we have, it can seem like it's not enough. My friend Marcella, mom to four adventurous boys, has a solid village, made up of her parents, who live next door; her sister; and a few friends from work. She also stays in touch with her other sister, who lives in Florida, and me, her friend from college, where we played field hockey together.

I look at Marcella's relationships, and I see a healthy, thriving, and frankly enviable village. And yet when I told her I admired her full life, she got quiet. "Melissa," she said, "I still get lonely sometimes. I can fall into a pattern where I sometimes go weeks without connecting with anyone. There are days when I don't have it in me even to call my sister, and I feel so alone." Right. Of course. A village is not a cure-all for every form of loneliness. But that's okay. Pervasive, unrelenting loneliness that lasts for months or even years will be damaging to your life, but occasional feelings of loneliness are part of the human condition. They are normal, natural, and nothing to be ashamed or afraid of. It's not always going to be the right moment for a party or even a coffee. Some days—when your baby is teething and you've been awake so long your eyelids burn—you are not going to want to talk to anyone. On those days, a little loneliness is not the end of the world. Sometimes, the right thing *is* to stay home and coddle yourself.

As a species, our social needs vary wildly. If you are an extreme introvert, your village will not look the same as the one built by the mom who has five people in her walking group. According to psychologist Susan Pinker, "Individuals differ in the amount and type of social contact they need to avoid feeling lonely. John Cacioppo has discovered that the subjective state of loneliness... is very much like other biological appetites, like the need for sleep, food, and sex. [It] varies from person to person and has a powerful genetic component."[1]

I know all too well how easy it is to calibrate your need for connection based on what you see other people doing. By the time my sixth child, Matthew, was born, I had already started thinking about villaging. I knew I was looking for connection, and I saw how much moms who post in the Latched Mama Facebook group got out of joining a mothers' group. So I decided to join a moms' group when Matthew was a baby, even though I hadn't joined one since my failed attempts with colicky Nathan. I was determined to find my people in this group—after all, I was joining something, and I had put on my sneakers! But with a newborn and five other kids, it was simply too hard to make a plan to attend consistently, and after two meetings, I quit. At first I chastised myself for not being able to do what those other moms were doing, but then I realized I was aiming for an unrealistic ideal. I needed to be kinder to myself and acknowledge that with six kids and a company to run, a moms' group just wasn't right for me at the time.

I also try to remember that life's demands come in waves. These intense years of motherhood, when I am neck-deep in diapers and Band-Aids and bedtime arguments, won't last forever. Lindi and I love to laugh about owning a seaside bed-and-breakfast someday when the kids get older. We'll finally be able to drink coffee and eat scones and finish a conversation uninterrupted.

SET REALISTIC EXPECTATIONS

Finding friendship and connection is always hard, but finding connection and support when you are also navigating a new identity as a mom can feel nearly impossible. Motherhood, particularly early motherhood, can be one of the hardest times to gather a village around you, even though that is one of the times when it's needed most. The massive changes we go through when we become mothers can leave us feeling wobbly and uncertain. Having a baby literally transforms our brains. We are flooded with estrogen. Oxytocin receptors bloom in the brain. Some regions of the brain grow larger. And a bumper crop of amygdala neurons emerges, making us hypervigilant and hyperaware of danger.[2] No wonder motherhood is such a hard state in which to connect with other people.

I've found that the key to getting through the thicket is to be compassionate with yourself. It's okay to mourn the person you were before you had children. It's okay to feel sad that your time is no longer your own. It's okay to mourn the difference between the mom you thought you would be and the mom you turned out to be and the life you thought you would have versus the life you do have. Your life has changed drastically. You have changed drastically. It's not fair to expect that the old methods of making friends will work. Or that the relationships you have will meet your old expectations for what a relationship should look like.

When I first became a mother, I was totally unprepared for the Mack truck that was headed for my life. I knew to expect soreness in my breasts and vagina, but I didn't expect the tenderness that came from not knowing who I was without the career that had defined me up until that point.

I will never forget the disorienting feeling of sitting in my car in the moments after I resigned from my job as a real estate agent, which I'd had for more than a decade. I sat in the parking lot, nursing Nathan in the front seat as I stared up at my old office, knowing my friends were in there enjoying a chatty lunch while I wrestled a sweaty baby between the steering wheel and my swollen breasts. Selling houses was what I had done from the day I graduated from college until the day I went into labor. And now it felt like all my hard work and accomplishments were being replaced by this little screamy baby. Who was this woman leaking breast milk and tears onto her pantsuit? She felt as unfamiliar to me as my new boobs. Like so many women, I didn't *want* to accept that not only was my life changing, I was also changing.

It reminded me of the feeling of going through puberty. In so many ways, motherhood is like a second adolescence. We have new bodies, new feelings, and new relationships, plus a surge of hormones. At least during puberty, we have health class to help normalize the mood swings and new feelings that accompany the big changes we are going through. Not so much with becoming a mother. We go to fourteen prenatal appointments but attend zero classes on how our identities will shift when we go through a transition that rocks us to our very core. Backup dancers get more training for performing in the Super Bowl halftime show than mothers do for a major transition in their lives. A halftime show lasts, what, half an hour? Being a mom is *for life*.

We humans are continually evolving, and our needs evolve, too, especially when we encounter major life shifts such as moving to a new city, beginning a new job, losing a loved one, meeting a new partner...or becoming a mother. If you are reeling from the ways you have changed since becoming a mom, keep in mind that it took you twenty or thirty or forty years to become the person you were before you had children. So of course it's going to take some time to get comfortable with the incredible person you are now as a mom. Be gentle with this new version of you. She is capable of amazing things.

Shifting my mindset to a village mindset has changed my life. I started this project absolutely terrified that I would not find my way. I was not a friendship or connection expert. And years later, I'm still not. I'm just a mom who believes that we can find happiness and progress by working together and supporting one another. But the overarching lesson I have learned on this journey is the importance of compassion. Compassion comes in many forms, and we moms are expert at offering compassion—to everyone but ourselves.

When I look at the small but mighty village I have created, I not only feel supported and seen, I also feel worthy of love and belonging. My village is not perfect. It's actually far from it. But when I take a mental roll call, the members of my village are always there for me. When I think about the fullness of my life and the support I now have, I have never felt more capable, more alive, or more loved.

We are all just trying to find our way—for ourselves and our little people. Every one of us is living through mind-boggling growth and change while we simultaneously pour our love and hearts into our tiny humans. That's a lot to ask of anyone. Be kind to yourself.

Build Your Village

This village-building thing is hard. Following are a few tips to help you remember to go easy on yourself.

- *Say it out loud.* If you are in a season of life when it is difficult for you to show up the way you would like to as a friend, instead of working maniacally to live up to unrealistic expectations, have a frank conversation with your friend. Tell her that you value her and wish you could respond to her texts immediately and not ever cancel plans, but right now you are running low on resources. Be sure to emphasize that it's not a reflection of how much you care—it's just a by-product of where you are. Chances are, if the person you're speaking to is another mom, she'll completely understand. You may even come to a "no hard feelings" agreement, in which either person can cancel plans without explanation at any time. By naming the problem, you save both of you the stress of wondering *Was it something I did?*
- *Let yourself off the hook.* If you are tempted to say yes to an invitation because you feel obligated to, not because you want to, take a moment and consider what might happen if you simply demurred. Could you respond that this isn't a good time? Imagine what it would feel like not to accept. You don't have to say yes to every opportunity for connection. You don't want to burn yourself out. Save your energy for a time when you can bring more of yourself to the table.
- *Catalog your wins.* Next time you find yourself envious of someone else's village and are tempted to succumb to shame about your own, ask yourself if you are selling yourself short. Look around you. Do you have someone you could call in an emergency? Have you made the effort

to reach out to a friend recently? Have you left the house and put yourself in a position to speak to another human being? Those are all wins.

The first time you tell your partner that you are going to Target and not taking the kids with you? Celebrate it. The first time you go into Starbucks and make eye contact with the barista and ask her how her day is going? Celebrate it. The first time you decide to sit on the bench at the park next to another mom and ask her what her name is? Celebrate it. You probably have more wins than you originally thought.

Conclusion

You've Got This

ISOLATION MINDSET: No one is coming to help me. I guess I have to navigate the difficulties of motherhood on my own.

VILLAGE MINDSET: Motherhood can be grueling, infuriating, and terrifying, but it doesn't have to be lonely. There are millions of women like us out there with hearts full of compassion and a need for connection. We've got this. We've got you.

Eleven months after my miscarriage, our farm baby, Matthew, was born. He arrived in our master bathroom, just inches away from the spot where I had cried on the floor almost a year earlier, knowing that I was about to lose a pregnancy. As before, the contractions came and went in waves. But this time, they resulted in a beautiful baby boy.

I joyfully emailed Donna, my therapist, after Matthew was born. Lindi came over with a basket of goodies for me and dinner for the family. My mom moved in a for a month, and my in-laws dropped by frequently to help. I had put a ton of work into trying to create a village during the eleven previous months, and it changed everything. What I had managed to construct wasn't large, but it was a start.

During Matthew's first year, the pandemic waned, and life started again. There was work for me and Eric and homeschooling and activities for the kids. Collectively, we were all trying to learn how to be back in a world that had seemingly reopened overnight. Summer came, and Matthew started sleeping through the night. Then there was another surprise: I was pregnant again—with a very much unplanned seventh baby.

During the weeks that followed, a battle waged in my heart. Why was I not feeling the unfettered joy I had felt with my previous pregnancies? I leaned on Lindi, who had welcomed surprise twins of her own five years earlier. She understood my ambivalence. Each morning as we walked, her first question was "Where are you at today?" She gave me the space not to feel like a terrible human for having mixed feelings about the little one growing inside of me. Some days I was excited, and other days I wanted to crawl into a ball and just cry. I was stretched so thin. I didn't know how I could give seven kids what they needed emotionally. And damn it, life was just coming into balance. I had even started fantasizing about the day I could go on a kid-free vacation with my husband. I met with Donna weekly. She listened to all my feelings and helped me see my way through. I was so very thankful for my (small) village.

When I was twelve weeks pregnant, we went on our yearly family beach vacation. I sat on the sand as the sun set and watched the kids dig in the sand, topple from their handstands, and chase the waves. We were having another baby. I was finally at peace. And my teeny-tiny village had helped me get there.

Eric and I told our parents the following night over dinner. We dropped hints to the kids so they would be prepared for the new baby's arrival months later. At the end of the week, sun-kissed and sandy, we packed up to head home. As we deflated the air mattress, Eric and I laughed about how on earth we would fit another kid in a one-bedroom beach condo like the one we were staying in. But we'd figure it out. We always did. We packed the car, got the kids in their car seats, and closed the back of the van. I ran up the stairs to use the bathroom one last time.

I was bleeding.

My heart dropped. With tears rolling down my face, I yelled, "Are you effing kidding me?" to the empty condo. I told Eric quietly as I climbed into the car. He reached over and grabbed my hand and didn't let go during the entire five-hour drive back to Richmond.

Once we were home, it felt like *Groundhog Day*. The same call to my midwife I'd made twenty-two months earlier. The same blood work ordered. The same ultrasound tech in the same dark room. The same "I'm sorry, but there isn't a heartbeat" confirming my worst fears. The same prescription for Cytotec.

I drove to our local Publix and took the same walk from the deli over to the pharmacy. The pharmacist asked for my name and then told me that she didn't have any Cytotec in stock. I bit my lip. I fought back the tears. I put my head down. I started to walk away. And then in a split second, I decided I was going to change the story. Somewhere in the year prior, in the hours of therapy, in the miles walked with Lindi, in the putting on of sneakers, in the embracing of my own worthiness despite imperfection, I had gained enough confidence to take a chance. I let the tears fall. "But I really need it," I explained. "I wanted this baby, and now it's gone, and I need it to be over." Holy oversharing, but I knew in that moment what I needed more than the drugs was connection.

The pharmacist came out from behind the counter and wrapped her arms around me. "I've been there. We will find you some. And we will find it tonight." I felt immediate gratitude and relief. She called every pharmacy within a ten-mile radius and had the medication put aside for me. I arrived home, Cytotec in hand. I texted my mom and asked her to watch the kids while Eric and I went out.

We went to our favorite ice cream shop and ordered to-go. With me in sweatpants and Depends, my feet up on the dash and a large waffle cone in my hand, Eric and I listened to '90s music and chased the sunset down the highway. I was actively miscarrying, exhausted from the emotional whirlwind of the previous two months, but I was getting through it with my partner, singing along to Green Day and watching a glorious sunset.

I mourned in solitude, sure, but I also decided to put the connections I'd cultivated to work, allowing them to help me heal. To give me something to look forward to, Lindi and I bought tickets to see Brandi Carlile, one of our favorite singers. Just two days later, an ultrasound confirmed that I hadn't fully completed the miscarriage. My midwife advised a second round of Cytotec. She gave me specific instructions. *Lie in bed. Don't get up. Text me in an hour.* I felt another pang of sadness. I took a beat, and then I asked her if it was safe to wait until later that night. My heart was yearning for connection. I marveled at the person I'd become, a person who knew that what my heart needed in that moment was just as important as what my body needed.

A few hours later, my bestie and I sat on a blanket at the Brandi Carlile concert. We breathed in the early fall air, soaked in the energy of hundreds of other women, and sang loud. We cried and laughed, and I came home with the fullest heart. I crawled into bed, with Brandi still playing in my AirPods, followed the directions, and by the next morning the loss was complete.

The difference in my two miscarriage experiences was so stark that it felt like I was living in an alternate universe. Not only was the experience different this time around; *I* was also different.

~

Do you ever have moments in motherhood when you feel like you're on a tightrope with no net underneath you? Before I built a village, that's how I lived most of my years as a parent. If I made a mistake, or if life went sideways and I fell off the rope, I had to somehow scrape myself off the ground and climb back up and keep walking even if I was putting myself at risk. Living with a net? It's a game changer. Not only does it catch me when I fall, but when it is tight and strong, it'll actually bounce me right back up onto the rope, and I'm walking again before I know it.

Our shared state of invisible isolation as mothers is not our fault. We didn't create the problem. But that doesn't mean we can't begin to solve it. Let's be clear: there is nothing easy about the work it takes to build a village. In many cases, you might need to rework your brain, shift your priorities, and advocate for yourself for the first time in years. It is *hard work* to deprogram decades of messaging that tells us that once we become moms, our needs don't matter. But if there is any group of people up to the challenge of breaking the patterns that have left us isolated and overwhelmed, that group is moms. No amount of policy failure or stereotyping can stop us once we've shifted our mentality.

We moms are human beings with needs—and one of the greatest of those needs is connection. We are *worthy* of connection. It doesn't matter how many times today we think we have failed—whether we've fed our family fast food all week or given our kids unlimited screen time, no decision we make will change the fact that we are worthy of love and support.

Let's collectively shift our mindsets to a village mindset. Let's agree that asking for help is not a sign of failure. Let's acknowledge that the only way to get rid of our shame about isolation is to talk about it. Let's muster the courage to show our true selves and celebrate other moms when they show us theirs. Let's use the knowledge that our shared experience of motherhood is a mighty bond to propel us to seek out a village of moms a million strong.

We all deserve connection. We all deserve support. We all deserve a village.

Now let's go out and build one.

Together.

Notes

Introduction
1. David Brooks, "The Nuclear Family Was a Mistake," *The Atlantic*, March 2020.
2. Roosa Tikkanen et al., "Maternal Mortality and Maternity Care in the United States Compared to 10 Other Developed Countries," Commonwealth Fund, November 18, 2020, https://www.commonwealthfund.org /publications/issue-briefs/2020/nov/maternal-mortality-maternity -care-us-compared-10-countries; "Working Together to Reduce Black Maternal Mortality," CDC, April 8, 2024, https://www.cdc.gov/womens -health/features/maternal-mortality.html.

Chapter 1
1. Caitlyn Collins, interview by Ezra Klein, "Opinion | the Deep Conflict between Our Work and Parenting Ideals," *The Ezra Klein Show*, March 22, 2024, https://www.nytimes.com/2024/03/22/opinion /ezra-klein-podcast-caitlyn-collins.html.
2. "New Survey Finds Loneliness Epidemic Runs Deep among Parents," n.d., Wexnermedical.osu.edu, https://wexnermedical.osu .edu/mediaroom/pressreleaselisting/new-survey-finds-loneliness -epidemic-runs-deep-among-parents.
3. Susan Pinker, *The Village Effect: How Face-to-Face Contact Can Make Us Healthier, Happier, and Smarter* (New York: Spiegel & Grau, 2014), 6.
4. Vivek H. Murthy M.D., *Together: The Healing Power of Human Connection in a Sometimes Lonely World* (New York: Harper, 2020), 37.
5. Pinker, *The Village Effect*, 29.
6. Alan Lightman, *The Transcendent Brain: Spirituality in the Age of Science* (New York: Pantheon, 2023), 136.
7. Murthy, *Together*, 14.

8.   "'Loneliness Predicts Self-Reported Cold Symptoms after a Viral Challenge': Correction to LeRoy et al. (2017)," *Health Psychology* 37, no. 7 (2018): 690–90, https://doi.org/10.1037/hea0000640.

9.   Murthy, 13.

10. Murthy, 13.

11. Murthy, 50.

12. John Leland, "How Loneliness Is Damaging Our Health," *The New York Times*, April 20, 2022, sec. New York, https://www.nytimes.com/2022/04/20/nyregion/loneliness-epidemic.html.

13. Kathleen Chin, Amelia Wendt, Ian M. Bennett, and Amritha Bhat, "Suicide and Maternal Mortality," *Current Psychiatry Reports* 24, no. 4 (2022): 239–75, https://doi.org/10.1007/s11920-022-01334-3.

14. Pinker, 5.

15. Eun Kyong Shin, Kaja LeWinn, Nicole Bush, Frances A. Tylavsky, Robert Lowell Davis, and Arash Shaban-Nejad, "Association of Maternal Social Relationships with Cognitive Development in Early Childhood," *JAMA* Network Open 2, no. 1 (2019): e186963. https://doi.org/10.1001/jamanetworkopen.2018.6963.

16. Jancee Dunn, "Day 2: The Secret Power of the 8-Minute Phone Call." *The New York Times*, January 3, 2023, sec. Well. https://www.nytimes.com/2023/01/02/well/phone-call-happiness-challenge.html.

17. Murthy, 32–33.

18. Robert Waldinger M.D. and Marc Schulz Ph.D., *The Good Life: Lessons from the World's Longest Scientific Study of Happiness* (New York: Simon and Schuster, 2023), 8–9, 15.

19. Waldinger et al, *The Good Life*, 10.

Chapter 2

1.   Kim Parker, "Modern Parenthood." Pew Research Center, March 14, 2013, https://www.pewresearch.org/social-trends/2013/03/14/modern-parenthood-roles-of-moms-and-dads-converge-as-they-balance-work-and-family/#:~:text=At%20the%20same%20time%2C%20roughly%20equal%20shares%20of.

2.   Rachel Minkin and Juliana Menasce Horowitz, "Parenting in America Today," Pew Research Center, January 24, 2023, https://www.pewresearch.org/social-trends/2023/01/24/parenting-in-america-today/.

3.   Gabor Maté, 2023. Review of Dr. Gabor Maté: "The Power of Connection and the Myth of Normal" video. Released 2022 by Wholehearted.org. https://www.wholehearted.org/title/the-power-of-connection/.

4. Ibid.
5. Andrea Fields, Chelsea Harmon, Zoe Lee, Jennifer Y. Louie, and Nim Tottenham, "Parent's Anxiety Links Household Stress and Young Children's Behavioral Dysregulation," *Developmental Psychobiology 63*, no. 1 (2021): 16–30. https://doi.org/10.1002/dev.22013.
6. Klein, podcast. https://www.nytimes.com/2024/03/22/podcasts/transcript-ezra-klein-interviews-caitlyn-collins.html.
7. Cassie Holmes, *Happier Hour: How to Beat Distraction, Expand Your Time, and Focus on What Matters Most* (New York: Gallery), 9.

Chapter 3

1. U.S. Bureau of Labor Statistics, "American Time Use Survey Summary," BLS.gov, June 22, 2023, https://www.bls.gov/news.release/atus.nr0.htm.
2. "Study Shows Moms Work the Equivalent of 2.5 Full Time Jobs," ABC13 Houston, March 20, 2018. https://abc13.com/moms-motherhood-family-working/3238071/#:~:text=Well%2C%20now%20a%20new%20study%20shows%20just%20how.
3. Eun Kyong Shin, Kaja LeWinn, Nicole Bush, Frances A. Tylavsky, Robert Lowell Davis, and Arash Shaban-Nejad, "Association of Maternal Social Relationships with Cognitive Development in Early Childhood," *JAMA* Network Open 2, no. 1 (2019): e186963, https://doi.org/10.1001/jamanetworkopen.2018.6963.
4. "Moms Spend a TON of Time Driving Their Kids, Survey (and Your Life) Confirms," *Motherly*, November 7, 2019, https://www.mother.ly/life/survey-confirms-moms-spend-a-ton-of-time-driving-kidsbut-there-are-alternatives/#:~:text=According%20to%20a%20survey%20by%20carpooling%20service%20HopSkipDrive%2C.
5. Nikki Campo, "5 Ways to Make the Workweek Feel Less Stressful and Draining," *SELF*, September 15, 2022, https://www.self.com/story/work-stress-tips.

Chapter 4

1. News.bbc.co.uk, "Perfectionism Hits Working Women," May 28, 2009, http://news.bbc.co.uk/2/hi/health/8072739.stm.
2. Interview with Dr. Jen Douglas, June 20, 2023.
3. Ibid.
4. Waldinger et al., 42.
5. Douglas, interview.
6. Douglas, interview.

Chapter 5

1. Waldinger et al, 42, 36–37.
2. "APA Dictionary of Psychology," n.d., Dictionary.apa.org, https://dictionary.apa.org/propinquity-effect.
3. Douglas, interview.
4. "How Long Does It Take to Make a Friend?" Greater Good, 2018. https://greatergood.berkeley.edu/article/item/how_long_does_it_take _to_make_a_friend.Chapter 7. Operation Mom Friends

Chapter 6

1. Priya Parker, *The Art of Gathering: How We Meet and Why It Matters* (New York: Riverhead Books, 2020), 1–4.

Chapter 7

1. Douglas, interview.
2. Pinker, 21–23.
3. Maya Rossignac-Milton and E. Tory Higgins, Review of "Epistemic Companions: Shared Reality Development in Close Relationships," *Current Opinion in Psychology*, Vol. 23, October 2018: 66. https://doi.org/10.1016/j.copsyc.2018.01.001.
4. Ibid, 67.

Chapter 9

1. Pinker, 36

Chapter 10

1. John Leland, "How Loneliness Is Damaging Our Health," *The New York Times*, April 20, 2022, sec. New York, https://www.nytimes.com/2022/04/20/nyregion/loneliness-epidemic.html.

Chapter 11

1. Murthy, 218–219.
2. Jeffrey Hall, "How Many Hours Does It Take to Make a Friend?," *Journal of Social and Personal Relationships* 36, no. 4 (2018): 1278–96, https://doi.org/10.1177/0265407518761225.
3. Kim Parker, Juliana Horowitz, and Renee Stepler, "Americans See Different Expectations for Men and Women," Pew Research Center's Social & Demographic Trends Project, Pew Research Center, December 5, 2017, https://www.pewresearch.org/social-trends/2017/12/05/americans-see-different-expectations-for-men-and-women/.
4. Jainish Patel and Prittesh Patel, "Consequences of Repression of Emotion: Physical Health, Mental Health and General Well Being,"

International Journal of Psychotherapy Practice and Research 1, no. 3 (2019): 16–21, https://doi.org/10.14302/issn.2574-612x.ijpr-18-2564.

5. Diane Dreher, "Why Talking about Our Problems Makes Us Feel Better," *Psychology Today*, June 11, 2019, https://www.psychologytoday.com /us/blog/your-personal-renaissance/201906/why-talking-about-our -problems-makes-us-feel-better.

Chapter 13

1. *The New York Times*, "The Typical American Lives Only 18 Miles from Mom," December 23, 2015, https://www.nytimes.com/interactive /2015/12/24/upshot/24up-family.html.
2. A. J. Baime, "When Grandparents Are Called to Parent—Again," AARP, March 2, 2023, https://www.aarp.org/home-family/friends-family/info -2023/grandparents-become-parents-again.html.
3. *The New York Times*, "The Typical American Lives Only 18 Miles from Mom."
4. CNN, Elissa Strauss, "How 'Alloparenting' Can Be a Less Isolating Way to Raise Kids," CNN, June 15, 2021, https://www.cnn.com/2021/06/15 /health/alloparenting-multiple-caregivers-raising-kids-wellness/index .html.

Chapter 14

1. Pinker, 29.
2. Sarah Menkedick, *Ordinary Insanity: Fear and the Silent Crisis of Motherhood in America* (New York: Pantheon, 2020), 15–19.

Acknowledgments

Writing a book is a lot like raising kids. My expectations of what this process would look like (weekend escapes to a little cottage by the sea where I drank warm coffee, went for runs, and lost myself in the joy of writing) were completely different from the reality. But writing this book has changed my life in more ways than I could ever put into words.

Thank you to Kevin Anderson and his team for shepherding this project and seeing value in it even during the early days. Thank you to Bethany Bradsher for a wonderful visit to the farm and for your attention and care to my story and the people in it. Thank you to Caitlin Matalone and Gusto for priceless PR help during the pandemic and to Ashley Angelo for doing such a brilliant job when we brought the task in-house.

Thank you to Leah Stiegler and the entire team at Wood Rogers Vandeventer Black, for all of their legal guidance and support. Leah, you are the absolute best at what you do and one of my favorite human beings in the world.

When this project found a home at Grand Central Publishing, something magical happened. The editorial mastermind Karyn Marcus created a village around this book. The final product is only what it is because of Karyn's vision and our book writing village.

Over the past two years, we tested the concepts written on these pages and cheered each other on as we adopted the mindset shifts ourselves. We shared our stories of success and failure with each other, some of them featured on the pages of this book. I am a better human, mother, and friend because of this unique process and these other women.

Karyn: thank you for taking a chance on a first-time author and believing in the importance of this project. And thank you for continuing to believe in me when I was deep in the muck of self doubt. Jessica Sindler: thank you for sticking with me, even through a pandemic and cross-country move.

Thank you to Dr. Gardner Campbell, the person who introduced me to the healing power of writing and showed me how to find my voice. In some magical English 101: Writing Workshop sorcery, you designed a class that found its way through even the deepest layers of my teenage angst. I carried your teaching with me as I wrote this book. I am grateful for educators and safe space creators everywhere.

I have so much gratitude for those who have shown up so beautifully for our family over the years. We are very lucky to be loved by so many. Thank you to Alli and Connor Sheehan, who saw our family through the pandemic with patience, humor, and grace. Thank you to Stefanie Froelich for being one of my favorite humans and loving us all so well. Thank you to Hannah Wright and Rebekah Cray for dealing with our mess and chaos with love and grace. Thank you to Rose, Jessica, Maddie, Scout, Bre, River, Paul, and Leonilda and so many others. Thank you for showing up and scrambling eggs, filling bottles, kicking soccer balls, breaking up fights, and for making my kids laugh on days when I have nothing left to give.

Thank you to Nancy Giglio for a decade worth of magical hours spent in your office. During our time together, it often sounded like you were reading from a storybook when you'd described the village you and Therese created together. There are many concepts in this book that came from listening and learning from you. Thank you for your attention and care and for bringing my babies safely into the world. You are a remarkable gift to all those who are lucky enough to have you in their life.

Thank you to every person (and I mean every person) who has ever worked at Latched Mama and shared their energy, creativity, and time with me. Our growth is the result of the effort of hundreds of people who have held the collective belief that we must do better for women, mothers, and families.

To my leadership team, Lauren, Lindi, April, and Megan, being on this small business roller-coaster ride with you all has been one of the greatest honors of my life. Getting to lead beside you all every day brings me so much joy. Sorry for all of the missed meetings for book calls, and the "Hey, does this sound right to you?" moments. Thank you for pushing back and challenging me, still believing in me when I fall flat on my face, and letting me feed you when I don't know what else to do.

Thank you to Kat, Emily, and Elizabeth, for your friendship and grace and coming back into my life during this project and a time when I needed you all the most. I am so incredibly proud of you all.

Thank you to Keri for being my forever bestie.

Thank you to my swimming peeps. You all have changed my life. I wrote much of this book in my head during distance sets, inspired by how happy and connected you all make me feel. This book is better because of you all.

Thank you to my three beloved sets of parents. Our little family is forever grateful for your love and support. Eric and I are so very grateful for all the wisdom and love you bring to our lives.

To Susan, it's safe to say a lot of these words would not have found their way out of my head and heart without your presence in my life. Thank you to you and Tim for loving me like you do.

I am grateful that I grew up with a writing and book-obsessed older brother and an older sister who could match my drive and intensity. Mark and Amy, thank you for always cheering me along, even though I was really obnoxious as a kid.

To my kiddos: Nathan, Alex, Caroline, Benjamin, Katherine, and Matthew, thank you for your patience and your grace. Thank you for always finding the bright side of having a large family and a mom who is stretched thin. Thank you for loving each other so well. Thank you for the dance parties in the kitchen and for always making everything else in life feel much less important. You all are simply all that matters, and I am so damn proud of you all.

A special thank-you to my oldest, Nathan, for graciously granting me the permission to share our early experiences together in the pages of this book. I become prouder and more in awe of you every single day. I look forward to crying tears of desperation together again during your teenage years, but even then, please don't ever question my love and the overwhelming amount of gratitude I feel toward you and our journey together. You have been my greatest teacher in life and for that I am forever grateful. Oh, and thank you for bringing Milo into the family; we didn't need another dog, but we absolutely needed him.

To Eric, thank you for not thinking that my dreams are silly and for always helping me move mountains to make them happen. Thank you for charging my phone at night, for making sure there is coffee creamer in the fridge, and for always devouring everything I cook. But most of all, thank you for making me laugh every day and for being the best dad to our little people I could dream of.

Lastly, to the Latched Mama community and mothers everywhere, this book only exists because of you. Motherhood is the hardest job in the world—Thank you for being my companions on this wild ride.

About the Author

Melissa Wirt is the CEO and founder of Latched Mama, a breastfeeding-apparel company that has been featured in media outlets ranging from *Business Insider* to *USA Today* to *CBS Mornings*. Melissa and her husband, Eric, and their six children live outside of Richmond, Virginia.